# THE DANCE OF OPPOSITES

# THE DANCE OF OPPOSITES

## Explorations in Mediation, Dialogue
## and Conflict Resolution Systems Design

KENNETH CLOKE

GOODMEDIA PRESS
DALLAS, TEXAS

GoodMedia Press
25 Highland Park Village, 100-810
Dallas, Texas 75205
www.goodmediapress.com

Book cover by Lindsey Baily of GoodMedia Press
Book layout by Christopher Rodriguez of GoodMedia Press.

The text in this book is set in Caudex, Futura and Georgia

Manufactured in USA

Cloke, Kenneth.
    The Dance of opposites : explorations in mediation , dialogue and
conflict resolution systems design / Kenneth Cloke.
    p. cm.
    ISBN 978-0-9911148-0-1
    Includes index.

    1. Mediation. 2. Conflict management. 3. Interpersonal relations. 4.
Negotiation. 5. Mediation --Study and teaching. 6. Conflict management
--Study and teaching. I. Title.

    BF637.N4 C54 2013
    303.6/9 --dc23                                    2013952763

*To my grandchildren, Orrin, Thacher, Tallulah, Oliver, Jonah, and Elias, in the hope that they will inherit a less conflicted world, in which opposites learn to delight in their dance.*

*By the very fact of his being human, man is asked a question by life: how to overcome the split between himself and the world outside of him in order to arrive at the experience of unity and oneness with his fellow man and with nature. Man has to answer this question every minute of his life. Not only—or even primarily—with thoughts and words, but by his mode of being and acting.*

~ Erich Fromm~

*We look at the dance to impart the sensation of living in an affirmation of life, to energize the spectator into keener awareness of the vigor, the mystery, the humor, the variety, and the wonder of life.*

~ Martha Graham ~

*I feel the other, I dance the other, therefore I am.*

~ Leopold Senghor ~

*Live at the empty heart of paradox. I'll dance there with you, cheek to cheek.*

~ Jelaluddin Rumi ~

# CONTENTS

# INTRODUCTION

## A New Vision for Conflict Resolution

*The purpose of a writer is to keep civilization from destroying itself.*

~ Albert Camus ~

CONFLICT RESOLUTION IS COMING of age, and as it matures, must come to terms with a violent, adversarial world, grapple with its unsolved problems and difficulties, discover new issues, and redesign or reinvent its values, ideas and practices, and make them match its new-found strengths and weaknesses. And in the process, it must realize, as Edith Wharton observed, that "True originality consists not in a new manner but in a new vision."

But how do we invent a new vision for a process that is as old as humanity? I believe we do so by re-examining our relationship to the worlds around and within us, by thinking deeply about the nature of our work and what makes it useful and effective. One way of doing this is to think more clearly about what it *means* for us to succeed and fail in mediation.

## SUCCESS AND FAILURE IN MEDIATION

It is not uncommon for mediators to become so preoccupied with success and failure that they lose sight of their vision and reasons for mediating, which paradoxically are the very things that help them succeed. So let us begin by considering what success and failure consist of in conflict resolution.

Winston Churchill, in the midst of war, famously defined success as "proceeding from failure to failure with undiminished enthusiasm." A similar definition can be applied to mediation, a process that routinely begins at impasse, which is a kind of failure, and remains there until, often for no clear or definable reason, an opening appears, and resolution occurs.

As mediators, we tend to define success as settling disputes. But doing so means constructing our definition of success externally around choices that are made by, and belong to, the parties rather than the mediator. Our desire for success can then encourage us to coerce others into promoting our success over theirs, forcing simple solutions onto complex problems, and not taking time to listen to what their conflicts are trying to tell us. In the process, as Virginia Woolf correctly perceived, we begin to lose touch with what connects us to them, and ultimately with our humanity:

> If people are highly successful in their professions they lose their senses. Sight goes. They have no time to look at pictures. Sound goes. They have no time to listen to music. Speech goes. They have no time for conversation. They lose their sense of proportion—the relations between one thing and another. Humanity goes.

Attitudes toward success and failure in mediation should therefore be less concerned with what we do as mediators and more about how much we can learn from every conflict by discovering its meaning to each participant; how deeply we can feel what they experience and bring it to the surface; how much skill we can bring to difficult and dangerous conversations; how much of ourselves we are able to manifest during the mediation; how openhearted, empathetic and honest we can be in the presence of anger, defensiveness, dishonesty and fear—in other words, who we are in the mediation.

The old models of success and failure are deeply deceptive, not only because failure as a "tough" negotiator might imply success as a collaborative one and vice versa, but because the outcome and effect of any success is generally to repeat whatever it was we did before, whereas our failure more frequently results in serious rethinking, greater willingness to experiment and approach problems creatively, and a shift from hubris to humility, all of which lead to learning and growth. So we may well ask ourselves, in reality, which is the success, and which the failure?

If our goal is to increase our own learning and skills and become more aware of what doesn't work in mediation without feeling badly about who we are, neither success nor failure will be particularly helpful in guiding us. What matters most is our willingness to try new things, experiment, and take risks without being afraid of failure. In this sense, failure means trying too hard to succeed, whereas success means being willing to accept the possibility of failure.

An alternative is therefore to shift our notions of success and failure from focusing on individual moments of elation and disappointment that every mediator experiences, to the creation of a collective vision of conflict resolution that allows us to imagine what we do in every mediation as part of a comprehensive global movement that is transforming and reshaping the world in which we live.

## THE ELEMENTS OF A NEW VISION

Tangibly, this means approaching conflict in brand new ways and coming to grips with topics that are difficult to analyze or rethink from a conflict resolution point of view. The chapters that follow are efforts to discover the elements of this new vision as it emerges, sometimes in the petty or sordid details of conflicts I have mediated over the last thirty years, and sometimes in the discovery, through other disciplines and lines of thought, of new techniques and ways of understanding conflict.

They examine, for example, our understanding of how language operates in conflict, how people tell stories about their disputes, how mediation interfaces with psychology, and how the brain responds to conflict. They attempt to wrestle with religion and spirituality, to articulate an approach to mindfulness in meditation, and to consider how we can initiate heartfelt communications in family and couple conflicts.

A new vision for mediation will also require us to understand the larger social and environmental conflicts that impact us daily, and learn how to engage in dialogue over climate change and other contentious political conflicts without destroying our relationships. It will require us to consider how to design, organize, and conduct dialogues on difficult, dangerous, and controversial issues; and how to mediate chronic organizational disputes. It will invite us to examine the ways other cultures, such as China, have handled conflict resolution, and the interface between mediation and politics or values.

At a deeper level still, a new vision for mediation means exploring how opposites combine in dialectical patterns, how movements for social change both create and resolve social conflicts, and how the relationship between mediation, law, and justice impacts our work, even in seemingly insignificant conflicts.

Each of these topics forms a chapter in this book. None is final and each is an invitation to all of us to discuss, investigate, and write about conflicts in these areas, and in others that have not been considered, in hopes that by doing so we will contribute, even in small ways, to Camus' project of keeping civilization from destroying itself and creating a fresh vision for our work that redefines our notions of success and failure.

More importantly, I believe we will discover by doing so that our youthful field is bursting with creative insights and immense promise. Beyond merely helping us avoid destructive adversarial contests, mediation, collaborative negotiation, dialogue, and conflict resolution systems design enable us to develop entirely different approaches to "the dance of opposites," ones that are able to build a more just, heartfelt, peace-able, and collaborative world.

## TOWARD A CONFLICT REVOLUTION

In his essay on Machiavelli, Isaiah Berlin reveals how the ability to recognize two simultaneous truths leads automatically to the values that lie at the heart of dispute resolution, including tolerance, pluralism, and an appreciation of diversity:

> So long as only one ideal is the true goal, it will always seem to men that no means can be too difficult, no price too high, to do whatever is required to realize the ultimate goal. Such certainty is one of the great justifications of fanaticism, compulsion, persecution ... If there is only one solution to the puzzle, then the only problems are first how to find it, then how to realize it, and finally how to convert others to the solution by persuasion or by force. But if this is not so ..., then the path is open to empiricism, pluralism, tolerance, compromise. Tolerance is historically the product of the realization of the irreconcilability of equally dogmatic faiths, and the practical improbability of complete victory of one over the other. Those who wished to survive realized that they had to tolerate error. They gradually came to see the merits of diversity, and so became skeptical about definitive solutions in human affairs.

As a result, we can see how conflict resolution can not only help individuals, families, couples, and organizations resolve their disputes and possibly rescue and rebuild their relationships, a new vision for mediation should also recognize that it can undermine intolerance and strengthen democracy. Mediation is therefore a critically important skill for us to learn, if we are to successfully overcome the global inclination to use force and violence whenever we disagree. As Hannah Arendt correctly points out in her essay on violence,

> The chief reason warfare is still with us is neither a secret death wish of the human species, nor an irrepressible instinct of aggression, nor, finally and more plausibly, the serious economic and social dangers inherent in disarmament, but the simple fact that no substitute for this final arbiter in international affairs has yet appeared on the political scene.

In other words, rather than reinforce pessimistic and fatalistic notions about the inevitability of warfare and human violence, it is now possible for us to suggest, and invite others around the world to consider that a genuine, *workable* substitute for brutal and murderous acts has indeed appeared on the political scene, in the form of conflict resolution.

We are increasingly facing problems that are international in scope and can no longer be solved by individuals, or even by consortiums of nation states, but instead require global cooperation, informal problem solving, and dialogue. We cannot solve these problems using military force or litigation, by violence or coercion, or by accusations and denunciations, but now require the use of mediation, collaborative negotiation, dialogue, and conflict resolution systems design in order to successfully collaborate in overcoming them.

What we need, in short, is a "conflict *revolution,*" a comprehensive, fundamental transformation in the way we argue, disagree, and resolve our differences as a species. We need a vision that is large, all-inclusive, human, and at the same time revolutionary enough to allow us to analyze all our institutions and relationships, families and couples, governments and workplaces, in order to identify the sources of chronic conflict within them and use heart-based conflict resolution systems design principles to reinvent them.

## ABOUT THIS BOOK

The chapters that follow are intended to encourage these deeper explorations in a variety of important fields. Each chapter was originally written as a "stand alone" article or essay, and many were circulated among mediators, especially at Mediate.com, and have been significantly revised or rewritten. They are experimental and designed to suggest ways mediators can learn from other disciplines, be they mathematics and physics, neurophysiology and psychology, spirit and wisdom traditions, politics and philosophy, law and justice, or organizational design and movements for social change.

I have included a few newly revised and updated passages from previous books I have written when I was unable to improve on an earlier description, but altered and retrofitted them to the framework and purpose of this book.

My hope is that these chapters will make it possible for any reader who is interested in mediation to learn innovative ways of resolving disputes, new and powerful techniques that can be adapted and applied in completely unexpected arenas of conflict, together with fresh insights into the ways we fight and novel ideas about how we might resolve our differences worldwide, without the costly consequences we witness every day.

Most importantly, I hope every reader will realize that it is possible for each of us working individually and collectively to re-imagine and re-envision what we do in conflict resolution, and to use these new understandings to learn and grow, become better human beings, celebrate and unite around our differences, revolutionize the way we respond to conflicts on all levels, and transform our differences into opportunities for individual and social improvement. It is up to us to make it happen. As George Herbert wrote, "The shortest answer is doing."

Kenneth Cloke
Santa Monica, California

# CHAPTER 1

# THE LANGUAGE OF CONFLICT

*We human beings belong to language. In language, we love and hate, we admire and despise. We interpret our crises as individual and social. We suffer, and exalt, and despair. In language, we receive the gift of being human. All the feeling, the thinking, the action, and the things of this world as we know it are given to us in language.*

~ Fernando Flores ~

*Remember how the naked soul
comes to language and at once knows
loss and distance and believing ...*

~ W. S. Merwin ~

**W**HILE EACH OF US experiences conflicts well below the level of language, for the most part, we recount, understand, mediate, and resolve them primarily through language. As a result, while words can never suffice to describe what or how we feel when we are in conflict, they form an essential part of our journey through conflict experiences.

As a result, every word in conflict is simultaneously a failure, because it does not reflect the deeper meanings of the dispute; an escalation, because it is distant and removed from the underlying emotions that have informed it; and a provocation, because it is nearly always presented to the other side as an accusation. Yet every word in conflict is also an expression of hope, because it is an attempt to bridge the gap that separates adversaries; an act of courage, because it is a plea for understanding; and an effort to re-connect, because it is a deliberate effort to move toward our opponents and away from the hostile assumptions that feed impasse.

There is an inevitable gap between experience and description, between what happened and how we choose to describe or label it. Yet the act of turning complex, indeterminate, multi-dimensional conflict experiences into simple, precise, single-dimensional words allows us, on the one hand, to separate them from the complex array of inchoate feelings, false expectations and inaccurate perceptions that gave rise to them, and thereby feel more confident in addressing them. On the other hand, it may also strip our experiences of paradoxes, enigmas, subtleties, and self-contradictions, allowing us to imagine what happened solely as a product of other people's intentions and to cast them as "The Truth."

Thus, while the experience of conflict is always deeper than words, it is primarily through words that we participate in disputes, reach impasse, and try to settle, resolve, transform, and transcend them. Language gets us stuck, but it also sets us free, by revealing new, unimagined paths out of our difficulties. Words translate our primal emotional responses to perceived threats and hostilities into language, which is the first significant step in resolving them. As Sigmund Freud astutely observed, "The man who first hurled a term of abuse instead of a spear was the founder of civilization."

Still, most words are inadequate to capture the intense emotions that are experienced in conflict. Novelist Jeffrey Eugenides writes, somewhat whimsically, about the inadequacy of emotional language:

> Emotions, in my experience, aren't covered by single words. I don't believe in "sadness," "joy," or "regret." Maybe the best proof that the language is patriarchal is that it oversimplifies feeling. I'd like to have at my disposal complicated hybrid emotions, Germanic train-car constructions like, say, "the happiness that attends disaster." Or: "the disappointment of sleeping with one's fantasy." I'd like to show how "intimations of mortality brought on by aging family members" connects with "the hatred of mirrors that begins in middle age." I'd like to have a word for "the sadness inspired by failing restaurants" as well as for "the excitement of getting a room with a minibar." I've never had the right words to describe my life, and now that I've entered my story, I need them more than ever.

While no words can capture the intense experience of rage, or fear, or loss, as powerful emotions easily distort the meaning of whatever words we decide to use, even in the pettiest of disputes. Words in conflict then turn into gestures, puzzles and smokescreens, designed to disguise and evasively, circuitously and indirectly communicate what we really feel and mean. Conflict language can then be seen as representation, as reflection, as symbol, as artifact, even as lies that are told in pursuit of some deeper truth.

For these reasons, it is axiomatic that in order to successfully resolve any dispute, we need to learn successful ways of communicating with each other, not only about what happened, but about how we felt and why, and endeavor to put our conflicts into words that can be heard and understood accurately, even by our opponents. For this reason, mediators, like psychotherapists, practice "the talking cure," and while every parent and pre-school teacher understands the value of instructing their charges to "use your words," the problem we confront in conflict resolution is: which words, used when, and how?

## WHAT IS LANGUAGE?

Hundreds, perhaps thousands, of volumes have been written about language in an endless effort to define it, and academics and linguists continue to disagree over various points, especially regarding the origins and operations of language. For our purposes as mediators and conflict resolvers, we can think of language as the use of sound, silence, bodily movement, context, and symbols to convey thoughts, feelings, and especially meanings from one person to another. The structural relationship between these elements and symbols can be thought of as grammar, their organization into sentences as constituting syntax, and the many ways of assessing meaning as comprising semantics.

Most languages consist of words, which are sounds or gestures that operate as symbols, meaning that they refer to something other than themselves. For this reason, there is a momentary neurophysiological delay in accessing the meaning of any word or gesture, and an inevitable separation between the expression and the thing it symbolizes. Thus, neurophysiological studies reveal that the meaning of words is assigned by the coordinated activity of a number of different areas in the brain, with measurable delays created by conflicts between its hemispheres and specialized functions. Thus, identifying the word "green" when it is written in red creates a momentary delay. And we all recognize that the word "water" can't be drunk, that "fire" doesn't burn, and that "money" can't be spent.

More fundamentally, language consists of sentences in which words are strung together to create even more complex meanings. Man-Booker Prize winning novelist John Banville writes, "Surely mankind's greatest invention is the sentence. Words may matter, but the sentence is form." By bringing words into formal relationship with each other, new meanings are created. This is especially true in conflict conversations, where meanings clash and contradict each other.

The desire of people in conflict to merge a set of words or symbols with their own unique experiences forces them to rely on symbols to communicate meaning, yet the use of these symbols inevitably removes the listener from directly experiencing the other person's reality. The present moment for each of us is wordless, yet full of meaning. In conflict, moreover, the search for meaning and ways of communicating what we have experienced inevitably force the listener to retreat from the deeper meanings that precede words. In Zen, this idea is central, and often conveyed simply, as in the phrase, "The sound of the rain needs no translation."

Social language is largely dependent on context to convey the meaning of words and sentences. As cultural anthropologist Edward T. Hall discovered, different languages require varying amounts of context to impart the correct meaning to words and expressions. For example, science and law require very little context to accurately interpret, whereas emotional, romantic and sexual communications require a great deal more, with identical words varying widely with small shifts in context. In this sense, we can think of the words used in conflict as inherently uncertain and "chaotic," since they are "sensitively dependent on initial conditions."

## CONTEXTUAL ELEMENTS IN COMMUNICATION

The adversarial context of conflict communications interferes profoundly with the usual ways we have of assessing meaning, generating an overarching distrust of ordinary meanings. The context of adversarial conflict actively generates a set of contrary meanings and negative interpretations, even for ordinary, conflict-free words like "hello."

Because of the presence of distrust, which is the first casualty in every conflict, nothing spoken by one side is likely to be accepted by the other side in terms of its ordinary meaning. Instead, meaning will be supplied, partly by subconscious association with memories gathered from past experiences with conflict, and with fear, anger, grief, guilt, jealousy, and similar emotions. These meanings will then become self-reinforcing, creating a cycle from which there is no obvious escape. Every word will be shuttled through the amygdala, which will detect a threat even when no overt action is being taken. Partly for this reason, mathematician Kurt Godel wrote, "The more I think about language, the more it amazes me that people ever understand each other."

Context, of course, includes everything that surrounds a communication, not just the environment in which it takes place, but the history, relationship, and culture of the people who are trying to communicate; the familial, organizational, social, economic and political systems in which they live; even their personal histories going back several generations, and the subtle chemistry and wiring of their brains.

More usefully for conflict resolution, we can describe a series of steps that can be taken by mediators to assess the impact of context on communication, and identify some of the elements that help to define it, including these:

- Express Meaning: In the absence of context, what is the literal meaning of the words that are being communicated?
- Intention: What does the speaker intend to communicate to the listener?
- Awareness: What level of awareness regarding the communication is present in the listener?
- Understanding: How much of what is being communicated does the listener actually understand?
- Acceptance: Which parts of the communication are acceptable to the listener and which are not?
- Medium/Process: How was the message communicated? What was the tone? What was the energy level? What was the body language?
- Systemic Context: What is the impact of the family, organizational, social, economic, and political context, the structures and systems in which the communication was made? What was the meaning of similar communications in the parties' experiences, back into their families of origin?
- Relationship: What is the relationship between the speaker and the listener? What is their history? What do they expect of each other? What are their assumptions? What are their unspoken needs and desires?
- Emotion: What is the emotional state of the parties and how has it influenced their speaking and listening, directly and indirectly?

- Culture: How have cultural norms and ideas influenced the communication, including definitions of what is appropriate or acceptable behavior, and even their ideas about time and space?

Context can also include the specialized languages that result from social divisions, including those between diverse groups and professions. Mikail Bakhtin, for example, described:

> ... the internal stratification of any single national language into social dialects, characteristic group behavior, professional jargons, generic languages, languages of generations and age groups, tendentious languages, languages of the authorities, of various circles and of passing fashions, languages that serve the specific sociopolitical purposes of the day, even of the hour (each day has its own slogan, its own vocabulary, its own emphases).

Each of these, of course, can be seen as generating conflicts through the proliferation of misunderstandings and contradictory messages. In addition, context includes the impact of non-verbal forms of communication, including the following:

## Some Forms of Non-Verbal Communication

| | |
|---|---|
| • Architecture and Space | • Context |
| • Setting | • Ambiance and Aesthetics |
| • Cultural Expectations | • Organization of Space |
| • Use of Time | • Distance and Orientation |
| • Seating and Separation | • Ownership and Territoriality |
| • Facial Expressions | • Eye Movements |
| • Gestures | • Posture |
| • Body Movements | • Energy and Presence |
| • Attitude | • Posture |
| • Balance | • Breathing |
| • Tone of Voice | • Loudness |

- Pitch
- Duration of Speaking
- Modulation
- Pronunciation
- Scent and Odor

- Pace and Rhythm of Speaking
- Quality of Voice
- Articulation
- Silence and Use of Questions
- Quality and Duration of Touch

All of these shape language, substitute for it, and assist us in interpreting ambiguous communications. We also interpret the meaning of communications, especially those involving conflict, by listening closely to inflection and tone of voice. Simply by altering where we place the emphasis in any simple communication we can completely alter its meaning, as in this example drawn from mathematician and science fiction writer Rudy Rucker:

### Subtle Variations in Communication

| | |
|---|---|
| I'm glad to see you. | (Even if no one else is.) |
| I'm glad to see you. | (What made you think I wouldn't be?) |
| I'm glad to see you. | (Instead of talking to you on the phone.) |
| I'm glad to see you. | (But not the shlub you came in with.) |
| I'm glad to see you. | (It's wonderful to be with you.) |
| I'm glad to see you. | (So stop asking me if I am.) |
| I'm ... glad-to-see-you. | (Are you glad to see me?) |
| I'm ... glad ... to ... see ... you. | (And I'm drunk, or I don't really mean it.) |
| I'm glad ... to see you. | (As an afterthought) |
| I'm glad-to-see you. | (Kiss me you fool!) |

## CONFLICT, CULTURE, AND LANGUAGE

Culture, we all recognize, has an enormous influence on the assignment of meaning in language. But what is culture, and how are conflict communications shaped by it? There are many definitions of culture, but for our purposes in mediation and conflict resolution, we can think of culture as a set of understanding that define:

- How we approach our environment;
- How we group and divide;
- How food is produced and consumed;
- How gender is perceived and displayed;
- The ways space and boundaries are established;
- How time is defined and used;
- How learning takes place;
- How and when people play and laugh;
- What people do when conflicts occur and when they do when their conflicts are not resolved;
- How goods are made, possessed, used, exchanged and distributed;
- Ways of perceiving and processing reality;
- Shared behaviors, beliefs, attitudes, customs or ways of life;
- How people satisfy their needs in a given environment;
- An accumulation of successful adaptations to each other and the environment;
- A way of differentiating ourselves from others;
- What everyone knows and nobody talks about;
- An agreed upon pattern of meanings found in symbols, events, sensations and behaviors.

From these examples, we can see that it is possible to for us to define all conflict as cross-cultural since it consists, for example, of differences between those who is always on time and someone who is routinely late, or someone with high status and someone with low status. Here are some cultural differences that can easily create chronic conflicts:

- Precision vs. ambiguity in communication;
- Open vs. closed about personal information;
- Verbal vs. written basis for traditions;
- High vs. low context in establishing meaning;
- Consensus vs. individualistic in decision making;
- Formal vs. informal in process;
- Hierarchical vs. collaborative in relationships;
- Direct vs. indirect in giving feedback;
- Authoritarian vs. democratic in organization;
- Deference vs. rebelliousness in relations to authority;

- Exclusive vs. inclusive with outsiders;
- Linear vs. non-linear emphasis in thinking;
- Gestalt vs. detail in orientation;
- Appropriateness vs. inappropriateness of in humor and play;
- Demonstrative vs. restrained in emotional expression;
- Permissive vs. directive in child rearing;
- Fixed vs. fluid attitudes toward time;
- Open vs. closed attitudes toward space;
- Individual vs. group orientation in norms and values;
- Interests vs. power or rights orientation in dispute resolution.

In the everyday, unspoken give-and-take of human relationships, "silent language" plays a vitally important role in setting cultural norms. Edward T. Hall analyzed some of the many ways that people "talk" to one another without using words. For example, he compared the pecking order in a chicken yard with the fierce competition in a school playground, showing how even unwitting gestures and actions contribute to the vocabulary of culture.

According to Hall, culturally defined concepts of space and time are ways of transmitting meaning through a kind of silent messaging that is common across species. Space, for example, is an outgrowth of the instinctive animalistic defense of the lair, reflected in human society by an office worker's defense of his cubicle, or residence in a guarded, gated community.

For the most part, conflict communications do not provide us with words that are adequate to convey these meanings, so we select words that can be twisted and reshaped to convey at least the essence of our underlying emotional experience, which is nearly always confusing to the listener. In *The Night Train to Lisbon*, novelist Pascal Mercier describes this confusion:

> Of the thousand experiences we have, we find language
> for one at most and even this one merely by chance and
> without the care it deserves. Buried under all the mute
> experiences are those unseen ones that give our life its
> form, its color, and its melody. Then, when we turn to
> these treasures, as archaeologists of the soul, we discover

how confusing they are. The object of contemplation refuses to stand still, the words bounce off the experience and in the end, pure contradictions stand on the paper. For a long time, I thought it was a defect, something to be overcome. Today I think it is different: that recognition of the confusion is the ideal path to understanding these intimate yet enigmatic experiences. That sounds strange, even bizarre, I know. But ever since I have seen the issue in this light, I have the feeling of being really awake and alive for the first time.

And again,

... not only do we reveal ourselves with words, we also betray ourselves. We give away a lot more than what we wanted to reveal, and sometimes it's the exact opposite. And the others can interpret our words as symptoms for something we ourselves do not even know. As symptoms of the sickness of being us. It can be amusing when we regard others like this, it can make us more tolerant, but also put ammunition in our hands. And the moment we start speaking, if we think that others are doing the very same thing with us, the word can stick in our throat and fear can make us mute forever.

Some "languages," such as those used in art, music and dance, seek to overcome this silence, muteness, and confusion, by conveying meaning through action, subconscious imagery, and direct personal experiences, without relying on words or sentences. We can then realize that all languages possess not only structure and ways of ascribing meaning but music and poetry as well. Focusing solely on the structure of a sentence, or strictly defining the meaning of words, stops the music and reduces the poetry to cant. We can see this quite easily in the language of love, but it is equally true in the language of conflict.

These deeper meanings and poetic resonances appear even in ordinary language and stretch back for millennia. Penelope Lively described it beautifully:

We open our mouths and out flow words whose ancestries we do not even know. We are walking lexicons. In a single sentence of idle chatter we preserve Latin, Anglo-Saxon, Norse; we carry a museum inside our heads, each day we commemorate peoples of whom we have never heard. More than that, we speak volumes—our language is the language of everything we have not read, Shakespeare and the Authorized Version surface in supermarkets, on buses, chatter on radio and television. I find this miraculous. I never cease to wonder at it. That words are more durable than anything, that they blow with the wind, hibernate and reawaken, shelter parasitic on the most unlikely hosts, survive and survive and survive.

If we want to preserve the music and poetry of conflict communications, it is necessary first for us to understand how conflict sentences are routinely structured, and how their syntax is shaped and distorted.

## THE STRUCTURE AND SYNTAX OF CONFLICT COMMUNICATIONS

The sentences we use in conflict are commonly structured as follows:

### PRONOUN + VERB + ACCUSATION (JUDGMENT)

These can be elaborated into:

### "THEY/HE OR SHE/YOU" + "DID/ARE" + "LAZY"

When we structure our conflict communications in these ways, they are more likely to produce the following primary "fight or flight" responses in the other party: denial, defense, and counter-attack. These can be expressed symbolically, omitting the verb for the moment, as:

**P (PRONOUN) + A (ACCUSATION) → [] (DENIAL), | (DEFENSE) and ⇥ (COUNTER-ATTACK)**

Or, more mathematically:

**P + A → [], |, ⇥**

A more accurate mathematical expression would include i, an imaginary number representing the square root of minus 1. This makes sense literally because conflicts can then be depicted as similar to complex numbers, with one part that is real and another that is imaginary. It also makes sense mathematically because imaginary operations can be diagrammed as circular rotations of 90 degrees around a central point. In this way, denial, defense, and counterattack can be seen as circular, moving from positive to negative and back again, and each complex point can be understood as having two distinct elements. We can therefore conclude:

$$P + A \to i \,([],\, |,\, \rightarrowtail) = C \text{ (CONFLICT)}$$

Or, using mathematical formalism:

$$P + A \to i \,(\,[],\, |,\, \rightarrowtail) = C$$

Each portion of these conflict communications contributes to misunderstanding and can be analyzed separately. The pronoun portion may seem minor, yet it is responsible for triggering the threat response and can be transformed by examining the form of communication and the likely outcome that will result from using each pronoun in connection with any problem or conflict. Thus:

# Pronouns and Conflict Resolution

| Pronoun | Form | Predictable Result |
| --- | --- | --- |
| *They* [Example: They are lazy and irresponsible.] | Stereotype | Prejudice |
| *You* [Example: You are lazy and irresponsible.] | Accusation | Counter-Accusation/ Denial |
| *He, She* [Example: He/She is lazy and irresponsible.] | Demonization/ Victimization | Blame and Shame/ Disempowerment |
| *It* [Example: There is a lot of work here – how shall we divide it so we can both pull our own weight?] | Objectification | Problem Solving |
| *I* [Example: I feel overworked and would like to take time off but won't let myself and am jealous when you do. / Could you give me a hand?] | Confession/ Request | Listening/ Responsiveness |
| *We* [Example: We haven't been clear about how to divide up the work. / What do you suggest we do?] | Partnership / Collaboration | Consensus / Ownership |

Clearly, shifting from accusatory to non-accusatory objective, subjective, or collaborative pronouns can have a beneficial, even transformative impact on conflict communications. Simply by using the first three pronouns, we send one or more of the following emotionally charged messages to the listener:

- Rejection: "Go away/Leave me alone/Back off!"
- Blaming: "It's your fault."
- Shaming: "You are bad/wrong/no good."
- Self-Defense: "Don't punish me, punish him/her."
- Pain: "You hurt my feelings."
- Fear: "I don't respect/like/love you."
- Sadness, Grief and Loss: "I wish it were different/miss you."
- Desire: "I want to have a better relationship with you."
- Confession: "Because of these responses I am emotionally vulnerable to your responses/behaviors and wish you could be different."
- Wish/Request: "Please stop/start acting differently."

Following the pronoun comes the verb, and while the verbal element in this model may seem innocuous, in many languages, verbs are used to represent processes or actions, while nouns are used to represent things or substance. However, every thing is a process, and every process is a thing. They are like quantum waves and particles that are dual and complementary to each other. The confusion that is created by separating them can easily result in a false assumption that they are different or even opposed to one another.

Verbs can also be used to describe action or being, as in "*you did*" as opposed to "*you are,*" which results in the formation of fixed judgments about someone by not separating who they are from what they have done, i.e., their personality or character from their actions or behaviors. In their classic text, *Getting to Yes*, Roger Fisher and William Ury recommend that mediators and negotiators "separate the person from the problem," so we can be "hard on the problem and soft on the person." Altering the verb portion of conflict communications helps to achieve this result, distinguishing personal judgments into descriptions of actions and behaviors.

The accusation portion of conflict communications can also be usefully broken down into three distinct components:

1. An indirect negative statement of interests
2. An indirect negative emotional communication
3. A deep-seated relational fear

Each of these can then be elaborated, defined, discussed directly, and reframed from negative to positive. As mediators, we can reframe positions as interests by asking "why" questions, or by, for example, turning "Don't do that" into "It would feel much more respectful to me it if you would ..."; or negative emotions as positive ones by turning "Stop yelling at me" into "I can see you care a lot about this issue, why is that?"; or addressing relational fears by asking "What kind of relationship would you like to have with me?"

Thus, ordinary conflict communications can be profoundly altered by mediators, or by the parties themselves, in at least the following seven ways:

1. Substituting It/I/or We as non-accusatory pronouns;
2. Converting judgments about people into descriptions of actions and behaviors, and being soft on people and hard on problems;
3. Turning accusations into interests plus emotions;
4. Surfacing underlying relational fears;
5. Presenting interests as requests;
6. Reframing from negative to positive emotions;
7. Converting statements into questions.

An example of the use of this conflict syntax analysis might be as follows. Starting from the initial statement:

**"THEY/HE OR SHE/YOU" + "ARE" + "LAZY"**

We can see that this accusation will typically result in the following responses:

- Denial: "I don't know what you're talking about."
- Defense: "No I'm not."
- Counter-Attack: "You're up-tight/a slave-driver/bossy!"

If we break the accusation portion of this conflict communication into its three distinct components, we can start to see several potential interventions:

1.  A Negative Statement of Interests: "I am working hard and need some help."
2.  A Negative Emotional Communication: "I'm sad/angry/frustrated that you don't care about my needs."
3.  A Deep-Seated Relational Fear: "You don't respect/like/love me."

The parties can then transform their conflict communications, purely at the level of syntax and choice of language, in the following six ways:

1.  Substitute It/I/We As the pronoun: "The work isn't divided fairly." "I wish I could take more time off." "We need to agree on a fair division of the work. What would work for you?"
2.  Convert judgments about people into descriptions of actions and behaviors, be soft on people and hard on problems: "I feel sad and angry when you don't help out when I ask."
3.  Turn accusations into interests plus emotions: "I need help." And: "I'm getting upset because I asked you for help, and you didn't respond."
4.  Present interests as requests: "Can you give me a hand?"
5.  Reframe from negative to positive emotional phrases: "I want to work with you and want both of us to feel supported."
6.  Surface the underlying relational fears: "When you don't help, I think it means you don't respect/care about/love me." "Is that true?" "What kind of relationship would you like to have with me?"
7.  Convert statements into questions: "Why didn't you help out when I asked?" "How would you like me to ask you in the future?"

## "YOU ALWAYS ..." "YOU NEVER ..."

Another example of the structure and impact of conflict communications can be found in the frequent use of the phrases, "You always ..." and "You never ..." Not only will the typical response be one of defense, denial, and counter-attack, but the communication will also be distorted by the amalgamation of two entirely different communications into one. The two communications are: "You are doing this too often/not enough for me," together with a negative emotional communication: "I am getting frustrated and angry because I've asked for this before, and I am starting to think you don't respect/care about/love me."

It is common in conflict communications for there to be an internal contradiction between two profoundly different statements that have been combined into a single merged statement, giving rise to multiple misunderstandings and miscommunications. The problem, however, runs even deeper, as we can see that simply by using these phrases, we predictably:

- Camouflage our requests as statements of fact;
- Exaggerate the truth;
- Stereotype the other person as unreasonable;
- Not take responsibility for communicating our needs;
- Ignore others' needs, explanations, or reasons for acting in their own self-interest;
- Fail to accurately describe what we really want from others;
- Miss opportunities to become vulnerable and invite others into more intimate conversation and relationship;
- Suggest that it is not acceptable to express deeper emotions directly;
- Infuse frustration and disappointment into the conversation;
- Convert desire into anger and hurt feelings into annoyance;
- Miss opportunities to collaboratively negotiate the satisfaction of mutual needs and diverse interests;
- Create a source of chronic conflict within our relationship.

We can also see that this analysis and the identification of these likely outcomes allows us to transform these conflict phrases by finding alternative ways of expressing the truths they conceal.

## HOW WE COMMUNICATE IN CONFLICT

When we are in conflict, we use an immense variety of adversarial expressions like "you always" and "you never" in order to express how we feel and what we want. These expressions are often highly satisfying in the short-term because they offer us an emotional release, but in the long-term produce only misunderstanding and an unending cycle of adversarial conflict communications. For example, here are some common ways we communicate in conflict, together with sample phrases:

- Judgmentally: *"You are a ... "*
- Moralistically: *"You should ..."*
- Insultingly: *"If you weren't so ..."*
- Disrespectfully: *"Who cares what you think."*
- Negatively: *"You don't understand a thing."*
- Demandingly: *"I insist that you ..."*
- Threateningly: *"If you don't..."*
- Adversarially: *"You are totally wrong."*
- Competitively: *"That's my ..."*
- One-Sidedly: *"The truth is ..."*
- Hierarchically: *"Because I said so, that's why."*
- Comparatively: *"I am much more ... than you are."*
- Absolutely: *"You always/never ..."*
- Humiliatingly: *"You don't get it, do you?"*
- Victimizingly: *"He did it to me."*
- Fatalistically: *"She's never going to change."*

From these phrases we can recognize a number of ways we can get stuck in conflicts, and why conflict communications turn in a circle, rather than spiraling upward into resolution. Beneath these phrases lies an idea that we are right, together with a number of feelings associated with pain and loss that turn what otherwise might be considered neutral or positive attributes into malevolent ones. For example, people in conflict often describe their opponents using words in column one below, but could as easily describe the same behaviors using similar words in column two:

## Which Description is More Accurate?

| | |
|---|---|
| Lazy | Relaxed |
| Micro-Managing | Detailed |
| Gossiping | Discussing |
| Yelling | Concerned |
| Conspiring | Planning |
| Bad Mouthing | Critiquing |
| Angry | Upset |
| Evil | Harmful |
| Two-timing | Playing the field |
| Egotistical | High self-esteem |

Here is another example, drawn from a mediation I conducted in which one group presented its grievances. After they presented, I wrote next to each complaint a different version presented below in italics, then asked them which of these two statements was true. Their answer, of course, was "they both are."

- "They don't understand." Or: "We haven't explained it to them."
- "They are angry and out to get us." Or: "We have not been listening to their complaints or responding well."
- "They won't change." Or: "We haven't explained clearly enough why change is necessary."
- "They don't respond to our requests on time." Or: "We don't follow up to make sure they understand our requests and are able to respond on time."

My object was to demonstrate that conflict is a relationship, and that the language of demonization and victimization can be reversed by each side describing the problem in a way that accepts responsibility for whatever is not working in their relationship. Beneath their selection of language to describe their conflict was an assumption that they were in a power contest with an opponent who is solely responsible for creating and fixing the problem. A different calculation occurs when we move from the language of power to that of rights, to that of interests where responsibility for the problem and its solution are shared.

## POWER, RIGHTS, AND INTERESTS IN LANGUAGE

It is common in conflict resolution analysis to distinguish three methods of resolving disputes. First, there are methods that are based on power, which use war, violence, and duress to resolve disputes. Power-based methods produce winners and losers, destroy important relationships, and encourage corruption in those who use it, and blind obedience, resistance, and revolt in those it is used against.

Second, as a result of these difficulties, there are methods based on rights, which use legislation, litigation, adversarial negotiation, bureaucratic coercion, rules and regulations, contractual agreements, and policies and procedures to resolve disputes. Rights-based methods also generate winners and losers, undermine relationships, and encourage corruption, but less so than power-based solutions. Uniquely, right-based methods give rise to bureaucracies that are needed to interpret and define competing rights.

Third, there are methods based on interests, which use informal problem solving, facilitation, open dialogue, collaborative negotiation, and mediation to resolve disputes. Interests reflect not merely what people want, but the reasons why they want it. Interest-based processes therefore do not require winners and losers, support relationships, and discourage corruption. As a result, they are able to prevent, resolve, transform, and transcend conflicts at their chronic sources; support collaborative, democratic relationships; and encourage peaceful systemic change.

Power-based processes rely on hierarchy, operate by command, and result in obedience; rights-based processes rely on bureaucracy, operate by control, and result in compliance. Power-based approaches encourage domination, resulting in personal arrogance, elitism, and contempt. Rights-based approaches encourage alienation, resulting in personal cynicism, apathy, and uncaring. Neither method seeks to prevent or transcend chronic conflicts, or dismantle them at their systemic source.

Interests, on the other hand, invite people to communicate at a deeper level, learn from each other, and work jointly and collaboratively to solve problems. They encourage parties to redesign the dysfunctional power- and rights-based systems and structures that continue to cause, aggravate, and sustain disputes. For these reasons, they invite deeper levels of resolution and support more complex, collaborative interactions, democratic relationships, and a deeper sense of community.

While these methods and processes are widely recognized within the dispute resolution community, they have not been seen as being supported by entirely different kinds of language. Yet it is clear that there is a distinct language of power, a language of rights, and a language of interests, as illustrated below.

## 1. The Language of Power

The language favored by power-based organizations such as the military, police, and monarchical states requires clarity, simplicity, and uniform interpretation in order to encourage unthinking obedience. The communications that emanate from these institutions therefore take the form of declarations, pronouncements, and orders, which reinforce hierarchy and command, and imply punishment and contempt for those who disobey.

## 2. The Language of Rights

The language favored by rights-based organizations such as legal institutions, bureaucracies, and formally democratic states, requires narrow distinctions, exceptions, and adjudicated interpretations in order to maintain control by permitting some behaviors and forbidding others. The communications that emanate from these institutions take the form of rules and regulations, policies and procedures, legislative definitions, and legal interpretations, which reinforce bureaucracy and control and imply coercion and censure for those who do not fit in.

## 3. The Language of Interests

The language favored by interest-based organizations such as teams, civil society, and radically democratic states, requires affirmation of diversity, dissent, and dialogue in order to encourage collaboration and participation. The communications that emanate from these institutions take the form of open-ended questions, public dialogues, value-driven rules, and consensus decision making, all of which reinforce social equality, economic equity, and political democracy.

Here are some trivial examples, translated into the language used in many families, relationships and organizations:

| | |
|---|---|
| Power: | "You must ... " "You shall ..." "You will ..." "... or else." "Because I said so, that's why." |
| Rights: | "You should ..." "You ought to ..." "You need to ..." "You have a right to ..." "You are entitled to ..." |
| Interests: | "You could ..." "You might consider ..." "What would happen if you ..." "What would you like to have happen?" "Why" "What do you think will happen if you ..." |

Here is a somewhat longer list of commonly used power and rights-based phrases that easily result in miscommunication, for example:

# Phrases for Miscommunication

| | |
|---|---|
| Ordering: | "You must... "You have to... "You will..." |
| Threatening: | "If you don't, then... "You'd better or else..." |
| Preaching: | "You should... "You ought... "It's your duty..." |
| Lecturing: | "Here is why you're wrong... "Do you realize..." |
| Giving Answers: | "What I would do is... "It would be best if you..." |
| Judging: | "You are argumentative... lazy... "You'll never change." |
| Excusing: | "It's not so bad... "Don't worry about it..." |
| Diagnosing: | "You're just trying to get attention... "What you need is..." |
| Prying: | "When? How? What? Where? Who? |
| Labeling: | "You're being unrealistic... emotional... angry..." |
| Manipulating: | "Don't you think you should..." |
| Egoizing: | "That's nothing. Here's what happened to me..." |

Here, on the other hand, are a few interest-based phrases that are often used in mediation to encourage open and effective conflict communications:

# Phrases to Encourage Listening

| | |
|---|---|
| Encouraging: | "Can you tell me more?" |
| Clarifying: | "When did this happen?" |
| Summarizing: | "Let me see if I understand what you just said ..." |
| Acknowledging: | "It sounds like you are really angry about that." |
| Open Questioning: | "Why? "What would you like to see happen?" |
| Responding: | "I see it this way ... How do you see it?" |
| Soliciting: | "I would like your advice about how we can resolve this." |
| Empathizing: | "How would you feel if it were you?" |
| Normalizing: | "I'm sure a lot of people would feel the way you do..." |
| Appreciating: | "I can appreciate why you feel that way." |
| Reframing: | "Do you feel _____when s/he_____." |
| Validating: | "I think I can understand now why you feel that way." |

The distinction between power, rights, and interests extends far deeper than mere words or phrases, and can also be found embedded in the narrative structure of the stories people tell about their conflict experiences, discussed in chapter two. To begin to understanding how conflict communications extend from individual words and sentences to entire stories, we need to first consider how they take the form of myths, archetypes, and metaphors, and how these forms of communication impact our ability to transform the language of conflict into a language of resolution.

## MYTH, ARCHETYPE, AND METAPHOR

Myths are the first stage in the metamorphosis of conflict feelings and experiences into mediative language. A myth can be thought of as a story about the past, or as a fable or fairy tale that attempts to communicate, without regard for factual accuracy, the *emotional meaning* of a significant experience. And when faced with a choice between factual accuracy and emotional accuracy in choosing words to describe our conflicts to others, we opt for emotional accuracy every time.

Myths are proto-stories, allegories, rituals, explanations, and sacred narratives, defined by University of Chicago Professor Bruce Lincoln as "ideology in narrative form." Otto Rank pioneered the psychoanalytic approach to myth and preceded Joseph Campbell in exploring the myth of the birth of the hero. Both explored deep psychic processes and spiritual yearnings in describing the ways that myths are fashioned out of conflict. Campbell believed there were four functions of myth:

1. The Metaphysical Function: Awakening a sense of awe before the mystery of being;
2. The Cosmological Function: Explaining the shape of the universe;
3. The Sociological Function: Validate and support the existing social order;
4. The Pedagogical Function: Guide the individual through the stages of life.

We can see that each of these can play a significant role in conflict resolution. If we consider conflict communications as myths, we can identify awe at the mystery of what happened in the dispute, efforts to explain why it occurred, attempts to validate and support the storytellers' experience, and ways of guiding the individual through the stages of conflict to resolution.

A somewhat different and more directly applicable approach to myth was adopted by structural anthropologist Claude Levi-Strauss, who found by studying myths in diverse, widely separated cultures, what he believed to be a universal principle: that "mythical thought always progresses from the awareness of oppositions toward their resolution." In his view, myths consist of two parts:

- Elements that oppose or contradict each other
- Elements that "mediate" or resolve these conflicts and contradictions

He cited, for example, the role of the "trickster," or raven or coyote in many indigenous myths, who served as a mediator by both embodying the conflict and reconciling the conflicting opposites, for example of life and death, agriculture and hunting, and similar forces. The idea that the mediator both embodies or internalizes and empathizes deeply with the conflict, and at the same time integrates, synthesizes and reconciles its opposite perspectives is quite accurate as a description of mediation practice, as is the expression of this duality in the transformation of conflict communications and stories.

## ARCHETYPES AND CONFLICT

Myths are closely related to archetypes, which represent recurring patterns, symbols, forms, and prototypes in human consciousness. Archetypes may signify events like birth, marriage, and death; or denote figures like mother, father, devil, and hero; or suggest motifs like creation and destruction. Carl Jung wrote, in The Archetypes and the Collective Unconscious,

> ... archetypes are not determined as regards their content, but only as regards their form and then only to a limited degree. A primordial image is determined as to its content only when it has become conscious and is therefore filled out with the material of conscious experience. Its form, however, ... might perhaps be compared to the

axial system of a crystal, which, as it were, pre-forms
the crystalline structure in the mother liquid, although
it has no material existence of its own ... The archetype
in itself is empty and purely formal, nothing but a ...
possibility of representation, which is given a priori. The
representations themselves are not inherited, only the
forms, and in that respect they correspond in every way
to the instincts, which are also determined in form only.
The existence of the instincts can no more be proven that
the existence of the archetypes, so long as they do not
manifest themselves concretely.

There have been many interesting applications and useful critiques
of Jungian archetypes, and each of these can be reformulated, extended
and adapted to conflict communications, helping us to define the patterns
and prototypes people adopt in describing their adversaries, allies, and
themselves. Over the course of several thousand mediations, patterns
slowly emerge in the ways we hear parties describe each other, and the
behaviors they find troublesome when they are in conflict.

Consider, for example, the archetypes and subconscious meanings
associated with the words "husband," "wife," and "marriage." Contained
within these words are a huge array of un-communicated images and
symbols, expectations and assumptions, myths and stories, any one of
which can trigger chronic conflicts within the relationship. The same can
be said of the words "family," "father," "mother," "daughter," and "son."

Thus, in couple and family conflicts, it is commonplace for one person
to accuse another of any number of sins against the relationship: one person
may, for example, be accused of being "bossy," while the other person is
accused of being "irresponsible." What is useful about every accusation in
conflict communications is that it simultaneously conceals and reveals a
deeper truth. In this case, the one who accuses the other of being "bossy"
conceals a deep feeling of being excluded, discounted, and disrespected,
yet reveals the presence of an archetype, expectation, or image of how the
other person ought to have behaved. Their expectation, image or desire
may be, for example, for the other person to act like a benevolent parent or
leader, rather than a dictator, and find out what the accuser wants before

making a decision. These expectations drive and inform the dispute, yet are only rarely communicated directly to the other person, and often exist only at a subconscious level.

By identifying the archetypes in conflict communications and bringing them to the surface, we allow them to be communicated and discussed openly and honestly, then they can be negotiated, modified and agreed to, then acted upon in the future in ways that encourage the parties not merely to resolve their disputes, but to transform and transcend them.

## METAPHORS AND CONFLICT

Metaphors are comparisons or connections that reach deep into the subconscious mind and contribute to the attribution of meaning in conflict communications. Much ordinary subject matter, from the most mundane to the most abstruse, can only be understood by means of metaphor. As George Lakoff wrote, in "The Contemporary Theory of Metaphor," they are the main mechanisms through which we comprehend abstract concepts and perform abstract reasoning.

Metaphors allow us to map and transition, as functions do in mathematics, from one idea, feeling, experience, or conceptual domain to another. They create a link, resonance or correspondence between a "source domain" and a "target domain," and connect both concepts and images. Metaphors are formed, for the most part, below the level of conscious attention, and mapped unconsciously. These mappings include interference patterns and culturally specific assumptions and experiences, although it is thought that some metaphors may be universal.

The reasons people cite for their conflicts are justified in terms of facts and logic, yet their experience of conflict is largely subconscious and highly emotional. And rather than participate in direct emotional communications with people they no longer trust, they transmit their feelings indirectly through the language they use to describe facts or express themselves logically.

For this reason, the language of conflict is highly charged, distorted, and full of allusion, metaphor and symbolism. For example, consider the following frequently cited example of commonly recognized metaphors for conflict:

## 1. Conflict as War

- "Your position is indefensible."
- "I shot down that idea."
- "We've got a battle on our hands."
- "She dropped a bomb on me."
- "He won't negotiate."
- "I won."
- "My enemy ..."
- "We blew him out of the water."

## 2. Conflict as Opportunity

- "This presents us with a real challenge."
- "Your feedback has given me some ways to improve."
- "We now have a chance to make things better."
- "What are all the possibilities for solving this problem?"
- "Let's work together to find a solution."
- "What could we learn from what happened?"
- "Let's find a solution that works for both of us."

## 3. Conflict as Journey

- "Your idea points to a solution."
- "This isn't getting us anywhere."
- "Where do you want to go with that?"
- "Let's do it together."
- "I think we've arrived at an agreement!"
- "Let's search for common ground"
- "Now we are getting somewhere."
- "What if we ... ?"
- "Let's try to find a way out of this."

In mediation, it is possible to introduce positive metaphors to replace negative ones, and thereby "nudge" the parties in the direction of engagement and collaboration, for example, by substituting "journey" metaphors for adversarial, war-like ones. Or if someone says they feel "trapped," we can ask if they would like to "open" the issue for "free" discussion and "expand" their "options" and "choices." In neurophysiology, this is known as "priming," which is explored in more detail in chapter three.

# MONEY AS METAPHOR

It is common in mediation, especially in litigated cases, for people to dismiss or devalue interest-based approaches by saying that conflicts don't require a great deal of interpretation, and in the end, "It's only about the money." But what is the meaning of money? Clearly, money is a powerful metaphor, with multiple meanings, each of which reveals a different set of ideas and interests. Money may, for example, be understood, defined, or experienced in at least the following metaphoric ways:

- As fixed, a repository of value, and a means of exchange. Thus, as a means of purchase and sale—but the purchase and sale of what? And why is that important to you?
- As transitory, a source of fluctuation, and a means of circulation. Thus, money as a breakdown of barriers, but which barriers would you like to move beyond and why?
- As a universal equivalent, equal to everything—thus, as a universal metaphor, but what would you want to spend it on?
- As filth lucre, a Freudian symbol for excrement, a source of corruption, greed, and craven, selfish behavior, but why is that behavior abhorrent to you?
- As a sexual object, an aphrodisiac, a symbol of potency and pleasure, but what pleasures can't you experience without it, and how will money help?
- As a source of status and power, but why are these important to you, what would you do specifically if you had them?
- As freedom, and the ability to realize one's dreams, but what would you do with your freedom, and what are your dreams?
- As a means of devastation, exploitation, and oppression, but what is the deeper means, and what would you do instead?
- As the reason for victory or defeat, political gain and loss, hope and despair, but how might it be possible without money to bypass victory and defeat, gain and loss, and what do you want to be victorious about, what gain do you want and why?
- As a means of survival, self-actualization, identity, and self-esteem, but how would you like to develop yourself and who would you like to be?

On the surface, money offers the appearance of being a simple, inherently adversarial topic, yet more deeply can be seen to conceal a variety of interests. These can often be revealed by asking questions, like "What does the money *mean* to you?" Or: "If a final resolution of the money issue is not entirely satisfactory to you, what would you want in exchange, in order to settle this dispute?" Or: "What does money represent or stand for in this conflict?" The list of possible metaphors for money is endless, and each one leads to a deeper, interest-based conversation that can transform conflicts over its allocation into collaborative negotiations and mediations, rather than into aggressive, adversarial battles for power and adjudication of rights. Yet, as Boris Groys wrote:

> Language is more universal and more democratic than money. It is, moreover, a more effective medium than money, for more can be said than can be bought and sold. But above all, the linguistification of social power relations gives to every individual human the possibility of contradicting power, fate and life – of criticizing them, accusing them, cursing them. Language is the medium of equality. When power becomes linguistic, it is compelled to operate under the conditions of the equality of all speakers—whether it wishes to or not.

In these ways, we can see that language, including not only grammar and syntax, but also myth, archetype, and metaphor, are essential elements in revealing the deeper meaning of the conflict to the parties. At the same time, as Mark Twain wrote, "Kindness is a language which the deaf can hear and the blind can see." It is therefore our *intention* that matters in conflict communications, sometimes more than our choice of words. A clear example can be found in the language of politics, which is both grounded in and distorted by conflict.

## POLITICS, CONFLICT, AND LANGUAGE

The deterioration, degradation and devaluation of language mark the closure of communication, reasoning and negotiation, and the transition to impasse, violence and war. As Margaret Atwood wrote, "War is what happens when language fails." The silencing of others, the inability to speak, and the conversion of civil conversation into insults and provocations is always a precursor to acts of violence. The return of speech, of dialogue and conversation, is therefore a way of returning to the difficult task of reconciling our differences.

Still, there is always a danger that the words we speak will be distorted, that they will lose in translation the real origins and essence of what we felt and experienced, along with the "trace minerals" and micro-features the listener needs in order to understand their exact meaning. For this reason, we often end up misunderstanding or missing the point, yelling and insulting each other, debating superficial issues, and ignoring the substratum of deeper meanings that precede language and alone can explain the intensity and character of complex conflict feelings. And, as George Orwell observed, "... if thought corrupts language, language can also corrupt thought." Novelist Octavio Paz brilliantly described how this happens:

> When a society decays, it is language that is first to become gangrenous.... Although moralists are scandalized by the fortunes amassed by the revolutionaries [in Mexico under the ruling party], they have failed to observe that this material flowering has a verbal parallel; oratory has become the favorite literary genre of the prosperous... and alongside oratory, with its plastic flowers, there is the barbarous syntax in many of our newspapers, the foolishness of language on loudspeakers and the radio, the loathsome vulgarities of advertising—all that asphyxiating rhetoric.

In response, it is necessary for conflicted parties to find or create an equivalent, commensurate, and common language, in which their isolated, complex, paradoxical, and individual meanings can become known, resonate, and influence each other, and to infuse their language, particularly political language, with complexity, honesty, humility, subtlety and meaning.

It is therefore useful to consider the ways we simultaneously express, disguise and reveal our conflicts through political language, together with the methods mediators and conflict resolvers can use to identify linguistic strategies, interventions and techniques that can assist conflicting parties in coming to consensus, or to resolution, including forgiveness and reconciliation. Doing so requires us to develop mediated, interest-based forms of language, not only for interpersonal disputes, but political disputes as well, since they have an impact on our "culture of conflict," and therefore on all of our communications, even the most trivial.

## FASCISM AND LANGUAGE

Victor Klemperer noted that the distortion of language by the Nazis was vital in creating fascist culture. He was repeatedly perplexed by how the masses, even those who opposed the Nazis, willingly ingested the linguistic poison the Nazis used to perpetuate collective self-delusion. "Words may be little doses of arsenic," he wrote. "They are consumed without being noticed; they seem at first to have no effect, but after a while, indeed, the effect is there."

There are, for example, generalizations that diffuse responsibility, as in President Nixon's memorable phrase, "mistakes were made," without mentioning what these mistakes were, who made them, or how they might be corrected. There are generalized emotional statements that lack specificity, as in "I'm mad as hell and I'm not going to take it any more." There is the attribution or assignment of blame to everyone, or to consumers or "the media" or "the public," as in "we are all at fault," allowing those who were responsible to hide and disappear. There are broad statements that are so abstract and meaningless they are impossible to oppose. Indeed, there is such a vast universe of diversions, disavowals, smokescreens and "plausible deniability" used by politicians and corporate executives that creating them has become an industry. For more on language and fascism, see chapter seven in my book, *Conflict Revolution: Mediating Evil, War, Injustice, and Terrorism*.

In these ways, language can become a tool of domination that reinforces prejudice and inequality, whether by distinguishing people through their accents and patterns of speech, or by jargon, as in corporate phrases, like "be a team player" (which means "be quiet and go along with the program"), or "accountability" (which is often intended to instill a fear of being found at fault and fired).

Perhaps worse from a mediation perspective, because mediators slip into it themselves, is the language of neutrality, which erases subjectivity, creates emotional distance, and most interestingly, as Semiologist Roland Barthes wrote, undermines "the paradigmatic, oppositional structure of meaning, [and] aims at the suspension of the conflictual basis of discourse."

Instead, we have political parties that use language to describe themselves, including their values and beliefs, if not neutrally, than absurdly as being on both sides of every major political divide. As Maurice Glassman, a senior analyst of the British Labor Party, wrote tongue-in-cheek regarding what he referred to as the "politics of paradox,"

> Labour is robustly national and international, conservative and reforming, Christian and secular, republican and monarchical, democratic and elitist, radical and traditional, and it is most transformative and effective when it defies the status quo in the name of ancient as well as modern values.

The problem with political language, as the French syndicalist George Sorel pointed out, is not that it is too messy, but that it is too neat, because it reduces politics, with all its complexity and subtlety, to winning elections. This ultimately requires political movements to sacrifice principles for the sake of expediency. It divides political leadership into two camps: one that seeks change and another that seeks power. Successful politicians are therefore required both to commit themselves personally to political values and ideals in their public speeches, while at the same time undermining and discarding them for the sake of personal gain.

In the US, political language combined with expensive campaigns results in the selection of wealthy candidates who claim to represent the poor and middle classes. This encourages vast amounts of information to circulate regarding political issues, yet simplifies the language that information is expressed in and removes whatever lies at the edges, both on the left and the right. Political debates between candidates define the issues in ways that create a "middle" ground that panders to the sentiments of the largest block of voters, rather than engaging honestly with them about complex issues.

As a result, chronic conflicts are encouraged, not just in the political realm, but more broadly as a result of the inability of political leadership to solve difficult or contentious social problems. In these ways we can see that the language of conflict has profound consequences that impact all of us. "Neutral" language becomes a cover for simply playing it safe and hiding from the consequences of what we do.

Yet our work as mediators and dialogue facilitators *implicitly* invites a shift from bureaucratic conformity and reflexive passivity to more creative, strategic and proactive approaches to conflict resolution, by encouraging people to examine their conflict language in order to reveal its deeper meanings.

# CHAPTER 2

# THE NARRATIVE STRUCTURE OF CONFLICT STORIES

*Stories matter. People die of pernicious stories, are reinvented by new stories, and make stories to shelter themselves. Though we learned from postmodernism that a story is only a construct, so is a house, and a story can be as important as shelter: the story that you have certain inalienable rights and immeasurable value, the story that there is an alternative to violence and competition, the story that women are human beings. Sometimes people find the stories that save their lives in books. The stories we live by are themselves like characters in books: Some will outlive us; some will betray us; some will bring us joy; some will lead us to places we could never have imagined.*

~ Rebecca Solnit ~

**M**YTHS, ARCHETYPES, AND METAPHORS can be identified easily in the individual words and sentences people use in their conflict communications, especially those they use to describe their opponents. Mostly, however, they emerge in the stories people tell about what happened to them, and their descriptions of what it felt like.

In conflict stories, it is possible for us to discover the deeper meaning, not only of words, phrases and sentences, or of myths, archetypes and metaphors, but also of the stories themselves. By analyzing their stories, we gain insight into what the conflict means emotionally and subconsciously to each person, revealing transformational interventions and pathways to resolution.

The most important element in conflict stories is their emotional significance to the storyteller. As Ludwig Wittgenstein wrote, "Each word strikes an emotional key," and nowhere is this more true than in conflict stories, where not only do tone of voice and body language and verbal choices express deep underlying emotions, so also does the narrative structure of the story itself.

What are conflict stories? From the point of view of people in conflict, stories are efforts to mend the fabric of their perceived reality, to create a consistent version of different, even contradictory events and information. When significant conflicts occur in our lives, we create stories to encompass them, stories that define and limit the chaos of what we think is possible, both for ourselves and for others.

The subconscious mind does not distinguish between what is vividly imagined and what is real, between metaphor and description, between what is objectively verifiable and what is intensely perceived, either as wish or as fear. We continually manufacture and process our realities as stories that we tell both to ourselves and to others, in order to make the world consistent with our attitudes, feelings, expectations, wishes, beliefs, and actions. We "create" the world in our self-image through stories.

Conflict stories begin with an event, an objective act someone engaged in, which is then filtered through a mode of sensory perception, molded by culture, distorted by negative and positive emotions, matched with pre-existing ideas, made consistent with self-image, and censored by personal paradigms to such an extent that it becomes unrecognizable to the other party to the conflict. The conflict is thereby differentiated and polarized, as it is reconstructed in the image of each of its participants and their antagonistic relationship, gradually taking the place of whatever facts may have actually led to the original dispute.

In addition to the "text" of a conflict story, there is also a "sub-text." Beyond its meaning, there is a "meta" meaning, a symbolic, emotionally laden message that is also communicated, often through intonation and facial expression, but also by the story itself. The subtext of the story needs to be examined, for the following reasons:

- The most important part of conflict communications is not what is said but what is meant.
- Most meanings are ambiguous, uncertain, over-determined, non-linear, and susceptible to more than one interpretation. Therefore, the same communication may have different, even opposite meanings to different people.
- The greater the ambiguity in the communication, the greater the potential gap between the speakers' meaning and the meaning attributed by the listener.
- Metaphors, symbols, myths, parables, and rituals that are often hidden or disguised and organized beneath the level of conscious thought, invest ambiguity with meaning.
- All words have hidden emotional meanings that become more powerful the more emotional they are, and the less they are revealed.
- Meaning in conflict stories is communicated directly through words, and indirectly through body language, tone of voice, and facial expression, among others. Indirect forms of communication communicate meaning more accurately than the words that are used.

- Meaning is established by the intention (frequently emotional and unconscious) of the speaker, the receptivity and attitude (also emotional and unconscious) of the listener, and the larger context in which the communication takes place.
- The speaker, the listener, and the context therefore form a system that interacts with itself to create the meaning of conflict communications.

Mediators intuitively recognize that the stories told by people who are in the midst of conflict differ radically from those told by the same individuals after they have resolved their disputes. Conflict stories that are told while the conflict is raging reveal a number of important elements that become increasingly divergent as the seriousness of the dispute increases and the more often the story is told. These elements constitute what we can think of as the narrative structure of conflict stories in general, which include the following elements:

- The storyteller is a victim who is more acted upon than acting.
- The opponent is the creator, initiator, and cause of the conflict.
- Whatever the storyteller did is related as rational and just.
- Whatever their opponent did appears as irrational and unjust.
- The symbolic and metaphoric content of the story points to its real emotional meaning to the storyteller.
- The story that is told collapses and combines all other perceptions, possibilities and versions into one. It appears to exclude all other stories.
- All stories about conflict are metaphorically true.
- The conflict stories people tell create their lives. As they tell their story, it happens to them.
- Conflict stories are rituals designed to comfort the storyteller with their rationalizations, justifications, formulaic content, and familiarity.
- The more conflict stories are repeated, the more they are believed to be true. As Lewis Carroll put it: "I've said it once, I've said it twice, I've said it thrice—it must be true!"
- The central purposes of conflict stories are to maintain the self-image and self-esteem of the storyteller and to justify whatever harm has been or may be done to the opponent.

- Conflict stories merge emotionally charged symbols with action and events so that it is nearly impossible to separate them.
- Stories help fulfill wishes, expectations, desires, and dreams, or to explain why they failed to occur.
- Conflict stories are organized around a central unstated myth about the nature of one's opponent, which is nonetheless subconsciously perceived by the storyteller to be only partially true.
- Conflict stories link together perceived facts to favor the teller. Inconsistent facts, or those that favor the other side, are denied, dismissed, and disconnected from the story.
- Conflict stories reveal in their imagery and choice of language a set of emotional assumptions that have more to do with the storyteller, and the real basis for the conflict than with the opponent or the narrative itself.
- In most conflict stories, it is made apparent that nothing can be done to resolve the dispute because otherwise the listener might consider the storyteller responsible for some part of the conflict and withhold sympathy or support.
- Most of the stories we tell about ourselves are compensatory, revealing in their search for satisfaction the existence of a deep underlying need.
- Most of the stories we tell ourselves about others are relational, creating our opponents as opposites, in order to define ourselves by negation and an antagonistic relationship with them. If our enemy is evil, we must be good.
- Thus, even the stories we tell about others often end up being about ourselves, about what we admire in them because we lack in ourselves, or what we dislike in others because we reject it in ourselves, yet are simultaneously drawn to it.
- Stories nonetheless create listening and a powerful empathic bond with the listener, even when the listener is an opponent or an adversary.
- The purpose of all stories is to create a suitable ending, one that allows the parties to reach release, completion and

closure in their conflict. This purpose can often be found by reversing the most powerful metaphors or symbols contained in the story.

For most listeners, storytelling creates a feeling of participation in the event, a deep willingness to understand, and a feeling of empathy and community that can be accentuated in mediation by summarization and reframing, or by the mediator's use of parable, ritual, symbolism, metaphor, and ceremony to create a common, agreed-upon version that ends in resolution.

Mediators try to help parties tell their stories in such a way as not to exclude the other side's version, and to encourage listening and empathy as a way of bonding and connecting with the meaning of the story and its teller. Forgiveness can therefore be seen as the creation through listening, emotional completion, and a common understanding of what went wrong and how to fix it, of the classic fairy tale ending "and they all lived happily ever after."

Conflict resolution can then be seen as the successful creation of a composite, dyadic story made up of the essential elements in both parties versions of what happened while eliminating all the efforts to demonize the other party and victimize the storyteller. It can also be regarded as the opening of what was originally presented as a private narrative through an alternative, collective interpretation. In mediation, two stories are generally better than one, since by combining different perspectives an average or synthesis can emerge that is richer, more detailed, fairer, and more "true" than either of the individual stories standing alone.

Conflict stories reveal a natural self-regulating structure that initially minimizes or denies the possibility of any resolution of the underlying conflict, other than by the storyteller winning and the opponent losing. One purpose of conflict stories is to justify a particular outcome. Where evil exists, the use of force is justified; where arrogance, there needs to be a humiliation; where theft, some form of restitution. These might be referred to as implied "positional" elements that can be contrasted with "interest-based" conflict stories that center on what the storyteller really wants for herself and why.

Conflict stories are also fairy tales, in which the storyteller becomes a princess (victim) describing the actions of a dragon (perpetrator) to someone they hope will become their prince (rescuer). In the fairy tale, the princess is primarily responsible for expressing feelings and being emotionally vulnerable, the prince is responsible for coming up with solutions, and the dragon is responsible for directing attention toward problems that might otherwise be unnoticed.

In order to elicit sympathy and support from the listener, the storyteller must be seen as powerless in the face of evil. The action of every conflict story is therefore one of trading power for sympathy. Instead, the mediator offers empathy and empowerment and shows each person how they play all three roles. This means refusing to become a rescuer, asking the princess to accept responsibility for being part of the problem, helping the dragon become more open and vulnerable, and encouraging both to participate in solving the problem. Rainer Maria Rilke writes:

> How should we be able to forget those ancient myths that are at the beginning of all peoples, the myths about dragons that at the last moment turn into princesses; perhaps all the dragons of our lives are princesses who are only waiting to see us once beautiful and brave. Perhaps everything terrible is in its deepest being something helpless that wants help from us.

The two most common resolutions that are implied or suggested by the adversarial structure of conflict stories are:

1. Victory over one's external enemies, vanquishing one's foes, triumphing over evil, plus a *retributive* form of justice that punishes the evildoer;

2. Victory over oneself, vanquishing one's weaknesses and temptations, triumphing over our own selfishness, anger, and willingness to be taken advantage of, plus a *restorative* form of justice that returns the parties to a more equal, fair and non-adversarial relationship.

The location of the "enemy," the conflict, or the problem within the story, as either external or internal, is crucial in attempting to resolve the dispute. For the most part, we choose our opponents, at least by lacking the skill to be able to handle their behavior effectively. Through our stories, we participate in bringing them into existence, we perfect them, and we empower them, so that we can become what we could not become without them: victims, heroes, irresponsible, guilt-free, justified in acting the way we want, inflictors of pain, sufferers, powerful, powerless, etc.

There can also be a political element in certain forms of conflict storytelling. Stories told in justification of racial, sexual, religious, and other forms of intolerance or inequity create entire populations as enemies, mythologizing and sentimentalizing ancient hierarchical and dominating relationships, falsifying and stereotyping the "enemy within," using the anger and tension created by unresolved intra-social conflicts to justify the suppression of rights, and exploiting a fear of differences or of an historic enemy to promote conformity, consolidate power, and de-politicize public life. As Nazi leader Joseph Goebbels wrote,

> ... it's always a simple matter to drag the people along whether it's a democracy, a fascist dictatorship, or a parliament, or a communist dictatorship. Voice or no voice, the people can always be brought to the bidding of the leaders. That is easy. All you have to do is tell them they are being attacked, and denounce the pacifists for lack of patriotism, and exposing the country to greater danger.

Creation of the other-as-enemy, whether by governments or individuals, requires the active suppression of empathy, and therefore the subtraction of logic and rationality from negative, fear- and anger-inducing stories about an enemy's behavior. The reconstitution of empathy, or creation of the self-as-other and the other-as-self, is thus a political as well as a personal act, since it reduces the potential for demonization and domination in response to inequality and social divisions.

All conflict stories are, however, disguised, distorted, and inherently ambiguous. They are all political in the sense that they are about power, and apolitical in the sense that they are distant from action and efforts to constructively improve communication, dialogue and relationships. They are concerned with what has already taken place and are therefore historical, yet they also take place outside history and are therefore "a-historical." They are literal in the sense that their meanings can be found in what is said, and non-literal since their meanings also lie in what is implied, and in what is not said.

# ADAM, EVE, AND THE SNAKE: THE FIRST CONFLICT STORY

Let us take, as an example, a simple story of conflict, one that is viewed by many as the first conflict story. In Genesis, God asks: "Adam, has thou eaten of the fruit of the tree whereof I told thee thou shouldst not eat" To which Adam replies: "The woman you gave me, she tempted me, and I did eat." God then propounds the same question to Eve, who answers: "The serpent, he beguiled me."

One can imagine the dialogue they might have had afterwards and the things they might have said to each other, before the advent of mediation:

| | |
|---|---|
| Adam: | Why should I suffer? You're the one who's at fault, you and that damn snake. You tricked me. |
| Eve: | There you go again, blaming someone else. You chose, didn't you? I didn't force you to eat it. Besides, you never warned me about the snake. |
| Adam: | You're too impulsive, too gullible. |
| Eve: | You're in denial. You refuse to take responsibility for your own mistakes. |
| Adam: | My biggest mistake was listening to you. |
| Eve: | You can go to hell. |

The problem with each of these versions is that they accept (post-apple) that their behavior is either good or evil, yet it is plain that they were set up, that any Omniscient All-Seeing Creator *must* have known in advance that His only prohibition would be violated. Why else would there have been a tree of knowledge within the Garden, other than for its fruit to be ingested? Why create a being endowed with curiosity, other than to encourage discovery? Why forbid eating its fruit, other than to focus attention and temptation in its direction?

By this reading, it was not God, but Adam and Eve who expelled themselves from the garden, through recrimination and blaming. Perhaps if Adam had answered: "Yes, and it was delicious," all would have been different.

Adam even tries to shift the blame to God, as in "the woman you gave me." Alternatively, Adam (or Eve) might have taken responsibility for their actions and said: "It was my temptation; it was I who gave in; it was my choice." Yet with knowledge came ignorance, and with good and evil, amorality. Denial of responsibility and blaming others go hand in hand. An alternate story they might have agreed on could go as follows:

> God didn't warn either of us about the snake or about the desire He placed within us to taste forbidden fruit. There's no sense in blaming the snake, each other, God, or ourselves for what happened. Instead of focusing on the past and blaming someone else, we should concentrate on the future and how we can work together in harmony with the snake (i.e., Nature) to get what we want. We can't make God responsible for our actions, and we need to be responsible for ourselves. I apologize to you for trying to shift the blame onto you, and to myself for being dishonest and feeling guilty about something that was no one's fault. A little knowledge can be a dangerous thing, and the more I learn about good and evil, the less useful they become and the closer we get to Eden. Want another apple?

If we look beyond the text to the sub-text and the hidden meanings of this story, several strands emerge. First, there is an abundance of sexual imagery and ideation, from the snake to the forbidden fruit, to "temptation," and the clearly incestuous brother/sister, husband/wife relationship of Eve and Adam. Translated into sexual terms, the story might be told differently:

> Eve, unable to resist her attraction to the externalized symbol of Adam's sexuality (the snake) and beguiled by lust, tasted the forbidden fruit of incestuous desire, with which she tempted Adam, who also succumbed.

Alternately, the story can be read as a projection based on men's fear of women's sexuality:

> Adam, being unadventurous and frightened of the externalized symbol of Eve's sexuality (the apple) and caught up in patriarchal abstractions (good and evil) was

only able to discover his own capacity for sexual pleasure
by creating a division between good and bad women (the
virgin and the whore) and blaming her for his cupidity.

A third set of meanings might find the story symbolic of intellectual awakening, of discovery and knowledge. It is not so much good and evil themselves, but the distinction and opposition between them that symbolize other oppositions, as between objective and subjective, rich and poor, powerful and powerless, true and false. The state of Eden is thus representative of a unity that synthesizes these polar opposites in a prehistoric dialectic, a yin/yang symbol of the interpenetration of opposites.

A fourth set of meanings might focus on spiritual loss, on the severance of an intimate connection with our own god-like nature, or with nature in general. In considering the fruit of knowledge, emphasis might be placed on the word "knowledge," as distinct from "awareness," "understanding," or "wisdom," and on the loss of sensual awareness and mindfulness.

A fifth set of meanings might be drawn from the punishment meted out to Adam and Eve in their expulsion from paradise, as symbolizing the rise of rules and regulations, policies and procedures, and with them, rule-breaking and punishment. Expulsion from the garden and an Eden of cooperation and consensus can be seen as symbolizing the rise of a punitive and coercive state, which supplanted a more collaborative and communal civil society.

Each word in the story contains additional meanings that extend far beyond the literal text, and we could continue to add meanings for some time to those that have been mentioned without exhausting the possibilities. What mediation and conflict resolution offer as an aid to interpretation is a set of understandings about the alternative meanings of the story, including these five:

1.  All stories and interpretations are potentially and relatively true, though none is exclusively or absolutely true. In other words, there are degrees and varieties of truth and all metaphoric truths are relative to the observer.

2.  If the meaning is believed, that makes it true, to the extent that it is believed. Or rather, believing and truth are the same for the listener.

3. A deeper level of meaning is one that arises when we ask why the story is told. What are we trying to convince ourselves of by telling this story? Our own innate goodness? Our lack of self-control? Our suffering? Our innocence? Our guilt or "original sin"?

4. Another layer of meaning is derived by looking at who the story is told to. For example, if the Adam and Eve story is told by a parent to a child, or a religious leader to a congregation, the message is clear: "Obey the rules or you will be punished and lose my affection and protection."

5. As between any two stories, a synthesis can be created that is also true. For example:

| | |
|---|---|
| A's Version: | "You said we could go to the movies." |
| B's Version: | "No I didn't. I said you had to mow the lawn." |
| Synthesis: | A wants to go to the movies. B wants A to mow the lawn. A can first mow the lawn, then go to the movies with B. |

Notice that the synthesis does not answer the question of whether B actually said A could go to the movies. This is because proving the "truth" of this statement is instrumental, designed to achieve a particular outcome, and pointless, because A cares more about seeing the movie than about being factually correct. By eliciting the deeper meaning of A's story it becomes possible for A's interests to be satisfied without excluding B's. Notice also that the key elements in both stories survive the synthesis, and that a false dichotomy has been replaced by a unity of intention and action. A set of hidden false assumptions ("If I let A go to the movie the lawn won't get mowed."/"If I mow the lawn I won't be able to go to the movie.") has been revealed and resolved in the new, synthetic story.

In the synthesized story, the other side has been de-villainized and made legitimate and whole again, permitting the story to end with a "happily ever after." Any conflict story that refuses to admit elements of the other side's story contains a deeper story that may need to be processed first, before resolution can become possible.

For example, notice that the story implies an element of unequal power and responsibility in the relationship between A and B, and a set of potential sources of conflict that stem from this relationship, which may be an underlying or real cause of the dispute. A resolution that simply involves going to the movies may settle the presenting dispute without allowing the parties to surface and resolve what is actually bothering them. Thus:

> Deeper Synthesis:  A really wants acknowledgement and acceptance from B. B really wants A's help around the house and willingness to accept responsibility. B thanks A for pitching in and asks to go to the movies with her. A agrees that she should take more responsibility for household chores and volunteers to take on a job B has not assigned.

Thus, each different form of storytelling creates the listener as a different person; it elicits through sympathetic vibration, an empathetic discovery of what it must feel like to live the story. At the same time, the story encourages the listener to respond supportively, yet may also seek to manipulate, win over, or hypnotize the listener, or to defend itself against less flattering stories. Janet Rivkin and Sara Cobb have considered conflict stories from the perspective of plot, character, and themes, all of which are rehearsed and improved in their ability to achieve these goals based on the listener's response.

A central purpose of conflict stories is to enable the storyteller to construct a safe version of reality through causal connection, one that allows the storyteller to feel good about himself, or less anxious about the world, or permit him to function in a way he perceives as necessary. The listener may be active or passive, supportive or reflective, sympathetic or empathetic, involved or committed. Mediators are then able to listen to these as "access points," or places where meaning can be shifted.

Marriage can then be seen as two individual stories coming together to create a third that is told by both. If so, divorce can be seen as the surrender, even the death of a common story, a common plot, predictable characters, etc. The marriage story is itself an expression of togetherness, of connection, trust and belonging. It is the communication form assumed by the relationship. In divorce, each partner struggles to create their own individual story, but finds it impossible to convince or reach the other person by telling it.

## STORIES AS ACCUSATIONS, CONFESSIONS, AND REQUESTS

While most conflict stories are framed as accusations or assertions of facts or feelings, they can also be heard as confessions of vulnerability and concern, and as requests to the listener to do something different, if only by offering sympathy, alliance, or advice. The accusation that forms the core of the story is intended to:

- Draw the listener into a close, sympathetic relationship with the storyteller, and a distanced, antagonistic one with the opponent;
- Describe, rationalize, and reinforce the tensions that separate them;
- Counter-balance or equalize the perceived power of the opponent while justifying the storyteller in failing to communicate more effectively or work harder to resolve the dispute.

Conflict stories are also acknowledgments of feeling discouraged, cries for help, confessions of powerlessness, and requests for forgiveness. The cunning or depravity of the opponent is simply the flip side of the storyteller's own powerlessness, vulnerability, pain, sadness, and frustration. Because people feel powerless in their conflicts, they seek comforting explanations, justifications for their failure to do more, and rationalizations for their adversarial reactions. When they experience pain at the hands of others, they are drawn to ask what could possibly have motivated someone to harm them. If they want others to respect them as decent people who do not deserve this kind of treatment, they are further drawn to characterize their opponents as wicked, malicious people who intended harm for no good reason, and to explain why the storyteller could have done nothing to prevent or resolve it.

In these ways, conflict stories indirectly discourage their own resolution. They "dress up" the facts regarding upsetting events, yet by doing so they create signposts that draw us inward to the hidden sources of conflict *within the* storyteller. Each story directs the listener's attention outward toward what the perpetrator did, partly out of a desire to minimize or deny the storyteller's complicity, and partly out of fear of confrontation, or a wish to prevent future attacks through the deterrent of a well-timed counterattack. The perpetrator's perfidy is magnified in proportion to the storyteller's desire to appear innocent. In these ways, conflict stories "protest too much."

Mediation provides people in conflict with an opportunity for full and satisfying storytelling; for a deeper level of listening than would otherwise be possible in the midst of their conflict; for validating both stories and storytellers, for surfacing the sub-texts and hidden meanings, the myths, archetypes, and metaphors contained within the story; for reframing or retelling the story in ways that encourage listening; for expanding the range of possibilities contained within the story; for revealing the deeper interests of both parties; and for synthesizing and combining both stories so as not to exclude the essential elements of either, and end, if possible, with a version that allows each of them to live happily ever after.

The narrative structure of any *complete* conflict story includes its resolution, transformation, and transcendence. Our culture contains many stories of triumph over others, but fewer that point to collaboration and mutual gain. Our ideas of resolution and victory are more solitary than collective, more competitive than cooperative. Yet when we understand that the true struggle is within ourselves, and in our refusal to dehumanize our enemies, we are able to create new stories and a new understanding: that no one needs to lose when someone else triumphs, and a greater victory is achieved when it ends in no one's defeat.

Here are twenty ways mediators can transform conflict stories and turn them in the direction of resolution:

## 20 Ways of Transforming Conflict Stories

1. Summarize what is true and useful in each party's story, leaving out the portions that demonize or victimize the other party.
2. Ask each party to write their own story, then the other person's story, and then combine them.
3. Ask them to tell a story that is positive and acknowledging.
4. Ask them to change the pronoun in their story from he or she to I or we.
5. Ask each party to clarify the context in which their story occurred.
6. Offer a contrary, empowering interpretation, i.e., if the person

says, "I was frightened," you say, "You were brave." Or if they say "I am so angry," you say "You must care a lot."

7. Clarify expectations. Ask: "What did you want him to say?"
8. Identify the hidden judgments in the story.
9. Map the evolution of the conflict, identifying steps 1, 2, 3, etc.
10. Ask the parties to correct the conflict step by step.
11. Ask the parties to compare the cultural influences on their perceptions and responses to each others stories.
12. Contrast their stories with what they want to achieve, with their goals.
13. Ask them to jointly or separately investigate their factual assumptions.
14. Identify the gaps in their stories. Ask them what was left out?
15. Reveal their assumptions about causation and suggest a joint need to improve skills and responsibility for outcomes.
16. Identify the larger systems, processes and conditions that impact their story, i.e., the absence of peer mediation, gender inequalities, etc., and extend the mediation to include the field" in which the conflict took place.
17. Clarify the "ghost roles" including organizational policies and procedures, parents, people who are apathetic.
18. Clarify the *meaning* of the story to each party.
19. Separate facts from interpretations.
20. Create a third story without demonization or victimization.

Stories can encourage open and honest conflict communication and promote community. Their object is to bring people together through imagination and empathy. They are a device for learning and a means of play. They are also a bridge permitting forgiveness and reconciliation to cross the invisible lines we create to defend ourselves against those we chose to treat as enemies. With mediation and a better understanding of the dynamics of conflict storytelling, a myriad of seemingly endless stories of adversarial contest can be retold to include resolutions and a happy ending. And each of us can be one of the tellers. [For more on conflict stories, see Kenneth Cloke and Joan Goldsmith, *Resolving Personal and Organizational Conflicts: Stories of Transformation and Forgiveness*; and Kenneth Cloke, *The Crossroads of Conflict: A Journey into the Heart of Dispute Resolution*.]

# CHAPTER 3

# BUILDING BRIDGES BETWEEN PSYCHOLOGY AND CONFLICT RESOLUTION

## Implications for Mediator Learning

*A layman will no doubt find it hard to understand how pathological disorders of the body can be eliminated by 'mere' words. He will feel that he is being asked to believe in magic. And he will not be so very wrong, for the words that we use in our everyday speech are nothing other than watered-down magic.*

~ Sigmund Freud ~

*Everything that irritates us about others can lead us to an understanding of ourselves.*

~ C.G. Jung ~

*... By empathy, warmth, genuineness, congruence and an unconditional positive regard, one can establish a therapeutic relationship which is not only curative but also enables parties to resolve their own differences.*

~ Carl Rogers ~

**O**VER THE LAST THREE decades, hundreds of thousands of people around the world have been trained in community, divorce, family, commercial, organizational, and workplace mediation, as well as in allied conflict resolution skills such as collaborative negotiation, group facilitation, public dialogue, restorative justice, victim-offender mediation, ombudsmanship, collaborative law, consensus decision making, creative problem solving, prejudice reduction and bias awareness, conflict resolution systems design, and dozens of associated practices.

Among the most important and powerful of these skills are a number of core ideas and interventions that originate in psychology, particularly in what is known as "brief therapy," where the border separating conflict resolution from psychological intervention has become indistinct and in many places blurred beyond recognition. Examples of the positive consequences of blurring this line can be found in recent discoveries in neurophysiology, "emotional intelligence," and solution-focused approaches to conflict resolution.

While it is, of course, both necessary and vital that we recognize key differences between the professions of psychology and conflict resolution, it is more necessary and vital, especially in these times, that we recognize their essential similarities, collaborate in developing creative new techniques, and invite them to learn as much as they can from each other.

Beyond this, I believe it is increasingly important for us to consciously generate a fertile, collaborative space between them; to discourage the tendency to jealously guard protected territory; and to oppose efforts to create new forms of private property in techniques that are able to reduce hostility and relieve suffering.

It is therefore critical that we think carefully and strategically about how best to translate a deep understanding of the emotional and neurophysiological underpinnings of conflict and resolution processes into practical, hands-on mediation techniques; that we explore the evolving relationship between mediation and psychology, and other professions as well; and that we translate that understanding into improved ways of helping people become competent, successful mediators.

Among the urgent reasons for doing so are the rise of increasingly destructive global conflicts that cannot be solved even by a single nation, let alone by a single style, approach, profession, or technique; the persistence of intractable conflicts that require more advanced techniques; and the recent rise of innovative, transformational techniques that form only a small part of the curriculum of most mediation trainings. [For more on mediating global conflicts, see *Conflict Revolution: Mediating Evil, War, Injustice, and Terrorism.*]

The present generation is being asked a profound set of questions that require immediate action based on complex, diverse, complementary, even contradictory answers. In my judgment, these questions include:

1.  What is our responsibility as global citizens for solving the environmental, social, economic, and political conflicts that are taking place around us?
2.  Is it possible to successfully apply conflict resolution principles to the inequalities, inequities, and dysfunctions that are continuing to fuel chronic social, economic, and political conflicts?
3.  Can we find ways of working beyond national, religious, ethnic, and professional borders so as to strengthen our capacity for international collaboration and help "save the planet"?
4.  Can we build bridges across diverse disciplines so as to integrate the unique understandings and skills that other professions have produced regarding conflict and resolution?
5.  How can we use this knowledge to improve the ways we impact mediator learning so as to better achieve these goals?

Locating potential synergies between psychology and conflict resolution will allow us to take a few small steps toward answering these questions. And small steps, as we learn in mediation, are precisely what are needed to achieve meaningful results. Why should we consider the possibilities of ego defenses or solution-focused mediation? For the same reasons we consider the potential utility of a variety of interventions—because they allow us to understand conflict and interact with it in unique and useful ways.

The logical chain that connects conflict resolution with psychology is simple yet inexorable and logically rigorous, and proceeds as follows:

1. It is possible for people to disagree with each other without experiencing conflict.

2. What distinguishes conflict from mere disagreement is the presence of what are commonly referred to as "negative" emotions, such as anger, fear, guilt, and shame.

3. Thus, every conflict, by definition, contains an emotional element.

4. Conflicts can only be reached and resolved in their emotional location by people who have acquired some emotional processing skills, or what Daniel Goleman broadly describes as "emotional intelligence."

5. The discipline that is most familiar with these emotional dynamics is psychology.

6. Therefore, mediators can learn from psychology how to be more effective in resolving conflicts.

This logical reasoning alone should be sufficient to prompt a deeper assessment of psychological research and technique. Yet, considering the problem from a deeper perspective, we know that no clear line can be drawn in life that would allow us to separate emotions from ideas, or neurophysiology from behavior. Quite simply, we are all emotional beings and must discover their inner logic if we do not want to be trapped or driven by them.

Deeper still, when we distinguish, simplify, or isolate different aspects of a problem, we can easily disregard their essential unity, and miss countless opportunities to resolve critically important conflicts and disagreements, simply because we have approached them with a pre-determined, single-minded, particular point of view, no matter how profound or useful it may happen to be.

We can conduct an equally simple, inexorable, and logically rigorous analysis based on a few simple philosophical assumptions that point us in a profoundly different direction. It goes like this: No two human beings are the same. No single human being is the same from one moment to the next. The interactions and relationships between human beings are complex, multi-determined, subtle, and unpredictable. Conflicts are even more complex, multi-determined, subtle, and unpredictable. Most conflicts take place beneath the surface, well below the superficial topics over which people are fighting, and are frequently hidden from their conscious awareness. [For more on this topic, see *The Crossroads of Conflict: A Journey into the Heart of Dispute Resolution*.]

Thus, each person's attitudes, intentions, intuitions, awareness, context, and capacity for empathetic and honest emotional communication has a significant impact on their experience of conflict and their capacity for resolution. As a result, no one can know objectively or in advance how to resolve any particular conflict, as anything that is chaotic or rapidly changing will escape successful prediction and routine management.

For this reason, it is impossible to teach anyone how to resolve a conflict. Instead, we need to build their skills, improve their awareness and self-confidence, and help them develop a broad range of diverse insights and techniques that may or may not succeed, depending on inherently unpredictable conditions. We have known at least since John Dewey that learning is accelerated when it is connected with doing, yet we continue to train mediators based on a set of false assumptions about how people learn emotionally based skills.

As an illustration of why it is important to take a different approach to mediator learning, consider these questions, directed primarily to those who are already experienced mediators:

- What have you learned since you began mediating that you wish had been included in your training?
- What are the training values that seem to you to flow naturally from the mediation process?
- Were these values reflected in the way your training was actually conducted? If not, how might they have been?
- How did you learn the art of mediation—and especially, how did you learn to be more intuitive, empathetic, openhearted, and wise?
- What skills would you like to be able to develop in the future,

and how might these be incorporated in the way mediation training is conducted?

Every mediator to whom I have asked these questions has easily identified a number of important topics that were not discussed in their training, yet were critical lessons they discovered only after they started mediating. Here are some of the responses mediators had in a training I conducted when I asked them what they wished they had been taught:

- Ways of using "brief therapy" and similar psychologically based methods in mediation;
- Detailed techniques for responding uniquely to each negative emotion; i.e., fear, anger, shame, jealousy, pain and grief;
- Coaching skills for working with individual parties in caucus;
- Procedures for increasing emotional intelligence;
- Ways of discovering what people think or want subconsciously and bringing them into conscious awareness;
- Facilitation and public dialogue skills for working with groups;
- Consulting skills for working with organizations on systems design;
- Better ways of analyzing the narrative structure of conflict stories and a list of techniques for transforming them;
- Better techniques for option generating and "expanding the pie";
- Learning when to take risks and mediate "dangerously";
- Ways of becoming more aware of and responding to the "energies" and "vibrations" of conflict;
- How to develop, calibrate and fine-tune intuition, wisdom, and insight;
- Techniques for surfacing, clarifying, and encouraging people to act based on shared values;
- Ways of gaining permission to work with people on a spiritual or heartfelt level;
- Methods for opening heart-to-heart conversations;
- Knowing how to strike the right balance between head and heart;
- Improved techniques for responding to negativity and

resistance;

- How to maintain the right balance between control and chaos;
- Helping people reach deeper levels of resolution, including forgiveness and reconciliation;
- Ways of addressing the underlying systemic issues and chronic sources of conflict;
- How to transition into positive action, prevention, and systems design in organizational conflicts;
- Techniques for maintaining balance and equanimity and avoiding frustration and self-doubt when conflicts don't settle;
- Ways of addressing our own unresolved conflicts and making sure our emotions and judgments don't get in our way.

Many of these directly concern the interplay between psychology and conflict resolution, but what is equally interesting about these responses is that the way we often teach mediation does not conform to the core values and principles we practice in the mediation process, or to what we know is successful in reaching people who are in conflict, or to what stimulates our learning, or even to how we would most like to be taught ourselves.

As I have described elsewhere, values are essentially priorities and integrity-based choices. They can be found both in what we do and what we do not do, in what we grow accustomed to and what we are willing to tolerate. They are reinforced by being openly and publicly expressed, acted on repeatedly, and upheld when they run counter to self-interests. In this way, they are creators of integrity and responsibility, builders of optimism and self-esteem, and definitions of who we are. They become manifest and alive through action, including the action of sincere declaration.

At a deeper level, we all communicate values by what we do and say, by how we behave, and by the kind of people we become when we are in conflict. While values are often inchoate and difficult to articulate, beneath many commonly recognized mediation practices we can identify a number of values, even *meta-values* that, in my view, represent our best practices as a profession. Our most fundamental values are expressed and become manifest to others when we:

- Show up and are present: physically, mentally, emotionally, and spiritually;

- Listen empathetically to what lies hidden beneath words;
- Tell the truth without blaming or judgment;
- Are open-minded, open-hearted, and unattached to outcomes;
- Search for positive, practical, satisfying outcomes;
- Act collaboratively in relationships;
- Display unconditional authenticity, integrity, and respect;
- Draw on our deepest intuition;
- Are on both parties' sides at the same time;
- Encourage diverse, honest, heartfelt communications;
- Always act in accordance with our core values and principles;
- Are ready for anything at every moment;
- Seek completion and closure;
- Are able to let go, yet abandon no one.

While not everyone will accept these values, merely articulating, debating, and engaging in dialogue over them, considering how to implement them, and deciding to commit and live by them, automatically gives rise to a higher order of values—the value of having values. Practicing them over time—not solely in what we say or do, but in how we say and do it, initiates a third and higher order of values—the value that does not lie in any assertion of values, but in *becoming* what we value.

By living our values, we become what we practice, integrating who we are with what we preach and do. This is the deeper message of mediation: that by continually and collaboratively searching for positive solutions to conflict, bringing them into our conscious attention, living them as fully as possible, and developing the theories, practices, processes, and relationships that allow others do the same, we enhance our relationship to the mediation process as a whole, build a collaborative community of reflective, emotionally intelligent practitioners, and become more *mediative* as people.

To be fully realized, our values must therefore be reflected not merely in our practice, but in all aspects of our personal lives, including the ways we ourselves handle conflicts, teach mediation, and interact with those who wish to learn it. Yet many mediators' lives are filled with intense adversarial conflicts, many mediation trainings are conducted in ways that do not conform to its core values, and many mediators interact with students in ways that undermine their ability to learn.

For example, when trainers do not acknowledge or respect differences between cultures, styles, and diverse approaches to conflict; when they try to promote one-size-fits-all models as applicable to all circumstances; when they downplay and ignore the role of negative emotions, or heartfelt communications; when they do not pay attention to the diverse ways people learn, or even to the ways people are seated in the classroom; when they ignore the systemic sources of conflict; or when they fail to listen and learn from those they are teaching, we can say that the processes they are using are not congruent with the values they espouse.

Howard Gardner at Harvard University has famously described the diverse ways people learn using the idea of "multiple intelligences." The core of his theory is a recognition that people think and learn differently. Gardner believes there is not "one form of cognition that cuts across all human thinking," but that traditional notions of intelligence are misleading because I.Q. tests focus primarily or exclusively only on two areas of competence: logic and linguistics. Instead, Gardner believes there are eight areas of intelligence that account for the range of human potential:

1. *Linguistic Intelligence,* or the capacity to use the written or spoken language to express ourselves;

2. *Logical-Mathematical Intelligence,* or the ability to understand scientific principles or logic systems;

3. *Spatial Intelligence,* or the ability to conceptualize spatial relationships;

4. *Bodily Kinesthetic Intelligence,* or the ability to use our whole body or parts of it to solve problems, make things, or express ideas and emotions through movement;

5. *Musical Intelligence,* or the ability to "think" in music, be able to recognize patterns, and manipulate them;

6. *Interpersonal Intelligence,* or the ability to understand other people and form and build strong, productive relationships;

7. *Intrapersonal Intelligence,* or the ability to understanding ourselves and know who we are, including our strengths and limitations;

8. *Naturalist Intelligence,* or the ability to see and understand the interrelationship and interdependence of all living things

and have a special sensitivity to the physical features of the natural world.

While many scholars have disagreements with this list and with Gardner's idea, and while we might wish to suggest other alternative forms of intelligence, such as emotional, heart, or political intelligence, it is clear that many mediations and conflict resolution training programs narrowly focus on linguistic and logical skills and ignore other forms of intelligence, alternative intervention styles, and diverse conflict processing skills that might contribute significantly to success in mediation.

Even the word "training" is problematic. There are, for example, fundamental differences between various approaches to teaching and learning, and these same differences can be found in the ways we seek to resolve conflicts. We can distinguish, for example:

- *Lecture and Recitation*, which involve rote memorization and recall of facts, and result in a transfer of information, yet often end in testing and forgetting;
- *Education and Courses*, which involve exposure to ideas, specialized theories and practical techniques that result in learning and understanding, yet often end in disputation and Talmudic clashes of opinion over minutia;
- *Training and Workshops*, which involve group discussion and result in improved technical skills, competency and confidence, yet often end in mechanical repetition, inflexibility, and inability to handle problems not addressed in the training;
- *Practice and Exercises,* which involve role plays and practical drills, and result in increased self-confidence and some degree of flexibility, yet often end in improving skills without also improving the understanding needed to successfully implement them;
- *Personal Development and Seminars*, which involve discovery, self-awareness, and self-actualization, and result in authenticity, integrity and personal transformation, yet often end in non-engagement with others;
- *Meditation and Retreats*, which involve insight and concentration, and result in wisdom, spiritual growth,

and transcendence, yet often end in nothing ever changing or being accomplished, and a lack of interest in practical commitment to improving the lives of others.

These diverse forms of learning invisibly shift our focus, activity, and forms of interaction from an orientation toward memorizing, to one of knowing, to one of understanding, to one of doing, to one of being. As we transition to deeper levels of capability in our practice, understanding and commitment to conflict resolution, we require learning methods that will encourage us to develop more collaborative, democratic, self-aware, and diversely competent skills as mediators.

While every learning process has a value and each has times and circumstances that justify it and make it successful, in my experience, those that improve our ability to work through the emotional, psychological, and heart-based underpinnings of conflict—especially our own—create the greatest leverage in terms of our development of values, integrity, and overall capacity to resolve disputes.

Approaching the problem of mediation competency, learning, and training design from this point of view suggests a number of interesting questions we can begin asking prospective mediators in order to improve their psychological awareness, develop their emotional intelligence, and facilitate the design of more advanced training programs. For example, we can ask:

- What are the most significant transformational learning experiences you have had?
- What made them significant or transformational for you?
- What did these experiences have in common that you might want to incorporate into a training experience?
- Why attend this training? What do you really want to achieve?
- What are your larger goals and priorities, and how might this training support them?
- What could block your ability to achieve these goals and priorities, and how could these obstacles be anticipated and overcome?
- What specifically do you want to be taught? How might you best learn to do that?
- What do you think will be the best way of teaching what you

most want to learn?

- Who else should be in the training? Why them? Who should not be in the training? Why not?
- Who would be the ideal trainer? Why? Who would not? Why?
- What values, ideas, and skills do you most want to learn?
- How might those values, ideas, and skills be built into the content and process of the training?
- How will the training actually result in changed behavior?
- How could you be supported in changing?
- How might others support you in changing?
- Will the training lead to improved systems, processes and relationships? If so, how?
- How will you learn the art of what you want to do?
- How can the training be organized in a way that encourages you to participate, think critically, and feel free to be yourself?
- How might your future needs and problems be anticipated in the content and process of the training?
- How will you know whether the training has been effective?

The answers to these questions may help stimulate the development of a number of collateral areas in the field of conflict resolution, such as marital mediations between couples who would like to improve their relationship; applying conflict resolution systems design skills to a broad range of social, economic, and political issues; mediating the connections between families, community groups, workplaces, organizations; integrating conflict resolution skills into team building and project management workshops; extending school mediations to encourage parents and teachers to work through their personal conflicts along with the children; working with a broad range of hospital and health care disputes that flow from the need to process grief, guilt, rage, and loss; and new ideas for resolving intractable international conflicts.

Part of the object of a mediative approach to mediator education would be to encourage students to become responsible for their own learning, and teachers to become responsible for finding the deepest, most profound and effective way of supporting them. One way of doing so, inspired by paradoxical approaches to therapy, is to ask students to complete the following questionnaire before their training, then discuss their answers.

# Pre-Training Evaluation

Please rate your expectations regarding the session we are about to have, and how you expect to participate on a scale of 1 to 10, 10 being highest. [Based on work by Peter Block]

1.  How valuable an experience do you plan to have? (1 = terrible, 10 = fantastic):

2.  How participative and engaged do you plan to be? (1 = asleep, 10 = extremely excited):

3.  How much risk do you plan to take? (1 = none, 10 = serious adventure):

4.  How open, honest and constructive do you plan to be? (1 = silent, 10 = painfully honest):

5.  How willing are you to listen non-defensively and non-judgmentally to others? (1 = doing email, 10 = completely open):

6.  How responsible do you feel for your own learning? (1 = not at all, 10 = entirely):

7.  How responsible do you feel for the learning of others? (1 = not at all, 10 = totally):

8.  How committed are you to implementing what you learn? (1 = amnesia, 10 = complete commitment):

Applying these ideas to conflict resolution, we know intuitively that mediators are not immune from conflicts, and that we will become better dispute resolvers by working through and resolving our own conflicts. It therefore makes sense for us to incorporate into every mediation training the emotional and psychological skills and processes that will allow people to work directly on resolving their personal disputes. At present, few mediation programs allow or encourage them to do so.

In the end, *we are the technique.* As imperfect as we are, it is who we are that forms the path to resolution, and that same path invites us to become better human beings, if for no other reason than simply to become better mediators. This realization returns mediation to its human origins and essence, as an exercise not exclusively in empathy and compassion, but also in creative problem solving, emotional clarity, heartfelt wisdom, and social collaboration.

Hopefully, these practices will encourage us to look more deeply and wisely at the world within, as well as the world without, and assist us in finding ways to translate our own suffering and conflicts into methods and understandings that will lead to a better, less hostile and adversarial world.

# CHAPTER 4

# BRINGING OXYTOCIN INTO THE ROOM

## Notes on the Neurophysiology of Conflict

*We do not see things as they are. We see things as we are.*

~ Anais Nin ~

**W**HILE PEOPLE IN CONFLICT commonly make reference to the facts, behaviors, feelings, personalities, or events surrounding their conflicts, for the most part they ignore the deeper reality that these experiences are all processed and regulated by their nervous systems, and are therefore initiated, resolved, transformed, and transcended by their brains. Yet only recently have mediators begun to consider how our brains influence our conflict behaviors.

It is clear that all conflicts are perceived by the senses, manifested through body language and kinesthetic sensations, embodied and given meaning by thoughts and ideas, steeped in intense emotions, made conscious through awareness, and then resolved by conversations and experiences and developed into character, expanding our capacity for openness and trust, and contributing to our learning and ability to change, and that all of these transpire or are processed inside the brain.

To explain the etiology of conflict, therefore, requires us to gain a deeper understanding of how the brain responds to conflict. This should include the ways distrusting personalities are formed, even among primates; the sources of aggressive character traits and the "fight or flight" reflex and how it dissipates; the wellsprings of emotional or spiritual malaise and hostile "gut" reactions; and the neurological foundations of collaboration, trust, forgiveness, open-heartedness, empathy, insight, intuition, learning, wisdom, and the willingness to change.

While conflict and resolution have yet to be reduced to a simple set of deterministic biochemical events taking place exclusively within the brain, research demonstrates that basic neurological processes provide all of us with alternative sets of instructions that can lead us either toward impasse or resolution, stasis or transformation, isolation or collaboration. For these reasons, it will serve us well as mediators to understand more about the neurophysiology of conflict.

We have yet to examine communication and conflict resolution very deeply from the perspective of neurophysiology, though we know that the presence of an empathetic listener, particularly one who is skilled in mediation, can by itself create a significant shift in conflict dynamics and alter, at a subtle level of awareness, the attitudes of parties in conflict. But why is this so, how does it work, and what does it imply for conflict resolution?

For millennia, our greatest sages—particularly those from the East, including Lao Tse, Confucius, and Buddha—have sought to convince us that the universe consists of opposites that, at the deepest level, merge into a single, unified whole. Yet it has taken until the 20th century and the discovery of quantum mechanics—initially by Planck and Einstein, then by Bohr and Heisenberg and others—to establish scientifically that observers and the things they observe are part of a single interconnected system, and reveal how and why the act of observation, at a subtle level, directly influences the object or process that is being observed.

I am not a trained neurophysiologist, but an avid lay reader, and have learned an immense amount of useful information regarding conflict resolution from reading scientific studies of the brain and how it functions. What follows is a brief synopsis of some of the more interesting and important ideas and news items I have read describing research and experiments in neurophysiology as they pertain to conflict and the mediation process. Much has been added and changed since I wrote it, and every day brings remarkable new research to light that is contributing to a revolution in our understanding of the brain.

## WHAT IS THE BRAIN?

Most conflicts are triggered by external events or experiences, and information regarding them is conveyed to us by sensory inputs that we have gathered from our environment. Our conflicts therefore seem to us to take place externally, yet everything we understand about the meaning of what happened, and all of our responses to the actions of others are initiated and coordinated internally within our sensory nervous system and our brains, which are not neutral, but directly influence the information we receive and how it is interpreted.

What, then, is the brain, how is it structured, and how does it typically respond to conflict? First, the brain is often analogized to a massively powerful parallel processing computer, more powerful than anything we have been able to design or create. As inadequate as this analogy is, we know that about one hundred billion nerve cells make up the brain, each of which can create up to ten thousand synaptic connections, and form a massive number of neuronal connections every second.

An average desktop computer is capable of sending 25 billion instructions per second, while a human brain can send over 100 trillion. An adult human brain, by some accounts, can make as many as 500 trillion synaptic connections per second, only a fraction of which emerge in conscious awareness. This, by itself, might explain what we commonly refer to as intuition, which can be defined merely as what we know that we don't know that we know.

Second, the brain is divided into two halves or hemispheres that are largely separate, but connected at the base in the center by a corpus callosum (in most people). Each hemisphere processes information regarding conflict somewhat differently: one side generally functions more linearly and considers problems individually and in detail, while the other side works more holistically and considers problems collectively and as a whole. One side favors logical reasoning while the other side favors pattern perception; one works by linear and rational thinking while the other practices emotional responsiveness. The right hemisphere, for example, has been shown to be more adept at discriminating between emotional expressions and processing negative emotions, while the left is demonstrably less so, and more involved in processing positive emotions. Language, mathematics, spatial relations and other elements of thought are also organized differently in each hemisphere.

Third, the brain is organized into regions, each of which processes different aspects of the information it receives related to conflict in specialized ways. For example, the ventral tegmental area reinforces the reward circuit; the prefrontal cortex allows for objectivity and logic; the nucleus accumbens, directly beneath the frontal cortex, is involved in the release of oxytocin, described in greater detail below; the hypothalamus produces testosterone; and, most importantly, the amygdala, an almond-shaped region near the brain stem, regulates immediate responses to conflict and change, especially anger and fear.

The three primary areas of the brain are the brainstem, responsible for our states of arousal and other physical functions; the limbic system that controls our basic drives and emotions, including relations and attachment, anger and fear, and via the pituitary gland, sends hormones throughout our body; and the cortex and prefrontal cortex that control higher order thinking.

## NEUROTRANSMITTERS AND CONFLICT

The brain is awash in chemicals, including hormones and neurotransmitters that accentuate or dampen its responses and influence its organization and operations. Neurotransmitters are chemicals that relay, amplify, or modulate signals that are sent between neurons and other cells. There are many different hormones and neurotransmitters, of which the most important are glutamate and GABA, which excite and modify synapses. With regard to conflict, the following compounds seem to be most active:

- Adrenalin, which triggers the fight or flight response;
- Testosterone, which stimulates aggression;
- Oxytocin which instills trust, increases loyalty, and promotes the "tend and befriend" response;
- Estrogen, which triggers the release of oxytocin;
- Endorphins, which reinforce collaborative experiences with pleasure;
- Dopamine, which generates a reward response and fortifies addiction;
- Serotonin, which regulates moods;
- Phenylethylamine, which induces excitement and anticipation;
- Vasopressin, which encourages bonding in males in a variety of species.

Many vertebrate brain structures involved in the control of aggression are richly supplied with receptors that bind with hormones produced by the endocrine system, in particular with steroidal hormones produced in the gonads. In a wide range of vertebrate species, there is a strong relationship between male aggressiveness and circulating levels of androgens such as testosterone, a hormone produced in the testes.

These aggressive behavioral patterns and the modulation of an animal's tendency to fight or flee are controlled by a hierarchical system of countervailing neural structures. Many of these are found in the limbic system—a part of the forebrain that is involved in emotionally based behavior and motivation. These neural structures interact with biochemicals that are produced inside and outside the nervous system. For example, it has been shown that serotonin injections cause lobsters and other animals to take a dominant or aggressive posture, while octopamine injections induce submissive postures, which favor cooperation. When serotonin levels are increased in subordinate animals, their willingness to fight also increases, and declines as they are reduced.

From fish to mammals, aggression levels have been shown to rise and fall with natural fluctuations in testosterone levels. Castration has been found to reduce aggression dramatically, while the experimental reinstatement of testosterone by injection restores aggression. Circulating testosterone also influences the responses and signals that are used during mating and fighting in many species. In stags, the neck muscles needed for roaring enlarge under the influence of testosterone, while in male mice, the scent of another male's urine, which contains the breakdown products of testosterone, elicits intense aggressive responses.

In pregnant female mice, the scent of urine from a male that is ill can even induce the formation of antibodies in their embryos, and the presence of stress chemicals that are increased by fighting or mild electrical shocks can be detected by females who are able to detect the smell of male urine, producing personality and behavioral changes in their unborn offspring. It is thought that stress chemicals like cortisone and epigenetic changes in methyl groups that turn gene expression on or off are responsible for personality changes into the second and third generation.

The experience of fighting has been shown to have a significant impact on brain biochemistry and therefore on brain structure, especially in the limbic system which is strongly associated with conflict. For example, among rainbow trout and lizards, dominant animals show significant transient activation of their brains' serotonin systems, whereas subordinate animals display a longer-term elevation of these systems.

Researchers have shown in several vertebrate species that electrical stimulation of the midbrain and hindbrain elicits stereotyped, yet undirected aggressive behaviors, while stimulation of the hypothalamus and a nearby pre-optic region in the forebrain elicits well-coordinated attacks on other members of the same species. Lesions in these areas have also been shown to reduce aggression.

The hypothalamus and pre-optic area of the forebrain are also involved in the generation of coordinated aggressive behaviors that are produced in lower brain regions. This activity is modulated by the brain's higher centers, including areas of the limbic system—in particular the septum, which lies above the hypothalamus and has an inhibitory effect on aggression, while the amygdala located deep in the temporal lobes has the opposite effect.

In a series of experiments, dogs and monkeys have been shown to respond negatively to favoritism and unfairness in experiments where certain animals have been given rewards without having performed, causing others to punish them, or refuse to cooperate with researchers.

The lateral habenula has been shown to react strongly when expected rewards are denied or replaced by mild punishments. Dopamine neurons are inhibited by the habenula, and since dopamine contributes to learning by producing positive sensations in response to success, many researchers now think the habenula may also contribute to learning by shutting off dopamine in response to disappointment, representing an internal form of "the carrot and the stick." Some research suggests that the habenula is implicated in depression. It has also been shown that the orbitofrontal cortex (OFC), located at the front of the brain behind the eyes, is implicated in various aspects of decision-making and choice evaluation. The anterior cingulate gyrus then reacts to mistakes and internal conflicts between intentions and outcomes and helps alter behaviors in response.

Researchers have established that the negative emotions we routinely encounter in conflict are triggered in more or less the following sequence:

- Sensory information from primary receptors in the eye, nose, ear, and other organs travels along neural pathways to the limbic forebrain.
- These stimuli are evaluated for emotional significance. Research by Joseph E. LeDoux has demonstrated that auditory fear conditioning involves the transmission of sound signals through an auditory pathway to the thalamus, which relays this information to the dorsal amygdala.

- The amygdala coordinates a "relevance detection" process that is rapid, minimal, automatic, and evaluative.
- Emotions are then activated in the subcortical thalamo-amygdala pathway and relayed from the thalamus to the neocortex for cognitive appraisal and evaluation.
- In some cases, the same information is simultaneously sent to the neocortex for slower processing, creating a dual, two-circuit pathway that permits reason to override an emotional response, or the amygdala to highjack the cortex and coordinate a response.

## PERCEPTION, MIRROR NEURONS, AND SUGGESTIBILITY

The brain notices changes in its immediate environment predominantly by contrast or comparison against a relatively static backdrop of unwavering familiarity, giving rise to expectation, desire, fear, and habit. Observing the contrast between what is moving and what is not is the principle way our minds attempt to simplify and predict what is likely to happen next. At a primitive level, there is an immense evolutionary advantage in being able to notice a potential threat by, for example, contrasting the mirror symmetry of a predator's face and eyes or a sudden movement against an asymmetrical, slower moving background. In a similar way, we are biased by evolution to credit threatening behaviors more than non-threatening ones.

A number of recent brain studies have revealed how perceptions and memories are profoundly distorted by emotions and by focused concentration, and how they can be reshaped by suggestion and subsequent events. Thus, areas of the brain that are linked with negative emotions and judging others are switched off, for example, when mothers look at photographs of their babies, and when even strangers view photographs of babies. Instead, the right prefrontal cortex lights up, not only in parents watching their children, but also in lovers and Buddhist monks who have been asked to meditate on loving-kindness and compassion. In other research, memory and awareness have been shown to decline dramatically in the presence of stress chemicals that are released during periods of intense emotion.

It has also been shown, in reverse, that the free expression through outward behavior of an emotion can intensify it, while repressing or not expressing it, as far as is possible, can soften it. Thus, experiments have shown that if people are able to control their facial expressions during moments of pain, there is less arousal of the autonomic nervous system and an actual diminution of the pain experience. The same result appears to obtain for anger and fear.

In one delightful experiment, a significant percentage of people were assigned to focus their attention on a single task, such as counting the number of individuals in a colored tee shirt to whom a basketball was passed. When they did so, the participants completely ignored and even vigorously denied afterwards that an unusual or bizarre occurrence had occurred, in this case, the entry onto the basketball court of someone dressed in a gorilla outfit, who walked and pranced across their line of vision.

Scientists have begun to trace the development of empathy in primates, including human beings, leading to the discovery of "mirror neurons," which fire in the brains of observers watching a given action, and replicate to some extent the experience of the one who is being observed. Similar neurons fire when we observe someone else suffering or frightened, reproducing those experiences in the form of empathy. Indeed, physical and emotional pains seem to trigger the same mirror neurons.

In one surprising recent experiment, "phantom limb syndrome," in which a lost limb can experience itching or pain, has been shown to dramatically disappear when a subject is allowed to observe a false image of the lost limb by means of a mirror, thereby tricking the brain's mirror neurons into thinking that the lost arm or leg had reappeared. Similarly, "out-of-body" experiences can be induced using video cameras and virtual reality equipment that gives the impression that the apparently different person viewed by video, is in fact themselves.

## PRIMING

Several studies have shown that the brain is highly responsive to suggestion. In a series of remarkable experiments it has been shown that the performance of simple, seemingly unrelated tasks can be increased or decreased merely by placing a briefcase or sports equipment nearby, triggering unconscious associations with work or play.

In an interesting study, subjects were made happy or angry, then shown happy and angry faces and friendly and hostile interpersonal scenes in a stereoscope. Happy subjects perceived more happy faces and friendly interpersonal scenes while angry subjects perceived more angry faces and hostile interpersonal scenes.

In addition, it has been shown that relatively small favors or bits of good luck (like finding money in a coin telephone or getting an unexpected gift) induced positive emotion in people, and that these emotions increased the subjects' inclination to sympathize or provide help.

At the same subtle level, a number of experiments have shown that behaviors can be modified simply by introducing background scents such as lavender or the lemony odor of detergent, and that consumers of different products will purchase different products more or less readily in the presence of discrete scents.

Equally dramatically, test results can be predictably raised or lowered merely by asking people of color, or those who have been discriminated against in their country, to identify themselves by their race or discriminatory categorization beforehand, or by giving indirect racial or emotional cues, or by priming teachers falsely in advance of a test regarding the innate intelligence or stupidity of their students, producing conformity with expectations and a well-established "Pygmalion effect."

In one remarkable study, when 12- and 13-year-old African-American students were asked to spend 15 minutes indicating which values, such as friendship or family, they upheld, the achievement gap between them and white students decreased by 40 percent. Similarly, when female college students read passages before a test arguing against gender differences in mathematical ability, their scores increased by 50 percent.

At a very subtle level, Yale University psychologist John Bargh found that when volunteers were "primed" with words associated with the elderly, like "wrinkle," they took significantly longer to walk down a hall than those who had not been primed. And interestingly, for conflict resolvers, Alex Pentland of the MIT Media Lab found that even without priming, watching body language and tone of voice for only a few minutes allowed researchers to predict with 87 percent accuracy the outcome of subsequent negotiations between strangers. Here are the results from some fascinating priming studies:

- Integrating words such as "cooperation" and "fairness" into sentences can result in a higher occurrence of these behaviors.
- When subjects were asked to think about the lowest and highest *fair* prices for a car before negotiating, they made conciliatory moves more quickly, were happier with the results, reached agreement in half the time, and were willing to negotiate again.
- Students primed with the word "rudeness" interrupted more quickly than others.
- People using a public bathroom were more willing to pay a fee on the honor system if the word "honesty" was posted, or to pay for coffee if a picture of a face or an eye was posted nearby.
- Seeing a briefcase or sitting in a hard chair caused negotiators to offer less than if they saw a backpack or sat in a soft chair.
- Scores in Trivial Pursuit were increased by thinking of a professor and decreased by thinking of a soccer hooligan.
- People who were primed with the names of their friends were more willing to help others, including strangers.
- Researchers at the Interdisciplinary Center Herzliya in Israel conducted a study involving 76 Israel-born Jews, 59 Israeli Arabs and 53 Palestinians living in the occupied Palestinian territories. Each individual was randomly assigned a reading – one portraying groups as having a fixed nature and the other describing them as flexible and open to change. Those primed to believe their adversaries were changeable were significantly more optimistic about their ability to reach a negotiated peace, suggesting they would be more willing to compromise to reach agreement.
- Group members primed with the words *dependable, helpful, share* and *support* were more cooperative within their group than others, even to their individual economic detriment.
- U.S. participants who listened to and mouthed the words of the "O Canada" anthem together showed increased feelings of being "part of the group," and made consistently cooperative

decisions in an economic game.

- William Cox has shown that, when presented with a depressed patient who "self-stereotypes herself as incompetent, a therapist can find ways to prime her with specific situations in which she had been competent in the past... Making memories of her competence more salient reduce[s] her self-stereotype of incompetence."

Nobel Prize winner Daniel Kahneman cites a number of interesting studies of priming in his excellent book, *Thinking, Fast and Slow*, among which are these:

- Exposure to a word makes it easier for people to recall it later. If you have recently seen or heard the word EAT, you are temporarily more likely to complete the word fragment SO_P as SOUP than as SOAP. The opposite occurs if you just saw the word WASH.

- The same is true if the word is presented in a whisper or a blurry font.

- Subjects asked to complete the word fragments W_ _H and S_ _P were more likely to complete them as WASH and SOAP if they had been primed to think about an action of which they were ashamed, and as WISH and SOUP if they were primed to think of food.

- Merely thinking about stabbing a coworker in the back leaves people more inclined to buy soap, disinfectant or detergent than batteries, juice or candy.

- This also connects to body parts. People asked to lie to an imaginary person over the phone preferred mouthwash over soap, while those who lied in email preferred soap.

- An entirely different set of associations and memories occur to us if we are asked "Is James friendly?" than if we are asked "Is James unfriendly?" In each case we easily slip into "confirmation bias" that leads us to memories and associations that confirm what the question primed us to think. The same is true for other negative and positive priming associations.

- Students were asked to walk around a room for five minutes at a rate of 30 steps per minute, about 1/3rd their normal pace. Afterwards, they were much quicker to recognize words associated with old age, like "forgetful, old and lonely." *Acting* old reinforces ideas and thoughts about old age.

- Similar reciprocal links include: being happy makes you smile and smiling makes you happy—even if only holding a pencil sideways in your teeth.
- People asked to squeeze their eyebrows together showed enhanced emotional responses to upsetting pictures.
- Nodding (yes) increases acceptance of editorials while shaking one's head (no) reduces it.
- A study of voting patterns in Arizona in 2000 showed that support for school funding propositions was greater if the polling station was in a school than in a different location.
- A different experiment showed that people exposed to images of classrooms and school lockers also increased their tendency to vote for school funding initiatives. This difference was greater than that between voters who were parents and voters who were not.
- On the other hand, words and images of money caused people to become more selfish, sit farther apart, and be less willing to help someone who pretended to be confused about a task, or to help pick up pencils a researcher dropped on the floor.
- Reminding people of their mortality increases the appeal of authoritarian ideas.

These studies suggest that the brain can be re-programmed by consciously selected practices. It has been shown, for example, that the ventromedial prefrontal cortex (which is responsible for empathy, compassion, shame, and intuitive emotional responses to moral dilemmas) can be significantly strengthened by the practice of meditation, or merely thinking compassionately for a few moments about the well being of others.

Other experiments have demonstrated that men become more loving toward their female partners as their ovulation approaches, that women prefer different forms of male attractiveness at different stages in their menstrual cycle, and that women make decisions about male attractiveness based on chemical indicators in their sweat indicating that they have immunities the women do not, as measured by genes for their major histocompatibility complex or MHC. Other studies have found that men also prefer women with dissimilar MHC genes, specifically with human leukocyte antigen, or HLA genes.

An important study from Stockholm suggests that lesbian women have more asymmetric brains, like heterosexual men, and that gay men have more symmetric brains, like heterosexual women. Moreover, in heterosexual women and gay men the amygdala connects mainly to areas of the brain that manifest fear as anxiety, whereas in heterosexual men and lesbian women it connects more strongly to areas that trigger the fight or flight (or freeze) reflex.

It has also been shown that sweat from women who watched violent movies was accurately rated by others as stronger, less pleasant, and smelling more "like aggression" than sweat from women who had watched a neutral movie. In an interesting study, researchers from Stony Brook University in New York taped absorbent pads to the underarms of 40 volunteers who went on their first skydive. In a double-blind experiment, a group of testers smelled sample pads from skydivers and non-skydivers while in an fMRI scanner. The testers showed increased activity in their amygdala and hypothalamus while breathing sweat produced by skydivers under frightening conditions, indicating that humans may in fact be able to smell fear in others, even if they have not experienced it themselves.

It has even be shown that liberals and conservatives use different parts of their brains when they make risky decisions, and these regions can be used to predict which political party a person prefers with over 89.2 percent accuracy. Specifically, when given a gambling task, Democrats showed significantly greater activity in the left insula, a region associated with social and self-awareness, while Republicans showed significantly greater activity in the right amygdala, a region associated with fear and the fight or flight response. Here is a summary of a number of other interesting studies revealing unexpected connections and associations:

- Israeli researchers, writing in the journal Fertility and Sterility, found that women undergoing in-vitro fertilization were almost twice as likely to conceive if they had been made to laugh by a hospital "clown" who entertained them as soon as their embryos were implanted.

- Using data from MRI scans, researchers at University College London found that self-described liberals have a larger anterior Cingulate Cortex associated with understanding complexity, while self-described conservatives were more likely to have a larger Amygdala, associated with fear and anxiety.

- A team at MIT ran tests to see if objects could influence judgments and decision-making. Passers-by were asked to judge a job candidate by looking at their resume. Half were given the resume on a heavy clipboard and half on a light one. Those with the heavy clipboard rated the same candidates more serious than those with the light one.

- Volunteers who sat on a hard seat were less willing to change their price in a hypothetical car purchase than those sitting on a soft seat. Textures associated with tactile metaphors may trigger linguistic links to behaviors.

- University of Southern California researchers asked male and female volunteers to put their hands in ice water, raising their levels of the stress hormone cortisol. They then looked at angry or neutral faces in a brain scanner. Men showed less activity in key face-processing regions of the brain and their ability to evaluate facial expressions declined. In women, this region became more active, as did an area of the brain linked to empathy and the ability to recognize others' emotions.

- A University of British Columbia researcher in Canada found that "the mere thought of having money makes people less likely to help acquaintances, to donate to charity, or to choose to spend time with others – precisely the kind of behaviors that are strongly associated with happiness." Spending as little as five dollars on someone else promoted greater happiness than spending money on oneself.

- When people have just seen an organic fruit salad, they think a cheeseburger has 1,041 calories, but only 780 calories after seeing a "decadent cheesecake."

- In offices with an honor system for coffee, people are more likely to pay on days when a photograph of human eyes is discretely posted above the coffee machine.

- People tip waiters an average of 140 percent more if the waiter repeats the order verbatim, as opposed to paraphrasing it.

- Sociologists at Tilburg University in the Netherlands interviewed travelers at a train station during and after a strike by janitors, and found that people in messy environments were more likely to accept negative stereotypes of Muslims and homosexuals. Travelers were asked to sit while filling out the survey, and those in messy environments chose to sit farther away from a black man than a white man.

- *The Swiss Journal of Psychology* reported a study in which women asked male passersby for directions to Valentine Street or Martin Street (neither exists). A moment later, they encountered a different woman struggling to retrieve her cell phone from a group of threatening guys. Those asked about Valentine Street were more likely to offer help than those asked about Martin Street.

- Yale University psychologists met volunteers and casually asked them to hold a hot or iced coffee while writing down their names. They later read a description of a fictitious person and answered questions about their character. Those who held an iced coffee rated the person as less warm and friendly.

- In a similar experiment, just thinking about being socially excluded can make a room feel about 3 degrees Celcius cooler.

- People who watched an upsetting film or a disturbing smell as opposed to a neutral one were more judgmental and severe about unethical acts, and those who read about an unethical act expressed a greater preference for cleaning products. Offering them an antiseptic wipe afterwards reduced their willingness to volunteer to help out a desperate student.

- Harvard University researchers created a public goods game in which players choose whether or not to contribute money to a common pool that is redistributed equally. They divided participants into three groups, one that could punish freeloaders, one that could reward contributors, and one that could do either. Rewarding people always gave the largest return, and when those who could chose opted to reward they received larger payoffs.

## OXYTOCIN AND DUAL PATHWAYS IN CONFLICT

The physical basis for collaboration, altruism, trust, forgiveness, and interest-based conflict resolution techniques, has been clearly identified with the "tend and befriend" hormone oxytocin. Oxytocin was discovered early in the 20th century and first synthesized by Vincent du Vigneaud in 1953, for which he received the Nobel Prize for Chemistry in 1955. It is secreted by the posterior lobe of the pituitary gland and can be made synthetically. Physiologically, it promotes the secretion of breast milk and stimulates the contraction of the uterus during labor. It cannot be reliably ingested orally, but can be administered intravenously, sublingually, or by nasal spray, although its strongest effects last only for a few minutes.

Oxytocin is widely believed to be responsible for prompting empathy, compassion, trust, generosity, altruism, parent-child bonding, and monogamy in many species, including human beings. Oxytocin has been dubbed the "bonding" hormone, primarily as a result of research involving voles. Prairie voles in the U.S. are largely monogamous and the males provide care for the young. Montane voles, on the other hand, are polygamous and the males are less caring of their young. Experiments that have deprived prairie voles of oxytocin and provided it to Montane voles cause a dramatic reversal in these behaviors.

In a number of duplicated extraordinary studies, participants are given a small amount of pretend money and encouraged to invest it with a stranger. On average, they initially invest only a quarter to a third of the money they possess. But after four sniffs of the neurotransmitter oxytocin, their trust levels skyrocket, and without hesitation they become willing to invest up to 80 percent or more. Here is a summary from the original study:

> Human beings routinely help strangers at costs to themselves. Sometimes the help offered is generous—offering more than the other expects. The proximate

mechanisms supporting generosity are not well understood, but several lines of research suggest a role for empathy. In this study, participants were infused with 40 IU oxytocin (OT) or placebo and engaged in a blinded, one-shot decision on how to split a sum of money with a stranger that could be rejected. Those on OT were 80 percent more generous than those given a placebo. OT had no effect on a unilateral monetary transfer task dissociating generosity from altruism. OT and altruism together predicted almost half the interpersonal variation in generosity. Notably, OT had twofold larger impact on generosity compared to altruism. This indicates that generosity is associated with both altruism as well as an emotional identification with another person.

Duke neuroscientist, Michael Platt found that when monkeys helped themselves, neurons in the anterior cingulate gyrus fired, but when they helped others, neurons in the orbitofrontal cortex that are known to be involved in reward processing fired, stimulating feelings of pleasure in altruism and helping others. He suggests that the orbitofrontal cortex encodes vicarious experiences that account for happiness and sadness and are "what actually drives giving behavior and perhaps drives charity in people."

Several experiments have shown that positive emotions facilitate creative problem solving. One study, for example, showed that positive emotions enabled subjects to name more uses for common objects. Another showed that positive emotions enhanced creative problem solving by enabling subjects to see relations among objects that would otherwise have gone unnoticed. A number of studies have demonstrated the beneficial effects of positive emotions on thinking, memory, and action in preschool and older children.

A recent study by a group in Zurich, Switzerland showed that oxytocin improves recognition and memory of previously presented faces, which were more correctly assessed as being "known," but the ability to recollect faces that had not been seen before was unchanged and there was no difference when recalling images of houses, landscapes, or sculptures. The researchers argued, "this pattern speaks for an immediate and selective effect of the peptide [oxytocin in] strengthening neuronal systems of social memory."

There is a considerable body of research that has linked oxytocin with collaboration and creative problem solving, and these with the release of endorphins, the brain's version of morphine. Creative problem solving has also been shown to increase with diversity, and a mathematical proof has been published demonstrating that more diverse groups predictably experience greater creativity, success in problem solving, and satisfaction as a result.

Thus, the brain possesses not one, but two systems for responding to conflict, and is capable both of adrenalin-based "fight or flight" responses, and of oxytocin-based "tend and befriend" ones. Just as, in biology, there are evolutionary advantages to aggression and "selfish genes," and there are also advantages to collaboration and altruistic efforts that aid others.

These opposing capacities are reflected elsewhere in the body and the brain. There are two bundles of nerves, for example, that connect the eye and other sensory organs with the brain. One travels directly to the amygdala where fight or flight responses are initiated, while the other proceeds to the neocortex where logical explanations can be discovered, allowing us to override costly adrenalin-based responses.

As we learn, develop language, mature, and accumulate long-term memories and experiences, these dual pathways to the amygdala and the neocortex become more developed and integrated, and we become able to process events in either or both pathways at the same time, and increasingly learn to shift from aggressive to collaborative responses.

This duality allows the amygdala pathway to specialize in processing information that may require a rapid response, while the neocortex pathway specializes in evaluating information that may be important in forming cognitive judgments or developing complex coping strategies. Duality allows us to learn how to choose either to by-pass the amygdala's initiation of the fight or flight response, or the less aggressive option of tend and befriend.

Moreover, the brain not only dictates how we respond to changes in our environment, it is actually shaped and molded by those changes. The brain requires sensory stimulation in order to develop, and repeated stimulation creates physical connections between neurons that strengthen the pathways and networks responsible for thoughts, feelings, and behaviors.

These stimulations have been shown to produce significant attitudinal changes. Indeed, several experiments have demonstrated that countless previous experiments on laboratory mice and rats over the course of decades have been deeply influenced by whether the animals were raised in rich or impoverished environments.

The environment in which a young animal is raised also has a significant effect on whether and how it fights as an adult. These environmental factors are not always directly related to social experience. For example, mice that are deprived of food during their early development become particularly aggressive as adults. On the other hand, environmental effects on the development of aggression may depend on social interactions in contexts other than fighting; for instance, mouse pups that have been roughly handled by their mothers are more aggressive as adults. Similar results have been found in a range of species that have been reared in social isolation.

More surprisingly, physical tests have revealed that babies are able to rewire their mothers' brains in utero, and that some of the genetic material and cells of each remain in the other throughout their lives and may influence a variety of behaviors, including a tendency to aggression or collaboration in conflict.

## IS AGGRESSION INEVITABLE?

Clearly, aggression and violence are "hard-wired" into the brain, but so are empathy and collaboration. Recent research has emphasized the cooperative aspects of warlike behavior, which forms a core element not only in gangs, but sports teams, organizations and nation states, which use internal cooperation as an aid to external competition. Indeed, modern warfare can be seen as requiring a high level of internal collaborative activity.

Yet it has been shown, for example by researchers at the University of Edinburgh, that men in war simulations tend to overestimate their chances of winning, making them more likely to attack and behave aggressively, leading to unnecessary losses that a more sober calculation might predict.

It has also been argued by evolutionary biologists at the University of New Mexico, based on data from 125 civil wars, that cultures become more insular and xenophobic when diseases and parasites are common, perhaps in an effort to drive away strangers who may carry new diseases. By contrast, cultures with a low risk of disease are more open to outsiders. They argue that when the risk of infectious diseases fell in Western nations following World War II due to antibiotics and sanitation, these societies became less hostile and xenophobic.

In one interesting experiment, cricket players on the Caribbean island of Dominica experienced a surge in testosterone and aggressive behavior after winning against another village, but did not experience the same surge when winning against a team from their own village. Similarly, it has been shown that an increase in testosterone typically experienced by men in the presence of a potential mate is muted if she is in a relationship with a relative or friend.

This suggests that building empathy and "identification with the enemy" may prove useful as techniques for countering aggressive behavior in mediation. There is also research suggesting that while women may be better at brokering harmony within groups, men may be better at making peace between groups. These techniques suggest that it may be possible to identify more precisely which approach will work best in a given setting to reduce warfare and aggression.

Biologist Robert Sapolsky is a leading challenger of what he refers to as the "urban myth of inevitable aggression." In studies of baboons in Kenya, when several aggressive males who fought others for food died as a result of food poisoning, the females chose to mate with less aggressive males who began to collaborate and groom each other, leading him to conclude that "there is a great potential for dramatically decreasing the frequency of war and getting a lot better at intervention, termination, and reconciliation."

## IMPLICATIONS FOR CONFLICT RESOLUTION

These are just a few of the more dramatic conclusions that have emerged from countless studies and experiments, from which I have culled only a few that seem most significant based on my experience as a mediator. What, then, does all this research suggest for conflict resolution?

In the first place, it reinforces the idea of brain "plasticity," which holds that the brain is not fixed but evolving, learning, and producing new synapses all the time, even among those who were previously considered elderly and incapable of doing so. Among other things, this gives us hope, and explains why it is possible for people to switch suddenly from aggression to collaboration. Recent research shows, for example, that it is possible to increase our capacity for empathy and compassion through meditative practices.

Second, it suggests that a variety of techniques might be useful in reducing adrenalin, increasing oxytocin, and stimulating collaboration and trust. One clear example is research that involves what we call "mirroring," and in scientific literature is called mimicry, but is sometimes included under the heading of persuasion. It has been demonstrated, for example, in human subjects, that mirroring body language after a two second delay (so it is not recognized as mimicry by the subject) improves the outcome of negotiations and encourages collaborative behavior.

In reading each of these studies and experiments, we can imagine a number of subtle ways we might go about encouraging a shift in the attitudes of disputants toward problem solving and collaboration. For example, it is clear by hindsight that a number of very common simple techniques, such as welcoming, introductions, reaching agreement on ground rules, caucusing, summarizing, and securing small agreements, can predictably reduce the release of adrenalin and stimulate the release of oxytocin. This may cause us to wonder: what deeper results might we achieve by better understanding how the brain processes and overcomes the fight or flight response?

Even basic information about neurophysiology can lead us to new techniques, for example, by allowing mediators to work directly with different hemispheres of the brains of conflicted parties, not only by presenting information in ways that are more accessible to one hemisphere or the other, but by focusing attention, for example, on the eye that feeds information to a particular hemisphere that may be more receptive to it.

Other quite subtle techniques might also have an impact on the brain chemistry of conflict, including the introduction of scents that remind people less of fear than of social connection, serving chocolate to stimulate the production of dopamine, placing objects that encourage positive emotions inside the mediation room, asking questions about values to orient people to their highest standards, using body language to trigger mirror neurons, or offering positive acknowledgments regarding something each party did or said. Here are some simple additional things mediators might do, based on brain research, to encourage parties to reach an agreement:

- Create an environment with objects that "prime" or encourage collaboration and dialogue. Use soft chairs, serve hot drinks or food, and create a welcoming atmosphere.

- Slow, soften and relax your tone of voice, and create a context of acknowledgement and appreciation. Thank them for coming.

- Listen closely to the words they use and search for ways of reframing them from negative to positive. Ask them, for example, what words they would use to describe the kind of conversation they want to have, or what they most want to say to each other, or hear the other person say in response.

- Use words repeatedly that emphasize the outcomes you want to achieve, like "fair" or "satisfying" or "creative." Try to avoid words like "tough" or "win" or "dissatisfied" or "hard."

- Speak to both hemispheres of the brain, and help translate between them. When a "left brain" point is made, see if you can translate it into "right brain" language.

- Look directly into the eye that can access information located in a particular hemisphere of the brain.

- Meditate regularly to build empathy and emotional balance.

- Avoid pictures or objects that denote fighting, imbalance, hardness, roughness, coldness. Favor items that connote balance, cooperation, unison of movement or rhythm, warmness, softness. Keep the temperature on the warm side.

- Bring emotional processing directly into the conversation by asking "How does that feel to you?" "Why is that important to you?" or "What does that mean to you?"

- Make unilateral, unexpected concessions yourself and ask the parties to do the same, for example by asking, "What would you be willing to offer, in a spirit of collaboration, without any expectation of return?

- Be "environmentally" generous, in attitude and demeanor.
- Seek ways of unifying both sides against the problem and its causes. Remind them of what they have in common.
- Find ways of encouraging them to act jointly, as in solving a common problem. Help them to act in synchrony.

None of this is meant to suggest that oxytocin should be administered in large and continuous doses to parties in mediation, or that we should slip into clever, yet inevitably crass forms of neuro-manipulation. Rather, it is to say that we have been working with brain chemicals unconsciously for many years, and it is now possible for us to begin thinking about conflict resolution more scientifically and proactively, using the information we gather to encourage more positive responses, and being careful to build transparency, empowerment, and authenticity into the process. Deep ethical issues need to be addressed to make sure we are not undermining mediation by adopting a cunning or unscrupulous approach to the use of brain science.

# CONCLUSION

Perhaps the most extraordinary thing about the human brain is its capacity to understand and alter the world, including itself. We have begun a period of rapid, perhaps exponential increase in understanding how the brain operates, and a growing ability to translate that knowledge into practical techniques. But without an equally rapid, equally exponential increase in our ability to use that knowledge openly, ethically, and constructively, and turn it into successful conflict resolution experiences, our species may not be able to collaborate in solving its most urgent problems, or indeed, survive them.

All of the most significant problems we face, from war and nuclear proliferation to terrorism, greed, and environmental devastation, can arguably be traced to our brain's automatic responses to conflict. Out of the last few years of neurophysiological research has emerged a new hope that solutions may indeed be found to the chemical and biological sources of aggression. These solutions require not only a profound understanding of how the brain works, but a global shift in our attitude toward conflict, an expanding set of scientifically and artistically informed techniques, a humanistic and democratic prioritization of ethics and values, and a willingness to begin with ourselves.

# CHAPTER 5

# HOW TO MEDIATE RELIGIOUSLY WITHOUT RELIGIOUS BELIEFS

## Spirit and Heart-Based Techniques for Atheists and Agnostics

*Religion is a defense against the religious experience.*

~ Carl Jung ~

*Keep your intelligence white-hot
and your grief glistening,
so your life will stay fresh.
Cry easily like a little child.
Do not seek any rules for worship.
Say whatever your pained heart chooses.*

~ Jelaluddin Rumi ~

OVER THE LAST DECADE, there has been a remarkable increase in the importance and influence of spirituality in the field of dispute resolution, and a growing awareness of the sweep and power of heart-based techniques. At the same time, less paradoxically than it may seem, there has been an explosion in the publication of books on atheism and open challenges to the sway of religion in society and politics.

Most noticeably, Richard Dawkins and Christopher Hitchens have recently leveled serious criticisms at religion that have gained widespread currency and support. These critiques have not been directed at the experience of awe and reverence, or the presence of profound and poignant truths about life and death, but at the unprovable nature of religious beliefs, contradictions in scripture, and the hypocrisy of religious organizations and practices over the course of centuries.

These critiques have highlighted a significant contradiction, based on two well-documented historical truths. First, all of the world's religions acknowledge the value of peace, forgiveness, kindness, compassion, and conflict resolution, and played a mediative role in resolving disputes. Second, these same religions have, on countless occasions, transgressed their values, fomented conflicts and wars, sanctioned murderous regimes, and become deeply mired in blood. All have used religious ideas for cruel and aggressive purposes; suppressed honesty, kindness and compassion; and waged or supported "holy wars" against innocence and diversity that we now regard not only as mistaken and disastrous, but may even view with horror.

We are now able to recognize that there is a third truth that is rapidly gaining ground. Surrendering the claim to exclusive religious correctness (which has done far more damage in my view than political correctness), and to the scientific accuracy of scripture and theology, allows secular spiritual practices to develop, cross-fertilize, and re-invigorate, fortifying their deepest, most ancient and essential tasks: improving our capacity to experience love, compassion, empathy, caring, kindness, and forgiveness; strengthening heartfelt communications and relationships; and making peace between adversaries in conflict.

The Dalai Lama has enthusiastically supported this effort, providing a useful set of criteria for distinguishing religion from spirituality:

> I believe there is an important distinction to be made between religion and spirituality. Religion I take to be concerned with belief in the claims to salvation of one faith tradition or another—an aspect of which is acceptance of some form of meta-physical or philosophical reality, including perhaps an idea of heaven or hell. Connected with this are religious teachings or dogma, ritual, prayers and so on. Spirituality I take to be concerned with those of the human spirit—such as love and compassion, patience, tolerance, forgiveness, contentment, a sense of responsibility, a sense of harmony, which bring happiness to both self and others.

The difficulty with many of the discussions and debates between atheists and religious adherents in recent years is that they fail to make this distinction, adopting instead the Aristotelian idea of the "excluded middle," in which only one of two opposing ideas can be true while the other must then be false, fanning passionate convictions that inflame intolerance on all sides.

In conflict resolution, by contrast, there is an explicit search for multiple truths, subtle connections, and spiraling, integrated, synergistic middle paths that neither require nor reject religious beliefs, but regard the existence of a deity or "supernatural" force as, at least for the moment, beyond our ability to convincingly answer. Yet conflict resolution is clearly able to affirm, and increasingly turn to practical use, our natural sense of awe and wonder, our capacity for love and heartfelt connection, our depth of spirit and soul, all of which can produce profound, miraculous experiences for those who have become stuck in conflict.

Clearly, compassion, forgiveness, mindfulness, and similar ostensibly religious virtues play a significant role in the discovery and development of these techniques. Yet so also do independent and secular virtues such as honesty, non-conformity, emotional availability, courage, support for diversity, dissent, and free scientific inquiry.

While Dawkins and Hitchens offer a sustained and detailed critique of religion, no less an atheist than Karl Marx wrote eloquently, interestingly, and with greater insight regarding the complex and subtle relationship between these virtues and organized religion:

> Religion is the general theory of this world, its encyclopedic compendium, its logic in popular form, its spiritualistic *Point d'honneur*, its enthusiasm, its moral sanction, its solemn complement, its general basis of consolation and justification. It is the fantastic realization of the human being, inasmuch as the human being possesses no true reality. The struggle against religion is therefore indirectly the struggle against that world whose spiritual aroma is religion.

> The abolition of religion, as the illusory happiness of the people, is the demand for their real happiness. The demand to abandon the illusions about their condition is a demand to abandon a condition that requires illusions. The criticism of religion therefore contains potentially the criticism of the Vale of Tears whose aureole is religion.

Even the following famous passage that contains Marx's most frequently quoted (and misunderstood) line orients conflict resolvers in a similar interesting and useful direction:

> Religion is the sigh of the creature overwhelmed by misfortune, the sentiment of a heartless world, and the soul of soulless conditions. It is the opium of the people.

These passages, of course, were written in a period of intense political conflict and retreat from suffocating religious orthodoxy, still singed by the fires of the Inquisition. If, however, we pick up the thread of these remarks and regard the search for human happiness as primary and the critique of it's otherworldly and often escapist religious manifestations as secondary, we can agree with the mathematician Pierre Simon Laplace, who is alleged to have replied, when asked by Napoleon why he had not mentioned God in his brilliant work on astronomy, "I have no need of that hypothesis."

In mediation, we can offer a similar rejoinder, and focus our attention on what works in resolving disputes rather than on divisive issues that are beyond our capacity to know or prove to those who will not in any case agree. We can then, for purposes of investigating how we might successfully transform the misfortunes and "sentiment of a heartless world," and the "general basis of consolation and justification" as experienced in conflict resolution into higher order practical solutions, demanding "real happiness" while at the same time recapitulating Ludwig Wittgenstein's well-known injunction, "Whereof one cannot speak, thereof one must be silent."

It is possible, however, to go much further and move through and beyond these critiques by regarding the misfortunes, the heartless world, and the soulless conditions as precisely a demand for real happiness, one that is not illusory, unfalsifiable, or other-worldly, but practical, down-to-earth, and available in principle to everyone in conflict through mediation. This demand makes its first appearance in the simple form of communicating the suffering that is experienced in every conflict. It makes its second appearance in the search for real, practical, heart-based, and spiritual solutions.

The problem for mediators is not whether to promote or disparage the tenets of any particular belief or religious practice, but how to become more skillful and courageous in the discovery, invention and use of entirely secular spiritual and heart-based techniques in conflict resolution that form part of, yet transcend the limitations of each *particular* religious tradition. The development of secular, poignant, non-religious ways of touching each party's deepest desires, opening their hearts to each other, shifting their attitudes and altering their energy in conflict, is of immense importance in mediation, and leads to methods for promoting real happiness. Here is why and how.

## CONFLICT AND SPIRITUALITY

In every conflict, "self" and "other" not only cease being united, but become divided and hostile to each other. The primary goal of conflict resolution is therefore to abate and reverse that antagonistic relationship. The rise of antagonistic relations between self and other is a deeply philosophical and neurological topic, but it is also a profoundly spiritual issue in all religious traditions, and, I would assert, a practical problem for mediators in every dispute. [Parts of the remainder of this chapter have been drawn from *The Crossroads of Conflict.*]

Countless efforts have been made to define spirit, all of which seem woefully inadequate from the point of view of spiritual experience. Partly, this is because definitions consist of words, which are inevitably self-referential, circular, and elusive. Partly it is because every definition is a limit, and no limit can explain something that, by its nature, feels limitless. Definition means to make finite, which automatically places anything non-finite beyond definition. Moreover, language is a way of pointing attention at things, feelings, and ideas. But who or what is doing the pointing? Is it possible to point at what is pointing? And what is the nature of an attention that is not pointed at anything?

On the other hand, we can try to define spirit by what it is not and distinguish it from other things. But if spirit is related to energy, as I believe it is, it is impossible to find anything that does not possess energy, and we again find ourselves unable to separate it from everything else. We can try to define spirit by comparing it to something to which it is similar, but if it is part of everything, how do we create a unique or meaningful contrast? How do we compare something that is not comparable to something that is? Against what background does it appear as foreground?

A number of plausible scientific justifications might be offered to explain this definitional difficulty. If we draw on scientific ideas currently being advanced to explain equally bizarre aspects of the physical universe, we can see that several might help explain spiritual experiences. A complete scientific explanation of spirit is beyond my expertise and the scope of this book, but having thought about the issue for some time, I am drawn to a number of intriguing possibilities.

For example, it might be that what we are trying to measure extends throughout the entire universe and is larger than any existing unit of measurement. It might be, as in quantum physics, that what is being measured is so small that the act of measurement substantially alters it, or is antithetical to its operation. It might be, as with quarks inside subatomic particles, that it is impossible to separate pieces of it because the gluonic forces holding them together increase asymptotically in strength as they are pulled apart. It might be that what is being measured is itself a quality of space or time or matter and energy, from which everything is formed and by which it is measured, so that it is indistinguishable from everything else. It might be that the addition of an "imaginary number" based on the square root of minus one creates a complex "world line," a path through space-time that allows for such phenomena. It might be, as with quantum "entanglement," that the wave-like nature of spirit allows information to be shared instantly across physical distances. It might be that what we want to measure cannot presently be detected because it is the size of the smallest "Planck" unit of space-time at $10^{-33}$ centimeters, and either wrapped up or extended throughout the universe like one of the 10 or 11 dimensional strings some physicists think may constitute all matter. It might be that what we are defining is not a thing at all, but a wave that collapses when we try to measure it. It might be that the left brain cannot know what the right brain is doing. It might be that the piece we are examining is holographically organized, indivisible, and therefore indistinguishable from a much larger whole. It might be that it is a four-dimensional quality beneath the three-dimensional surface of a membrane, or "D-brane," or a tiny fifth dimension that separates two four dimensional branes. It might be that it is the by-product of an "compactified" or infinitely large, warped fifth dimension. It might be, as believed by physicist David Bohm, that it is a quality of "wholeness" or "implicate order" that has been "enfolded" into the structure of the universe and cannot be detected.

The point of these speculations is that there are a number of plausible scientific explanations for the existence of spirit that do not require divine intervention, mystical suppositions, religious doctrine, moralizing attitudes, or muddled "new age" thinking. Spirit is not the same as religion, morality, or ethics. It does not require belief in any kind of supernatural deity. While spirit forms the basis for much religious experience, religious beliefs have little in common with spiritual experiences, which precede and transcend them. Instead, as has been noted, religious beliefs often lead to the silencing of spirit and the suppression of doubt and curiosity that feed it

Moreover, certain qualities seem to disappear the moment we try to analyze, quantify, distinguish, measure, or enumerate them. For example, what happens to the feeling of love when we undertake to scientifically specify its nature? Is it possible to reason from a list of objective characteristics of love to a full description of what it feels like? Can the idea of love ever be satisfactorily explained to someone who has never experienced it? What is in common between the experience of happiness or joy and the five or 10 elements a scientist may cite as making them up? Who is unable to recognize the fragrance of a rose, or the sound of raindrops, or the feel of a lover's touch? But who can accurately describe them to someone who has never experienced them? The English writer, G. K. Chesterton described it a little differently:

> The real trouble with this world of ours is not that it is an unreasonable world, nor even that it is a reasonable one. The commonest kind of trouble is that it is nearly reasonable, but not quite.... It looks just a little more mathematical and regular than it is; its exactitude is obvious, but its inexactitude is hidden; its wildness lies in wait.... Everywhere in things there is this element of the quiet and incalculable.

Creativity and counting do not mix, Eros and Logos are non-translatable, and calculating a bottom line to love is as absurd as employing the pleasure principle in accounting, or judging a work of poetry, music, or art by strictly mathematical standards. This difficulty led poet John Keats to define "negative capability" as a state of mind in which a person "is capable of being in uncertainties, doubts, without any irritable reaching after fact and reason." Or, as Timothy Leary famously yet accurately remarked, "You have to lose your mind to come to your senses."

Even at a physical level, it is not possible to use quantitative measures or reductionism to define qualities or things that are holistic, or entirely different, or emanate from everywhere. This idea has gained wide currency. Where, for example, in the schematic diagram of a television set's electronic circuitry is there anything that could predict MTV or Star

Trek? Can one take apart the engine of a car and discover the thrill of racing, or locate the single organ responsible for sustaining life in the human body? As Antoine de Saint-Exupery wrote: "How could the drops of water know themselves to be a river? Yet the river flows on."

These scientific and philosophical ideas suggest that there is something in nature, conflict, and spirit that are both finite and infinite, simple and complex, predictable and chaotic. While there may appear to be nothing in common between complexity, chaos, and predictability; or between infinities and seemingly normal, finite equations in mathematics; unpredictability routinely arises from conditions that are determined and in equilibrium, and infinite results appear unexpectedly even in simple, finite mathematical calculations. Chaos and disorder are continuing sources of complexity, innovation, and higher levels of order, both in natural and human conflict.

Consequently, it is important to recognize that conflict and spirit are not only intrinsic, indispensable, creative properties of the universe *as a whole*, but that the more deeply we understand the subtle, complex, chaotic, infinite, and contradictory elements of conflict, the closer we come to understanding and being able to use spirit—not as a belief, wish, source of solace, or imaginary construct, but as a wellspring of practical technique, and an integral, holistic component of the art and science of resolution.

## WHICH ONE IS MOVING?

In defining spirit, it is customary to begin by associating it with mind and contrasting it with body, following philosopher Rene Descartes' famous declaration, "I think, therefore I am." Yet as the Buddhist monk Katagiri Roshi humorously pointed out:

> I have been reading your Descartes. Very interesting. "I think, therefore I am." He forgot to mention the other part. I'm sure he knew, he just forgot: "I don't think, therefore I'm not."

Descartes considered the mind, which he associated with the soul, to be a separate, distinct, disembodied, non-physical entity:

> ... a substance, the whole essence or nature of which is to think, and that for its existence there is no need of any place, nor does it depend on any material thing; so that this "me," that is to say, the soul by which I am what I am, is entirely distinct from body, and is even more easy to know than is the latter; and even if body were not, the soul would not cease to be what it is.

Considerable scientific research, however, has demonstrated that Descartes' "soul" and the body are inseparable, integrated parts of a whole organism that is, in turn, an inseparable, integrated part of its entire physical and social environment. Neurologist Antonio R. Damasio has summarized this research, finding, in opposition to Descartes, that:

> ... love and hate and anguish, the qualities of kindness and cruelty, the planned solution of a scientific problem or the creation of a new artifact are all based on neural events within a brain .... The soul breathes through the body, and suffering, whether it starts in the skin or in a mental image, happens in the flesh.

Whether we regard the brain or the spirit as primary, or the soul as the thing that connects them, together they form an undifferentiated whole, containing the entire movement of each into the other, their integration, and ultimate harmonization on a higher level, which we can analogize to spirit. In this sense, spirit is what transcends the effort to separate wholeness into categories, thereby lying beyond categorization.

At the risk of making this perplexing point more confusing, consider the ancient Zen problem of "which one is moving," in which two monks are avidly debating which is moving, the flag or the wind. They ask the Sixth Patriarch, who answers that it is their minds that are moving. In the language of physics, we can only know what is moving by comparing its change in location to something that is not moving. However, as Einstein explained, if our point of reference is the universe as a whole, everything is in motion relative to everything else, and we cannot know which is moving because there is no fixed or absolute point of reference we can use for comparison.

Accordingly, if there is one object, we can only measure its movement against the background of space, which is itself in motion. Black ink is noticeable only against a white page, the page against a book, the book against a scenic background, the background against a horizon, and the horizon against the whole of space. But against what do we contrast the whole? If spirit is a quality of the whole, we will be unable to distinguish it by comparing its motion against a moving background of which it forms a part.

Or consider a movie projected onto a screen. We lose ourselves in the movie by ignoring the screen on which it is projected. If the screen is bent, moving, or has its own color or shape, it distorts the movie. Spirit can be thought of as the screen on which our sensations, thoughts, and feelings are projected, the space in which they move, the background of everything. Ultimately, however, the screen is no different from the movie that is playing on it, space from the objects moving in it, or background from foreground.

This is therefore described in Zen as "not one, not two." It is neither the whole nor any of its parts, neither unity nor diversity, but greater than both. As Lao Tze wrote in the Tao Te Ching, "The Tao that can be spoken is not the true Tao." In relation to conflict resolution, this can be thought of as the undifferentiated unity that precedes conflict and follows its transcendence. It is the truth of who we are when we are one, two, and one again, but at a higher level, and therefore not exclusively either, both, or neither. This indivisible, holistic quality transcends all opposing categories and is the energy and animating principle that unites and divides them. The arising of sensation is concurrent with the separation of opposite forms, while its cessation is their coming together, transcendence, and disappearance.

Differentiation into categories for purpose of analysis does not imply actual separation. Thus, while waves can be subdivided into peaks and troughs, there are no naturally occurring waves that can be said to possess peaks in the absence of troughs. Similarly, what is material cannot be distinguished from what is spiritual, just as matter cannot be contemplated separate from energy, and as Einstein famously demonstrated, they are fundamentally the same.

We can therefore analogize spirit to the movement, rhythm, and unimpeded flow of the energy of life within, around, and between us; the backdrop or screen against which our physical sensations, mind, and emotions are projected. Spirit is anything left over after our physical, mental, and emotional sensations become silent; a combination of intense awareness and unfocused concentration; and undifferentiated direct experience, as in the Zen adage, "The sound of the rain needs no translation."

## EXPERIENCING SPIRIT THROUGH MINDFULNESS

Even if we find it difficult to define spirit, we nonetheless experience it directly and materially in countless ways. We may experience spirit when our energy shifts as we interact with different people; or as we transition from being focused to being distracted, angry, or frightened; or when someone withdraws, or decides without physical or verbal signaling that it is time to leave. We may experience it as our conversations grow shallower or deeper, or our attention is diverted from the past or future into the present. We may experience it intentionally by moving closer to someone, starting from four or five feet away, and sensing how the quality and depth of our energy, communications, and relationship shift as we approach the invisible boundary that defines their "space." We may experience it unexpectedly at the moment of death of someone we love, allowing us to sense the difference between a living, even comatose being, and lifeless flesh; as what it was that disappeared.

Whether we call it spirit, soul, life force, energy, awareness, or chi, we may feel it anytime, all the time, as it arrives, increases, declines, and leaves. We may experience it as open and joyful, or closed and sad, or compressed and fearful, or expanded and courageous. We may experience it in silent meditation by finding a still, soundless space inside that is neither body sensation, thought, nor emotion, but an undirected energy of awareness and equanimity, a state of being that is empty yet full, stable yet constantly changing, a nowhere that feels like home. We may experience it by tracking our breath or body sensations, or shifting attention, say, from our feet to our hands, and considering what exactly it was that moved from one to the other. We may experience it by observing physical, mental, or emotional sensations and watching as they interact and flow. We can consider: Who is the one watching, and who is being watched? And who is now watching the watcher?

As Leonard Riskin has written, mediators can use mindfulness meditation to break up conflict-hardened physical responses, ideas, and emotions, and form a clear, self-reflecting awareness of conflict experiences, become conscious of their impermanence, accept their emotions with ease and equanimity, watch as they move toward completion and closure, and learn to respond more skillfully as they arise and disappear.

Meditation can also help parties in conflict dissolve the grasping, aggressive and defensive behaviors that have kept them locked in impasse by noticing these qualities silently and peacefully within themselves and disarming them through empathetic listening, collaborative negotiation, and openhearted communications. They can do so by finding a place of stillness, like the calm in the eye of a hurricane, and becoming more focused, calm, and present, even in the midst of raging, adversarial arguments. [For more on meditation, see Chapter 6.]

Spirit has a quality of timelessness to it, allowing mediators to slow the pace of conflict communications and move the parties' awareness into the present, as happens in moments of intense love or joy, in the presence of great art, in meditation, in nature, in danger, in moments of deep awareness and realization, and in heartfelt moments. We can create a sense of timelessness in mediation by:

- Listening without aim or intention to each person;
- Observing moment by moment what is happening inside ourselves and others, especially in moments of intense emotion;
- Expanding empathy and compassion toward others;
- Encouraging them to speak honestly from their hearts, and act with unconditional integrity and skill;
- Recognizing that their conflicts have something important to teach them;
- Working collaboratively in a committed way to transform and transcend what got them stuck.

In each stage of resolution and location of conflict, it is possible to reduce the amount of conflict or friction by calming or slowing its energy. We can stop people from fighting and deescalate their confrontations using physical calming techniques, as by sitting down with them, slowing the pace of their speech, and listening peacefully. We can settle issues using intellectual calming, as by brainstorming creative ideas, caucusing, and open-mindedly exploring options. We can resolve underlying issues using emotional calming, as by acknowledging feelings, empathizing, and satisfying interests. We can encourage forgiveness using spiritual calming, as by encouraging them to learn from their conflicts, apologize, design rituals of closure, and let them go. We can reach reconciliation through heart calming, as by opening heart-to-heart communications, rebuilding trust, and encouraging acknowledgement and expressions of affection. And we can help prevent future disputes using systemic or environmental calming, as by identifying the systemic sources of chronic conflict and designing systems that prevent or respond more effectively to them.

There are three main reasons for mediators to learn how to directly experience spirit. First, by doing so, we will become increasingly aware of the quality of our energy and notice what happens to it when we do, think, say, or experience anything. We will become more aware at a sensitive level of how it shifts as conversations move from conflict to resolution, from lies to telling the truth, from anger to compassion, from defensiveness to open-heartedness, and the reverse. This will allow us to notice more readily when the parties we are working with do the same.

Second, directly experiencing spirit, energy, or life force can make us more skillful in directing or channeling it. We can discover how to make it stronger, clearer, and brighter, and avoid what makes it weaker, blurrier, and darker. We can more quickly reconsider the insulting remark we are about to make and speak respectfully, even to someone who does not do the same to us. We can watch angry judgments form and choose to listen with an open heart, even to people who are upset with us.

Third, the experience of spirit can help us recognize that conflicts exist partly to teach people who they are and might become, by helping us identify and resolve the underlying issues that are dissipating their life energy. Every conflict is simply a place where people are stuck and unable to be relaxed and authentic in the presence of others. By learning to become unstuck and authentic, they can discover how to transcend—not only that particular conflict, but all similar conflicts, liberating themselves from the confused ways of thinking and inauthentic ways of being that got them stuck in the first place. In this sense, every conflict is fundamentally a spiritual path leading to higher levels of conflict and resolution.

Resolution can be understood as altering the content or substance of conflict, transformation as altering its contour, shape or form, and transcendence as altering its context or meaning, thereby reducing its overall energy and attractiveness and disabling its underlying causes and cohesiveness. Transcendence occurs when people gain insight into the attitudes, intentions, and perceptions that sustained their conflict; improve their ability to learn from it, work collaboratively to prevent its' reoccurrence, and evolve to higher levels of conflict and resolution. Transcendence implies rising above, no longer participating in, overcoming, moving beyond, evolving, growing, leaving behind, learning and letting go. In conflict, it means releasing ourselves from negative, closed-hearted, antagonistic, withholding, impasse-generating attitudes toward our opponents and ourselves, and as Rumi suggests, crying easily and saying whatever our pained heart chooses.

To achieve transcendence, it is necessary for us to work through the deeper issues in our conflicts and learn the lessons that lie concealed in each of the places they are located. If conflict is present in our bodies, minds, emotions, spirits, hearts, and systems, is it not apparent that the deeper lessons they contain must also be located in these areas, and that each must be identified, discussed, resolved, transformed, and transcended in its own unique ways? If our conflict is primarily based on intellectual differences, rational dialogue will likely cure it. But if it is emotional or heart-based, no amount of intellectualizing will succeed in resolving, let alone in transforming or transcending it.

## TOWARD A PRACTICAL SPIRITUALITY

Beyond these ideas about spirit in conflict resolution lies what we might think of as a *practical*, ordinary spirituality, or what can be thought of in connection with mediation as "everyday spirituality." From this perspective, it then becomes possible to translate common religious practices into secular mediation techniques.

In the set of all possible conversations between people, there will naturally be some that are richer, more complex, nuanced, poignant, profound and meaningful than others. These are conversations in which the deeper meaning of the communication is allowed to emerge. These conversations are transformation points—places where openings and passageways appear to a fundamentally different level of communication, relationship, dialogue, and shared meaning. Where do these transformation points occur? How do we find them? How do we expand them and turn them to use?

In a wonderful Native American story, an elder tells a child he has two warring wolves inside him, one filled with hatred, fear, and distrust, and the other filled with love, compassion, and acceptance. The child asks which one will win, and the elder tells him, "Whichever one you feed." Every time we insult our opponents, we feed something insulting within ourselves. Every time we hate someone, a wave of hatred gathers and coalesces inside us. When we act without conscience, it is always ourselves we betray. And when we extend love, compassion, or forgiveness, love, compassion, and forgiveness grow within us. These are spiritual choices with life consequences that determine not only what we do, but who we become through our conflicts.

In the Cherokee version of this story, the elder adds, "If you feed both, they both win."

> You see, if I only choose to feed the white wolf, the black one will be hiding around every corner waiting for me to become distracted or weak and jump to get the attention he craves. He will always be angry and always fighting the white wolf. But if I acknowledge him, he is happy and the white wolf is happy and we all win. For the black wolf has many qualities – tenacity, courage, fearlessness, strong-willed and great strategic thinking – that I have need of at times and that the white wolf lacks. But the white wolf has compassion, caring, strength and the ability to recognize what is in the best interest of all... Feed them both and there will be no more internal struggle for your attention. And when there is no battle inside, you can listen to the voices of deeper knowing that will guide you in choosing what is right in every circumstance.

It can be argued that religions encompass these life choices, but our problem as mediators is to turn their practice in a secular direction and use it to drive technique. For example, here are some ancient religious practices that can be adapted to secular purposes and used to encourage spirituality and transcendence in mediation, illustrated by simple phrases that capture, in miniature, the essence of the practice:

| | |
|---|---|
| Confession: | "Yes, I did it." |
| Repentance: | "I'm sorry I did it." |
| Righteousness: | "I agree to act differently in the future." |
| Renunciation: | "I won't be your enemy." |
| Surrender: | "You're totally right." |
| Affirmation: | "I'm sure we can work this out." |
| Forgiveness: | "Please forgive me." |
| Reconciliation: | "I love you. Can we start over?" |
| Purification: | "I now understand why I did it and promise not to do it again." |
| Prayer: | "I wish you the best." |
| Ritual: | "Let's shake hands on it." |

In addition to these, there are dozens of methods of strengthening spirit and heart that do not require a religious gloss or connection, many of which are used by different religious traditions, that might prove useful in mediation:

| | |
|---|---|
| Acting on principle | Taking risks |
| Giving to others | Cultivating awareness |
| Radical acceptance | Paying attention |
| Sharing | Teamwork |
| Empathy | Loving ourselves and others |
| Forgiveness | Passion |
| Humor | Silence |
| Self-discipline | Making choices |
| Changing patterns | Surpassing our limits |
| Rituals and ceremonies | Surrendering attachments |
| Unconditional caring | Being authentic |
| Dedicating or consecrating | Sacrifice |
| Being Completely Present | Dedication to a higher purpose |

## TEN PATHS TO TRANSCENDENCE

Transcendence cannot be encompassed in ten, twenty, or a hundred paths. Nevertheless, we all transcend conflicts throughout our lives. For example, we do not so much resolve the conflicts we experienced as children on the playground, or as teenagers with our parents over curfew, as we outgrow and thereby transcend them. We do so by learning skills the conflict took place in order to teach us, because we could not perform them. In this way, the child on the playground discovers how to move from parallel to cooperative play, and the teenager becomes responsible for his or her own safety.

Here are some generic methods mediators can use to discover where some of these "points of transcendence" appear. I have tried to make them as brief, easy, practical, and effective as possible, though many are complex and difficult in practice. They are presented sequentially to encourage a sense of discernment and inquiry about how they occur, whereas in mediation practice they often resist ordering. Here, then, are 10 paths to transcendence for mediators, each of which will afterwards be explained in detail.

1. Engage in committed, openhearted listening, as though your life depended on what you are about to hear.
2. Use a spotlight of narrow, focused attention and a floodlight of broad, sweeping awareness to clarify what is taking place beneath the surface.
3. Use dangerous empathy to search for the center of the conflict within yourself, then ask questions to discover whether the same might be true for others.
4. Use dangerous honesty to communicate your deepest understanding to others.
5. Use your heart to locate a heart-space in the conversation, then open and expand it.
6. Craft a question that asks people to speak and listen directly from their hearts.
7. Work collaboratively to redesign and reform the cultures and systems that produced or reinforced the conflict.
8. Clarify and reinforce what was learned from the conflict, and use it to improve and evolve to higher levels of conflict and

resolution.

9. Move the conversation toward forgiveness and reconciliation.
10. Design and execute a ritual of release, completion, and closure.

It is important to recognize three limitations before reviewing these paths. First, it is impossible to pin heart-based communications down precisely, and at a certain level of exactness, every additional effort to do so will only make them more jittery and uncertain. Second, it is possible to follow each path faithfully, yet fail because we did not go deep enough into our own hearts, or may have harbored personal judgments, or perhaps sent mixed messages. Third, other people's decisions to participate in heartfelt conversation do not belong to us, and they may not be ready to follow any of the paths we open. Our role is to create an alternative path, invite them to walk it, and then let them choose whether they will follow it.

## 1. Engage in Committed, Open-Hearted Listening

Committed listening originates in the heart and is oriented toward poignancy and meaning. This is fundamentally different from routine listening or hearing, which originates in the mind and is oriented toward objectivity and facts. Most listening in conflict is adversarial, as when we listen for holes or openings in people's arguments or for what is wrong with them and what they are saying. Listening in mediation is collaborative, as when we listen for what is right about them and what they are saying and. Listening is a matter of intention and can be done in a variety of ways.

- Contextual Listening, as when we listen for background information, unspoken assumptions, and unmet expectations.
- Active Listening, as when we actively participate in discovering what others are trying to tell us and communicate our interest in their remarks.
- Responsive Listening, as when we engage in conversations or dialogues that flow back and forth between us.
- Creative Listening, as when we search for innovative solutions, or try to come up with novel approaches to solving a problem.
- Empathic Listening, as when we listen as though we were the one who is speaking.
- Undivided Listening, as when we are no longer aware of our

presence as a listener, but completely merge with the speaker and their story.

- Committed Listening, as when we listen as though our lives depend on understanding what others are saying.
- Listening with the Heart, as when we listen with an open heart to the heart of the one who is speaking.

As people tell stories about their conflicts and describe what happened to them, listening in these ways can help us locate the heart of their story and transform. Mediator Ken Dvoren wrote the following description of what listening with the heart means to him:

> When I'm conversing with someone, I find myself wanting to be listened to more than I want to listen. The person I'm talking with appears to want the same thing, and so a subtle competition ensues. When I decide to listen to the other with interest and empathy, I move beyond myself and notice that rather than feeling neglected or diminished, I'm actually expanded. My identity, who I sense myself to be, now includes them, so that as I give to them, I am also receiving.
>
> When I'm in conflict with someone, the stakes are even higher. I not only want to be heard but also to be agreed with and to be right. And it's even harder to listen to the other, because if I do I might understand them, and if I understand them I might agree with them, and if I agree with them I might think I have to give them what they want, and if I do then I won't get what I want. But if I take what feels to be the very real risk of truly listening, the same remarkable event occurs. As my identity expands to include them, I start to appreciate their values and interests, and when I consider meeting their needs, I realize I will also be meeting my own. And I have finally met my brother.

## 2. Use Narrow, Focused Attention and Broad, Sweeping Awareness

A second path consists of using a narrow spotlight of pinpointed, focused attention, and a broad floodlight of sweeping, unfocused awareness to clarify what is taking place beneath the surface of conflict. Awareness can be divided in two parts: pointed, laser-like concentration on a narrow, critical area; and expansive, generalized awareness of a wide-ranging, undivided whole. Both are useful, especially in combination. For example, imagine crossing a busy, two-way, pothole filled street with a full glass of water without spilling a drop. The only way to succeed is by merging these two forms of awareness, focusing simultaneously on each car and pothole and on the task as a whole. This may sound simple, but even a small loss of attention may make it impossible. The most important source of lost attention in conflict is ego, along with its ablest enforcers, anger, fear, shame, guilt, jealousy, and pride.

When we feel ashamed or proud of what we did in the past, or angry or frightened about what will happen in the future, we withdraw energy and attention from what is happening in the present and lose concentration. To communicate with the heart, we need to cultivate curiosity, attentiveness, agility, and acceptance in the present. The poet e.e. cummings stated this idea more eloquently as a wish: "May your mind walk around hungry and fearless and thirsty and supple."

### 3. Use Dangerous Empathy

Using dangerous empathy means searching for the heart of the conflict within ourselves and vividly imagining what it might have been like for others. This means understanding what might cause us to feel or act the way they did. The information gained through empathy will not provide us with an answer, but sometimes it will give us a question that can take us into the heart of a conflict.

While ordinary empathy is easily extended to people we regard as similar to ourselves, dangerous empathy stretches our identity to include those whose behaviors we find incomprehensible, burdensome, or abhorrent. For mediators, this means dropping our pretense of objectivity, neutrality, expertise, and professional truth, admitting our humanity (including distasteful qualities within ourselves), and endeavoring to become omni-partial, or on both people's sides at the same time, no matter how difficult this may seem.

At a heart level, there is no such thing as objectivity, neutrality, expertise, or abstract truth. These are professional disguises, used to create a safe emotional distance from our clients, camouflage fears, conceal biases, discount criticisms, and dress up subjective ideas in order to impose them on others. By presenting ourselves as objective, neutral experts who know what is true, we limit our capacity for empathy, discount subjective information, and minimize the value of dissenting perspectives. And, as Shakespeare has Macbeth proclaim, "Who can be wise, amazed, temperate and furious, loyal and neutral in a moment? No man."

Historically, objectivity and neutrality emanate from the law, where any combination of power and subjectivity may lead to tyranny, injustice, corruption, or oppression. The law makes a conspicuous display of objectivity, neutrality, expertise, and abstract truths, partly because these qualities advertise formal independence from powerful vested interests, and partly because people might otherwise refuse to obey. Yet while judges routinely exercise power in the name of objectivity, neutrality, and abstract truth, they also inevitably rely on their own conscious and subconscious subjective experiences, values, and ideas, transforming these into universal standards that allow them to lecture litigants from the bench on how they ought to behave.

Mediators, on the other hand, operate by consensus, placing the power to resolve conflicts in the hands of the parties. As a result, we are permitted to be subjective, vulnerable, human, and wrong, which are essential for opposing parties to experience us as unbiased and empathetic, and trust that their heart-based communications will be heard, honored, and appreciated.

When I find myself thinking judgmentally and unable to place myself on both people's sides at the same time, it is usually because they have pushed my emotional buttons, making it more difficult for me to find their hearts inside my own, reach out to them, understand their deeper issues, or work through mine. When I notice and own my judgments and biases, I become more effective in understanding theirs, am better able to perceive what lies at the heart of their dispute, and know what I need to do to mediate more effectively.

Many people resist or are frightened of empathy because they do not want to become vulnerable in the presence of their opponents, or be forced to surrender their anger, or dissuaded from behaving badly. Many mediators believe that exercising empathy and opening their hearts will make them appear unprofessional, denying them the safety of neutrality, expertise, and distance. The opposite is true. Neutrality, expertise, and professional distance close our hearts, blind us to the subtler sources of conflict, and make us less skillful in reaching people and assisting them in reaching resolution, transformation, and transcendence.

There are many varieties of empathy. There is, for example, physical empathy, which allows us to experience sympathetic bodily pains and pleasures; intellectual empathy, which allows us to identify with other people's thoughts and ideas; emotional empathy, which allows us to resonate with their feelings; spiritual empathy, which allows us to recognize their intentions, sincerity, and life energy; and heart empathy, which allows us to access wisdom and heart-truths.

## 4. Use Dangerous Honesty

After using dangerous empathy to learn what is in people's hearts, we can use dangerous honesty to communicate what we learned. Ask yourself honestly: have you ever gained a useful insight while listening to someone describe a conflict and said nothing? Most of us are reluctant to tell painful truths to others, partly because we believe they will interpret our comments as judgments or hostility. Yet our inability to communicate what we observe can prevent them from learning what their conflict took place to teach them, and us from becoming more skillful in communicating potentially painful information.

Telling the truth in conflict requires a "Golden Rule," inviting us to communicate, as we would have others communicate with us. Often, this means framing insights as questions, asking them in gentle and supportive ways, making sure we establish strong empathetic connections before we speak, listening with our hearts for what the other person most wants to say, lowering our voices, slowing our pacing, and being prepared to accept a greater, perhaps less skillful honesty in return.

The more dangerous it feels to communicate something, the more likely it may be to trigger transcendence, since what we fear most in conflict is change that may result in loss. For this reason, the most dangerous truths are those we already subconsciously know to be true, but deny, disguise, resist, and defend against, precisely because of their far-reaching implications. None of this would make any sense if the truth were not dangerous. And in conflict, as in society, as Oscar Wilde observed, "An idea that is not dangerous is unworthy of being considered an idea at all."

### 5. Locate and Open a Heart Space

A fifth path is to use your heart as a sense organ to locate a heart space in the conversation, then open and expand it. The only practical instruction I can offer is to focus attention on opening your own heart, then listen as it responds to whatever is being said and ask yourself what you think that person most wants or needs to hear. When your heart vibrates with some poignant truth, or another person's pain or pleasure, or wants to shout or laugh or cry, it is likely that their heart just opened and revealed its innermost secrets.

### 6. Craft a Question that Asks People to Speak and Listen from Their Hearts

A sixth path to transcendence is to ask a question that emanates from your heart, and invites the parties to speak and listen from theirs. The deeper purpose of listening and empathy in conflict resolution is to lead us to questions that can touch people's hearts and encourage open, honest communication. There is no single question that will work in every situation, and it is necessary to design each question using empathy, honesty, and intuition to probe what lies beneath seemingly superficial statements.

### 7. Work Collaboratively to Redesign and Reform Cultures and Systems

A seventh path to transcendence is to work collaboratively to redesign and reform the dysfunctional conflict cultures, contexts, environments, and systems that caused or reinforced the conflict. Many conflicts reappear after having ostensibly been resolved because the hostile cultures, contexts, environments, and systems that triggered or supported them were not also transformed. Preventing future conflicts requires us to collaboratively examine the behaviors and conditions we have accepted as necessary or taken for granted, accurately identify the systemic elements that contributed to our conflict, apply design principles to increase the possibility of early resolution, and act to improve these elements, even in small ways.

As an illustration, chronic conflicts regularly occur in health care facilities between doctors, nurses, staff, administrators, patients, and families. Most of these flow not from substantive disagreements over how to achieve medical goals, but from administrative hierarchies, bureaucratic procedures, insulated departments, physician/nurse miscommunications, racial and cultural differences, high-risk outcomes, overwork, low wages, lack of training in handling intense emotions, abrasive or manipulative personalities, unmet expectations, labor/management disagreements, and a lack of robust conflict resolution alternatives.

These conflicts directly impact the quality of health care and productivity. They undermine teamwork and morale, increase resistance to improvements, raise costs, waste time, alienate patients, interfere with healing, and occupy the conscious and unconscious attention of everyone at work, creating additional burdens on a system already groaning under the weight of reduced resources and increasingly stressful work.

Instead of trying to resolve each isolated, seemingly interpersonal conflict that emanates from these complex, compound sources, it makes sense to treat them as chronic and use a systems design process to staunch their flow. Systems design techniques can activate not only individual, but collective transcendence through organizational learning and evolution based on the lessons distilled from conflicts.

## 8. Clarify and Reinforce What Was Learned, and Use It to Improve and Evolve

An eighth path to transcendence consists of clarifying and reinforcing what was learned from the conflict and using it to improve and evolve to higher levels of conflict and orders of resolution. In my experience, every conflict contains a hidden, metaphorically coded lesson that the parties either already subconsciously know, or quickly recognized once it is clarified and their defenses are dropped.

It is possible for mediators to ask people directly or indirectly what they think their conflict is trying to teach them, or what they have already realized or learned as a result of their dispute. I sometimes ask people, after resolving their issues, if they would be willing to meet with others who did not participate in the mediation to describe what they learned from their conflict, how they came to resolve it, and what they think might be done to prevent future conflicts.

Learning from conflict sometimes means working collaboratively with their opponents to make improvements or take simple corrective actions that could make a difference. Occasionally it means apologizing for their thoughtlessness, or acknowledging the other side's good intentions. Sometimes it means inviting their opponents to ask questions about things they don't understand or can't surrender. Sometimes it means helping them microscopically alter their behaviors, so they no longer act in ways that can be interpreted as hostile, unpredictable, or inauthentic.

I call this "micro-surgery," in which people minutely and precisely analyze the sources of their conflict, approach each sub-issue separately and meticulously, microscopically, and painstakingly identify tiny collaborative steps they can take, individually or collaboratively, to prevent them from occurring again. I write these up as agreements, and ask the parties to sign and post them, and meet periodically to assess their progress.

### 9. Move Toward Forgiveness and Reconciliation

A ninth path to transcendence is to move the conversation in the direction of forgiveness and reconciliation. [This step is addressed in greater detail in my book *Mediating Dangerously: The Frontiers of Conflict Resolution*.] In this context, it is important to recognize that every heart-based conversation points finally and fundamentally in the direction of forgiveness and reconciliation, which are each essential for people to complete their conflicts, reclaim their energy, and move forward in their lives.

Forgiveness and reconciliation are not only large-scale outcomes, but small-scale openings and transformations that often go entirely unnoticed. In many intimate relationships, small "forgivenesses" and reconciliations may occur several times a day, often without much skill or forethought. What is most important is for people to *complete* their conflicts, leaving nothing left over to make their next dispute more difficult to resolve. To do so, they need to not only do and say whatever will allow them to reach closure, but to *become* people who are able to learn from their conflicts and successfully transcend them. Ultimately, this requires self-forgiveness, self-reconciliation, and a positive re-integration of their opponents within themselves, in the form of wisdom, learning, empathy, and evolution, leading to transcendence.

## 10. Design and Execute a Ritual of Release, Completion, and Closure

A tenth path to transcendence consists of designing, collaboratively if possible, a ritual of release, completion, and closure. Without rituals, it is easy for people to fool themselves into thinking they have transcended their conflicts, allowing old patterns to draw them into renewed hostilities.

In the end, transcendence cannot be predicted or compelled. While these ten techniques have worked for me, they may not work for you. It is important to find your own way of *being* in conflict; and if possible, to open your heart and help others do the same. In doing so, I hope you will discover, as I have, that the heart is a reliable source of insight, uniquely capable of revealing who we are and showing us what we most need to know.

With these tools, we may ultimately recognize that what divides us is less important than what wraps us in a common embrace, whether what divides us is grand or petty, international or familial, profound or silly. We may then discover that at the heart of every conflict we encounter lies the possibility of its conversion into forgiveness, reconciliation, and love.

## WHY MEDIATE WITH THE HEART?

At the core of mediation lies a deceptively simple proposition: No one gets into conflicts over things they don't care about. Therefore, every conflict involves an element of caring—sometimes about content, process, individuals, or relationships; sometimes about how they have been perceived or treated; sometimes about expectations, attitudes, and intense emotions that have been triggered but remain unresolved.

Thus, nearly every conflict triggers anger, frustration, anguish, grief, betrayal, and distrust, induced by the loss or destruction of something each person cares deeply about, together with a desire—not only for the relationship or object of caring, but for a quality of self that emerges only when we are able to love and be loved in return. For this reason, every conflict breaks our hearts. Indeed, for this reason, every conflict reflects a spiritual crisis in which we are asked to overcome our anger, fear, guilt, grief, and pain, and open our hearts—not merely to other people, but to repressed parts of ourselves, and thereby discover our capacity for unconditional empathy and compassion.

We can think of heart as a metaphor for caring, as well as for the center or essence of an issue over which people act out during their conflicts. Yet conflicting parties generally avoid these issues and confine themselves to superficial conversations, even when they are highly emotional. They focus on facts or issues rather than on collaborative processes, dysfunctional systems, deep desires or heartfelt relationships. For what generally seem like good reasons, they avoid the risk of becoming open and vulnerable in the presence of their opponent who they do not trust.

Yet it is possible for all of us to engage in deeper, more poignant, profound, and dangerous conversations that reveal who we actually are, and what we care about most intensely. These deeper conversations require a higher order of skills on the part of mediators—not just settlement, problem solving, or even emotional processing skills, but heart-based skills that are grounded in empathy and compassion, in order to search for the soft center and underbelly of the conflict, and invite the parties to open their hearts in the presence of people they may not trust or like.

Our most intimate relationships are selected, shaped, and shattered at a level far beneath that of conscious attention. No one decides, on the basis of intellectual criteria alone, to fall in love or terminate a relationship. Neither do we make these "decisions" only on the basis of isolated intellectual, emotional, or physical inputs. Instead, these seemingly intellectual, emotional, and physical decisions supplement, support, and rationalize choices we have already made in what we euphemistically call our hearts. As G. K. Chesterton wrote, "There is a road from the eye to the heart that does not go through the intellect."

The difficulty is that once our hearts have been shut or broken, we do not readily open them again, especially in the presence of those who shut or broke them. Yet by hardening our hearts, we justify hard-heartedness in return, allow the damage they caused to live on inside of us, and encourage them to do the same. Still, in spite of this damage, whatever is genuinely heartfelt inside us endures and continues to seek communion, even in the form of pain. The reason is simple, and expressed powerfully by Alexander Solzhenitsyn:

> If only it were all so simple! If only there were evil people somewhere else insidiously committing evil deeds, and it were simply necessary to separate them from the rest of us and destroy them. But the line dividing good and evil cuts through the heart of every human being. And who is willing to destroy a piece of his own heart.

A different way of saying the same thing can be found by answering a simple question: What is the very first part of you that shuts down when you are in conflict, and what is the very last part of you that opens up again once it is over? For me, and for most of the people I mediate with, it is our hearts.

Here is another question suggesting the same answer: Of all the possible conversations you could have with your opponent, what kind of conversation would you most want to have? For me, and most the people I mediate with, it is a heartfelt conversation, not one that is trivial or solves a superficial problem.

Every open-hearted conflict communication is therefore dangerous because no one gives unambiguous permission to transform their conflicts, because permission to stop a fight or settle a dispute does not translate into permission to resolve the underlying reasons that gave rise to it or reach forgiveness and reconciliation; because every transformation or transcendence represents a breakthrough that could not have been imagined or consented to at the time the permission was given; and because every genuine breakthrough dramatically alters people's lives, changing even what is considered acceptable.

Heartfelt communications have the unique ability to neutralize and overcome the accusations, defenses, trivialities, and smokescreens that fill ordinary conflict speech, allowing people to communicate directly with the hearts of those they have hurt, or who have hurt them. They allow us to re-draw the boundaries that separate adversaries, making them smaller, closer, and more porous, and enlarge the concerns that divide us, reframing our caring as shared.

While this may sound imprecise or idealistic, it has been my experience over three decades of mediating thousands of disputes that every one of us can become more skillful in speaking to people's hearts in dispute resolution without becoming imprecise, sentimental, or romantic. Indeed, I have become a better mediator by doing so, even in disputes where heart issues are not immediately apparent or recognized.

We can develop heart skills by regarding them as practical, involving clearly identifiable methods and techniques, and grounded in roughly replicable experiences. To develop heart skills we need to learn how to open our own hearts, identify the clues dropped in people's communications that reveal their desire for heartfelt interactions, and design questions and interventions that invite our opponents into heart spaces, reinforce heartfelt responses, and enlarge or expand them.

## HEART AS THE CENTER AND CROSSROADS OF CONFLICT

Every conflict is a crossroads, revealing radically different life choices. Think of it this way: if we are stuck at a certain place in our lives and cannot grow, evolve, or become who we otherwise might be, would it not make sense for our subconscious minds to find an opponent who can point out to us exactly where we are stuck, pressure us to become unstuck, and clarify through negative behavior what got us stuck in the first place so we can free ourselves?

Every conflict presents the parties and the mediator with a continuing choice. We can cling to safe territory, keep the conversation focused on relatively superficial issues and avoid mentioning deeper topics, thereby remaining locked in impasse and placing our lives on hold. Or we can take a risk, adopt a more open, honest, empathic approach, and initiate deeper, more dangerous, heartfelt conversations that could change our lives and result in transformation and transcendence. Which path we take depends partly on our willingness to invite heartfelt communications. As Sri Aurobindo wrote, "The mind creates the abyss, the heart crosses it." Try crossing it, and see what happens.

# CHAPTER 6

# MEDIATION AND MEDITATION

## The Deeper Middle Way

*Now, there are many, many people in the world, but relatively few with whom we interact, and even fewer who cause us problems. So, when you come across such a chance for practicing patience and tolerance, you should treat it with gratitude. It is rare. Just as having unexpectedly found a treasure in your own house, you should be happy and grateful to your enemy for providing that precious opportunity."*

~ The Dalai Lama ~

CONFLICT IS EVERYWHERE, NOT only between human beings, but throughout nature, from quantum mechanical particles to dark energy and the soap bubble structure of galactic superclusters. Nonetheless, we each take our conflicts personally, and far from being happy or grateful to our enemies, we often allow ourselves to be thrown off balance by them and drawn into unpleasant ideas, negative emotions, and destructive behaviors.

So what is the solution? How do we return to balance and equanimity, perhaps even to happiness and gratitude? One option is to reframe the way we understand and experience conflict by examining them through the lens of meditative practices, starting with the "four noble truths," as originally taught by the Buddha. For example, we can acknowledge first, that our lives are filled with conflict and the suffering it produces; second, that our suffering is caused by attachment, perhaps to unrealistic outcomes or our own false expectations; third, that we can stop, settle, resolve, transform, and transcend our conflicts by letting go of our attachment; and fourth, that the best way of doing so is by following a middle path—in other words, not merely by meditation, but mediation as well.

However, as we quickly learn, following a middle path in conflict may seem simple, yet it often conceals a number of deep, profound, and complex truths, one of which is that are skills and methods that look simple at the beginning, and become simple again only after passing through a period of complexity and confusion. As the famous Zen saying puts it,

> Before I started meditating, blue mountains were blue mountains and white clouds were white clouds. After meditating a while, blue mountains were no longer blue mountains and white clouds were no longer white clouds. But after meditating further, blue mountains are blue mountains and white clouds are white clouds.

When we engage in conflict, we can easily delude ourselves into thinking we are following a middle path, but are actually, in a simple way, merely withdrawing from our opponents, remaining silent, becoming apathetic or accommodating, compromising to get it over with, or avoiding engagement and controversy. If we want to become "Bodhisattvas of conflict," we need to follow a different path, one that leads through, and to the other side of the complexity of our conflict.

There are actually two fundamentally different middle paths in conflict, leading to entirely different outcomes. The first consists of compromise, as when we add two sums and divide by two to find their average, or when we combine hot water with cold water to produce water that is neither hot nor cold but lukewarm.

A second "middle" path consists of engaging with the conflicted parts of ourselves and our opponents, and discovering through awareness and the experience of authentic relationships, a deeper source of compassion than the abstract, purely meditative one that is often devoid of genuine experience with real, sometimes difficult people, and as a result, does not require us to grapple with or overcome our attachments at their source.

This second middle way consists of combining entirely different things in a synergistic and creative way, as when we combine water with flour and heat to create bread, which is not an average, but an outcome that is completely new and different. The same transformation takes place in conflict when we ask questions that reveal the underlying reasons for a dispute, which often have nothing in common with the issues we are vigorously fighting over.

This deeper, *transformational* middle way can be accessed through "skillful means," which include not only meditation techniques that assist us in becoming more centered, compassionate, and aware of ourselves and others; but mediation techniques that enable us to engage in authentic and committed listening, openhearted communication, empathetic dialogue, creative problem solving, collaborative negotiation, and genuine forgiveness and reconciliation. These quintessential conflict resolution skills allow us to escape the ruts our conflicts draw us into and reveal to us that it is the mind, and not just the flag or the wind that is waving. How do we reach this awareness?

Within Buddhism, there are not only mindfulness or awareness practices, but concentration and insight practices. These ultimately merge into a single practice that encompasses every part of us. As the great Rinzai teacher Hakuin wrote:

> What is the true meditation? It is to make everything— coughing, swallowing, waving the arms, motion, stillness, words, action, the evil and the good, prosperity and shame, gain and loss, right and wrong—into one single koan.

A koan, of course, is a brief story, question, or dialogue that conceals a paradox, or to paraphrase, a conflict that contains two truths, and does so in such a way as to illuminate their essential unity. The most commonly referenced koan is "What is the sound of one hand clapping?" To rephrase this paradox in relation to conflict, we might ask: "What is the disagreement between one party?"

Therefore, if we act in such a way that there are no longer two parties, but only one, the conflicts between them must dissipate, lose their energy, and begin to disappear, simply because there can't be a conflict without two or more sides. Yet there is a still deeper truth about the duality of conflict. The brilliant physicist Neils Bohr, in describing the paradoxes of quantum theory, coined the useful expression "complementarity," which he defined as "a great truth whose opposite is also a great truth."

When we apply this idea to conflict resolution, we discover that a far more profound outcome than the simple disappearance of conflict is the unification of sides that we formerly regarded as opposite. But if all the individuals and ideas that are locked in conflict, at a deeper level, simply represent partial expressions of a deeper underlying truth, what is the point or purpose of their conflict, if not to lead them to this truth? Doesn't all their yelling and posturing seem a bit silly and pointless? Perhaps it was this realization that led Hakuin to write:

> As for sitting in meditation, that is something which must include fits of ecstatic blissful laughter—brayings that will make you slump to the ground clutching your belly, and even after that passes and you struggle to your feet, will make you fall anew in further contortions of side- splitting mirth.

What is the source of this laughter and mirth, as applied to conflict? I believe it is the profound recognition that all our fuss and bother amounts to precisely nothing; that it is simply a cleverly disguised opportunity for transformation and transcendence; a chance to be grateful to our enemies and learn from them, and happy that they finally brought us back to sanity, unity, and equilibrium.

Practicing this koan, we can now easily understand that there is indeed a deeper "middle" path, one that opens for each of us when we transform and transcend our conflicts by finding a synergistic middle way that includes both of our opposing truths, integrates mediation and meditation into a single koanic practice, and merges both into a single, undifferentiated whole. Zen writer Bernard Phillips suggests:

> In Zen, the effort and the result are not two different things, the means and the goal are not separated, the finding occurs in the very seeking itself. For ultimately, what is sought is the wholeness of the seeker, and this emerges only in the wholeheartedness of the seeking.

In other words, the "simple," lesser, trivial middle path that lies on the simple side of complexity disappears when we "walk the talk," and become not just the resolution, and not just the integrated expression of both sides legitimate interests, but the creative force of the conflict itself, as revealed in the way that we approach and engage in it. Jean Genet was once asked, if there were a fire in his home what would he save. His response was, "Why the fire, of course." Perhaps for us it is the conflict.

As mediators, we routinely enter the conflicts of others, but do not always understand that, as a consequence, their conflicts also enter us. As Friedrich Nietzsche wrote, "When you look into the abyss, the abyss looks into you." Meditation is a way of looking into the abyss of conflict and allowing it to enter us without overwhelming our equilibrium, but instead, pointing us in the direction we need to go—not only to assist others in stopping, settling, resolving, and transforming their conflicts, but to finally and completely transcend them within themselves. How can meditation assist mediators in achieving these outcomes?

There is a natural affinity between mediation and meditation, inasmuch as both recognize the simultaneity of unity and opposition;

both acknowledge the presence of diverse and multiple truths; both seek a middle way; and both encourage us to have a complete experience of our conflicts, allowing us to evolve, become both, and then leave them behind. As the 12th century Chinese Zen monk Ta Hui (Dahui) wrote, "When a person is confused, he sees east as west. When he is enlightened, west itself is east." In practical terms, what does this realization mean for conflict resolution?

While there are dozens of personal benefits that flow from meditation, experienced mediators may find, as I have, that mindfulness, awareness, contemplation, and insight practices can enhance our professional skills as well. It is not uncommon, for example, for mediators who meditate regularly to experience the following benefits:

- Improved ability to remain calm and balanced in the presence of conflict and intense emotions;
- Greater willingness to move beyond superficiality in conversation and enter into the heart of whatever is not working effectively;
- Expanded sensitivity to the subtle clues given off by the parties, indicating a shift in their thoughts, feelings, and attitudes;
- Deeper insights into the nature of suffering and what might be done to release it;
- Greater awareness of what apparent opponents actually have in common, though they emphatically disagree with and even dislike each other;
- Improved creative problem solving skills and ability to invent or discover imaginative solutions;
- Expanded capacity to calibrate and fine-tune insights and intuition;
- Greater sensitivity to the natural timing of the conflict;
- Increased willingness to engage in "dangerous" or risky conversations and raise sensitive issues without losing empathy;
- Decreased investment in judgments, attachments, expectations, and outcomes;
- Increased ability to be completely present, open, and focused;

- Reduced stress and burnout.

Of course, this does not mean that meditators always make superior mediators. Buddhists have not always been the best role models in conflict, and Buddhism has, in my experience, fallen short in developing the social practice of what we can describe as "inter-mindfulness," or what meditation teacher Shinzen Young calls "the monastery of relationships," which is an essential part of many conflict resolution practices.

Nonetheless, it is clear that within meditation, as within mediation, lie a clear set of instructions on how each of us can improve our skills in handling conflict and untangling the knots they create inside us. What are these instructions, and how exactly do we develop these skills?

While meditation is traditionally oriented to internal sensations, awareness is a generic source of skillful techniques and insights—not only into ourselves, but into others and our relationships with them; and as a result, into the nature and sources of conflict. Meditation and conflict resolution can therefore both be said to operate by improving awareness, which can easily be applied to a wide range of difficult conversations, interactions, and relationships.

Whereas meditation focuses attention primarily internally, for example on the breath, noticing thoughts, emotions, and internal bodily sensations, then letting them go; mediation focuses attention primarily externally, for example on communications and interactions between conflicted parties, noticing and discussing what is not working in their relationship and asking what might be done to improve or let go of it. By combining these approaches creatively, we are able to produce fresh combinations.

We can say, for example, that mediative forms of meditation consists of using awareness to expose the false expectations, self-judgments, and suffering that lie hidden beneath the surface of our conflicts. These keep us attached to our opponents and the issues, and create the sensation of a solid, separate "Self" that congeals quickly around unresolved antagonisms. Awareness encourages us not simply to imagine or verbalize loving-kindness, but to act and make it real.

Meditative forms of mediation, on the other hand, can be said to consist of becoming keenly aware of what is taking place inside us in the midst of conflict, using empathy and compassion to increase our awareness of what is happening internally within ourselves and the parties, and helping to bridge the gap between them so they can discover a way out of their antagonism, attachment, and suffering. These combined practices enable us to move beyond merely settling, or even resolving disputes to discover insightful ways of transforming and transcending them.

We can do so, for example, using mediation techniques such as empathetic storytelling, conflict coaching, and private reflection; by creatively reframing differences to reflect underlying unities; by asking conflicted parties to empathetically imagine what it might have been like to have experienced what the other person experienced; by asking them to speak directly to each other from their hearts; by drawing their awareness to what they are experiencing right now, or the way they are talking to each other, and asking each what the other person could do that would help them listen or speak more openly, then doing that, and using feedback to reinforce awareness and on-going practice.

It is one thing, of course, to use these techniques in mediation with complete strangers, and quite another to avoid losing our balance when we are the ones in conflict. How do we use these skills in such a way as to remain authentically ourselves, and become unconditionally openhearted and aware in the presence of our opponents? Even a strong intention to practice compassion and loving-kindness may not suffice to achieve this goal, so it is useful to ask ourselves some difficult questions that will help us draw our attention to what really matters. Here are a few to start with:

- What do I really know about my opponent?
- What would make *me* decide to speak or act like that?
- What is true for him/her?
- What questions could I ask to find out?
- What am I doing that is helping to fuel the conflict?
- What am I not doing that is helping to fuel the conflict?
- What is the crossroads I am at right now in this conflict?
- What is the deeper "third path" or "middle way" in this conflict?
- How might changing my attitude, behavior, or response help me resolve, transform, or transcend it?
- What would it take for me to do so?
- What is preventing me from moving forward or letting go?

- Can I maintain awareness of my breath and what is happening in my body, mind and emotions while I am in the midst of conflict? What is stopping me?
- What price have I paid for this conflict? What has it cost me?
- How much longer am I prepared to continue paying that price?
- What is the most difficult aspect of this conflict for me? What makes it difficult?
- What would it take for me to let it go completely and open my heart to the person I am fighting with?
- What is one thing the other person could do that would change my entire attitude toward the conflict? What is one thing I could do?
- Is there anything I would be willing to apologize for, or offer, without any expectation of return?
- On a scale of one to 10, how sincere and deep was the apology I gave or the gesture I made?
- What would it take to make it a 10?
- What does my heart tell me to do?

The opportunities for integrating awareness, insight, and contemplation practices into dispute resolution, both personally and professionally, are limitless. Yet the modern world makes it much more difficult to sustain these attitudes and practices. The highly respected Zen scholar and practitioner D. T. Suzuki, who was invited to speak in London in 1936, noticed the contrast between traditional contemplative practices and the demands of modern life:

> How can I construct my humble hut right here in the midst of Oxford Circus? How can I do that in the confusion of cars and buses? How can I listen to the singing of birds and also to the leaping of fish? How can one turn all the showings of the shop window displays into the freshness of green leaves swayed by the morning breeze? How am I to find the naturalness, artlessness, and utter self-abandonment of nature in the utmost artificiality of human works? This is the great problem set before us these days.

The problem today is even greater, as it includes an additional difficulty: How we do so not just in the midst of our internal conflicts, or even the deeply upsetting interpersonal conflicts that transpire in our families, workplaces, and neighborhoods, but in response to wars, bombings, genocides, ethnic prejudices, religious intolerances, mistreatment of women and children, and seemingly endless international conflicts over environmental choices, economic policies, and political beliefs that affect us all deeply, no matter how far we may imagine we are from the turmoil and terror.

Sometimes, as May Sarton wrote, "One must think like a hero to behave like a merely decent human being." But sometimes one must also think like an ordinary human being, merely chopping wood and carrying water, in order to be heroic enough to find ways of transcending the conflicts that separate us.

In order to escape the downward gravitational tug of antagonisms on any level, and resolve, transform, or transcend them, we require a combination of inner and outer skills. If we do not transform ourselves, we will find it much more difficult to transform the world; and if we do not transform the world, we will find it far more arduous to transform ourselves. In meditation as in mediation, inner and outer increasingly merge and reveal themselves as one.

These are just a few of the important lessons we are able to learn by seeking the places where meditation and conflict resolution intersect. What is fascinating to me as a practitioner of both over the course of many years are the ways they call out to each other, invite each other in, and increasingly require the skillful practice of the other. Trying to meditate without addressing underlying conflicts makes our practice superficial, frustrating, and incomplete. Trying to mediate without cultivating awareness traps us at the surface of our conflicts and ignores what is taking place in their depths. When we combine these practices, we are led to the deeper middle way, and to profound insights, both for ourselves and others.

These are difficult tasks and a lifetime's work, but there are lots of resources that can help you make a start. I want to go further, however, and encourage all mediators to learn more about meditation as a practice and start or continue a regular practice of sitting meditation, as an integral part of your work in dispute resolution. As the great Buddhist sage Dogen wrote, "Practice and enlightenment are not two." Neither are mediation and meditation.

## WHAT IS MEDITATION? A FEW IMPRESSIONS

Meditation is sometimes described as the practice of mindfulness, which has been variously described as:

- Bare attention
- Mirror-like thought
- Non-judgmental observation
- Impartial watchfulness
- Non-conceptual awareness
- Present-moment awareness
- Non-egotistical consciousness
- Awareness of continual change
- Participatory observation

In my experience, meditation is simply the concentrated observation and sensuous experience of life energy as it breathes, flows and evolves within us, including the one who is observing and experiencing and the difficulties encountered in doing so. It is then the gathering of insights based on this process and the transformation of those insights into life changes.

There are two basic varieties of meditation: first, concentration on an *object* of meditation, such as the breath or a mantra; and second, awareness or mindfulness without a particular object, as by observing the *flow* of attention or experience as it moves within and around you.

By continuing to focus your attention inward and carefully observing your breath or the quality of your moment-by-moment experience, you become more aware of the nature of awareness and more precise about the methods and qualities of mindfulness.

Countless attempts have been made to define meditation, yet the experience of practice resists all of them. Rather than attempt another unsuccessful definition, I offer the following *impressions*. These are meant, like a painting, to convey its shape, texture and meaning, more as art than science. I encourage you to write your own.

- Meditation is experiencing yourself and what surrounds you as one.

- Meditation is falling like a rock, deeper and deeper into a bottomless lake.

- Meditation is grabbing on to something until it turns into nothing, then letting go and allowing it to grab you.

- Meditation is realizing that all efforts to define meditation are empty and pointless. In the Zen phrase, "Once the mind is clear, the very word *clarity* is like a snowflake on a red hot stove."

- Meditation is sinking slowly into the sweet, loving arms of the self, and then discovering that the Self, as an indivisible entity, does not exist.

- Meditation is stopping the wind of thoughts from creating waves on the surface of the lake of consciousness, slipping beneath the surface, and letting the current take you where it will.

- Meditation is seeing what lies beneath surface appearances, but without looking; it is hearing what is unspoken, but without listening; experiencing what is changing, but without sensing; being mindful of what is present and aware of your thoughts, but without thinking.

- Meditation is letting the bathrobe of the self slip effortlessly from your shoulders and fall to the floor, leaving you naked inside and out.

- Meditation is feeling like a kitten, picked up by the scruff of its neck.

- Meditation is feeling tiny champagne bubbles of ecstasy percolate through every cell of your body.

- Meditation is experiencing your entire body as though it were made of honey, and being able to taste it.

- Meditation is living completely, like a bonfire, leaving no trace of your self.

- Meditation is finding a place of complete stillness, with no moving parts other than the breath and impermanent processes of life.

- Meditation is "leaping like a tiger while sitting."
- Meditation is unconditional loving-kindness. It is "environmental generosity," without any expectation of return.
- Meditation is radical self-acceptance and non-engagement with the flow of experience, allowing a far deeper engagement to occur.
- Meditation is what happens when you move from swimming on the surface to diving deep beneath it.
- Meditation is dismantling not only the meaning of experience, but the scaffolding and the system that support and generate it.
- Meditation is letting the beauty that surrounds you become who you are.

## 30 Varieties of Meditation

1. Sitting, standing, lying, or walking in silence
2. Observing or counting the breath or heartbeat
3. Repeating a mantra or nonsense word
4. Humming or chanting
5. Sweeping awareness through the physical body and sensing each part of it
6. Observing moment by moment changes in bodily sensations
7. Noticing and correcting posture
8. Focusing and concentrating sight, smell, hearing, taste, or touch
9. Thinking about the meaning of a *koan* or perplexing, paradoxical question
10. Practicing *mudra* or gestures
11. Cooking, washing dishes, gardening, or cleaning house
12. Practicing yoga, *tai chi*, or *chi gong*
13. Probing the nature of impermanence
14. Understanding that you *are* the Buddha
15. Drawing or observing a *mandala* (complex circular drawing)
16. Noticing the flow of objects in nature
17. Watching a candle, fireplace or similar object of meditation

18. Observing as much detail as possible while looking at a complex natural scene
19. Dancing, swimming, running, or other athletic activity
20. Tracking the flow of intense emotions inside you, or within others
21. Practicing the *jhanas* (meditative absorptions)
22. Becoming aware of the nature of awareness
23. Noticing the subtle shifts of energy that flow between people as they interact, especially in conflict, in casual conversation and during sex
24. Observing what happens inside your body when you get into conflict, or lose mindfulness and balance
25. Observing what happens in your body when you resolve your conflict and regain mindfulness and balance
26. Practicing compassion, loving-kindness, or *tonglen* (sending joy and well-being to others)
27. Experiencing the indefinite, composite nature of the self
28. Letting go, disengaging, and releasing yourself from attachment
29. Living completely in the present
30. Finding the place inside yourself where all of the above intersect

All of these experiences can be seen to consist of self, awareness, and some object of awareness. In meditation, these elements increasingly merge and become one.

## STARTING ALONG THE PATH

There are two fundamental approaches we can take to understanding ourselves. The first is to interact with others and bounce or reflect ourselves off other people, objects, ideas, feelings and experiences, then see who we become as a result. This is the method of activity or *doing*, which includes the ways we express ourselves through art, relationships and conflict.

The second is by doing nothing, but sitting in silence, watching, and gaining insight into our deepest, most essential nature. This is the method of insight or *being*, which underlies the many ways we express ourselves through activity and doing.

Meditation is the moment-by-moment experience of our own deepest self, of our life-energy in its simplest possible form. It is pure being. It is being fully awake, aware, and unattached to the flow and impermanence of experience. This may sound simple, but takes considerable practice, in the course of which our brains actually re-wire themselves.

Here are the most important elements, based on my personal experience, in how to begin to meditate:

## A. Setting-Up:

1. Find a quiet spot to meditate in – or, after you have practiced awhile, a noisy, busy one can deepen your practice.
2. Choose a time to begin. The best time is a few minutes after waking up and before the distractions of the day begin, but it is possible to meditate at any time.
3. Pick a length of time to meditate, starting easy with 5-10 minutes and stick to it. Then gradually extend it, moving gradually toward 45 minutes to an hour or more each day.
4. If possible, sit cross-legged without your back resting against anything. This will allow you to center your body more easily, feel less pain, and notice torpor.
5. Sit on a cushion that rotates your body slightly forward, and dress warmly. This will make it easier to sit for longer without back pain.
6. Place a blanket over your legs and tuck it under your knees. This will keep you warm and help keep your legs from falling asleep.
7. Keep several tissues handy.
8. While you can meditate with your eyes open, in my experience, beginners do much better with their eyes closed.

## B. Beginning:

1. Close your eyes, center yourself within your physical body, scan the various parts of your body, and release any tension you may feel within your body.
2. Center yourself within your mind and let go of any thoughts you may have.
3. Center yourself within your emotions and let go of any feelings

you may have.

4.  Center yourself within the flow of energy that connects your physical body, your mind and your emotions, and let go of any knots or blockages you may find.

5.  Select one of the following methods as a place to begin:
    - Observe your breath, perhaps counting each breath from one to 10.
    - Repeat a mantra like "Om."
    - Observe and label body sensations as they come and go.
    - Watch the flow of your thoughts and feelings as they come and go.
    - Do a lengthy, detailed scan of your body from the tip of your toes to the top of your head.
    - Notice the changing nature of your experience each moment.
    - Focus on pleasant sensations as they arise, or on positive thoughts and feelings, like love for a person or animal.

6.  Be aware of your posture, of how your mind is constantly changing, and most important, of who it is who is aware of these changes.

## C. Tips and Trouble Shooting:

1.  In the beginning, it will be difficult to keep your "monkey mind" still. It may help to give yourself five minutes when you begin to let your mind roam – then return to concentration.

2.  When you lose focus, gently, compassionately, and good-humoredly return your focus and your practice, and notice what brings you closer to who you are when you are doing nothing, and no one is looking.

3.  If you are counting your breath, try repeating each number for several breaths, to slow your thinking process by giving it something meaningless and repetitive to latch onto.

4.  If this doesn't work, instead of focusing on the breath or a mantra, try forming a mental picture of a person or animal you love. Allow the feeling of love to fill you. Now let go of the mental picture and the person or animal, and just concentrate on the feeling of love inside you, letting it expand and fill you.

5.  If thoughts keep arising, watch them, and ask yourself: "What does the *experience* of thought feel like?" Then get ready to feel your next thought. If you are 100 percent focused and waiting to see what the next thought will feel like, it won't arise.

6.  If this doesn't work, shift your attention to your *lack* of attention, and watch your mind as it jumps from idea to idea or sensation to sensation.

7.  Relax. As your mind experiences what it feels like to concentrate without an object of concentration, in time it will automatically begin taking you there.

## D. Deepening:

1.  At a certain point in your meditation, the quality of your moment-by-moment experience may begin to grow heavy, thicken, deepen, and feel viscous. Go with that feeling.

2.  Your body and mind may begin to merge and seem as one, and the various parts of your body/mind – arms, legs, thoughts, feelings, may start to form a single mass of sensation. This sensation is the *field* of your being. Go with it.

3.  If you then observe your breath or count it or repeat a mantra, it will feel significantly different to you, and you will recognize that these actions were not the point of your practice, but designed to take you deeper, and to reveal have far you have gone.

4.  As you experience the energy of your body/mind, you may become aware of what feel like cellular "pinpricks," a bit like the feeling when your leg falls asleep, but not painful. Or, you may experience "champagne bubbles," each of which may feel like a microscopic burst of pleasure or ecstasy.

5.  A feeling of deep and intense pleasure often accompanies this experience. You can imagine that your entire body and mind were made of delicious dark chocolate, and you can taste it. Sink into it, enjoy it, and then let it go. Whatever you hold on to holds on to you.

6.  Notice that there is a space of complete integration, in which self and other, outer and inner, doing and non-doing merge

and become one. Rest in that space, and let it expand.

**E. Strengthening:**

1. Try meditating in the worst possible settings. I call this "dental chair meditation," "conflict meditation," or "noisy crowd meditation." When you are in a dental chair, close your eyes and notice your moment-by-moment feelings and responses. Find a bus bench at a busy intersection, or stop for a moment on a noisy street, close your eyes, and allow the sounds and experiences to pass easily through you, enjoying your ability to find a still, quiet space in the midst of noise and chaos.

2. Gradually extend the length of your practice and find moments throughout the day when you can have "mini-meditations," especially in distress.

3. Remember that every meditation session is unique and will range from superficial to deep, yet beneath each of these experiences a gradual deepening is taking place. Consider it a lifetime practice.

4. Try a Tibetan practice called "tonglen," in which you breath in all the suffering and pain in the world and breath out all the love and courage and compassion inside you to those who are suffering. This counter-intuitive practice will help you discover that these are renewable resources, and that you don't need to grasp or hold on to them.

5. Allow the work you do in meditation to seep into every aspect of your life. Become more aware of what it feels like to be off-center or out of sync, and re-center yourself.

6. There is no destination, it is all journey, so relax and enjoy the ride.

## FINAL ADVICE

Don't panic, don't worry, don't beat yourself up, don't give up, but keep trying. Progress is slow at first, but accumulates, and over the course of years, your body and mind will gradually learn, in spite of all your lapses and distractions, how to find their own natural resting state.

Read books, listen to tapes, join others, attend meditation sessions and retreats, and follow whichever paths appeal to you. As you do, however, recognize that meditation is friendly to *all* paths, and it is the places where they overlap and intersect that the deepest truths lie.

Finally, don't turn it into a drudge, a chore, or a source of anxiety and attachment. Take joy in everything you do, and that will be enough.

## A Summary: How to Meditate in Nine Not-So-Easy Steps

1. Wake up!
2. Center yourself.
3. Pay attention, especially to what is paying attention.
4. Let go of everything you possibly can.
5. Let go of letting go.
6. Discover the one within the many.
7. Expand your capacity for love and compassion as much as you can.
8. Rest inside it.
9. Enjoy!

## The Parable of the Mountaintop

Imagine for a moment that you live in a city and would like to climb to the top of a mountain. You can't see the mountain from the city and don't know how to get there, but are determined to try. You climb inside your car, pack everything you think you might need, and begin to drive. At first, you have lots of errands to run and are not even sure how to get out of the city, so you spend a lot of time stopping and starting, getting lost, and driving around in circles.

At last, you reach the outskirts of the city and start to relax. The further you get from the city the more relaxed you become. Off in the distance, through the smog and haze, you can just make out the presence of a mountain and begin to drive in its direction. You may stop along the way to rest or picnic and pick the flowers, and may think that this is as far as you really want to go.

After a while you decide to keep going anyway, and the mountain becomes clearer and closer as you drive. At last you reach the base of the mountain and discover that as long as you continue driving, you will circle the mountain without getting any higher or closer to the top. The mountain is quite beautiful, and you may again think that this is all you really want, and besides, leaving the security, comfort, and familiarity of your car feels risky.

You are now in the spell of the mountain, however, so you grab your backpack, leave your car, and begin hiking along a trail. You are now on the mountain and amazed at its beauty. You notice things you could not have seen from a distance, and your relaxation becomes deeper the further you go into the forest. Still, you find yourself circling the mountain at the same modest altitude, and could easily continue wandering amidst its beauty, but decide to keep on climbing.

Sooner or later, the trail begins to peter out and the climbing becomes more difficult. The trees grow fewer and the rocks more numerous, and you again stop and could decide not to go any further. Nonetheless, you reluctantly leave your backpack, put on your daypack, and begin scrambling over the rocks, relying on your awareness and instincts, with no trail to guide you. You feel yourself becoming more fit, and taking pleasure in the challenge of the climb.

Inevitably, you come to a sheer precipice that offers no clear way forward. Even so, you ditch your daypack, keeping only your pickaxe and rope, and start to scale the precipice hand-over-hand. There is now no room for idle thoughts. Every inch is a struggle, exhausting, and at the same time exhilarating. Every moment is ecstasy. You are completely alive, awake, focused, and relaxed. Once again, you might easily remain, but decide instead to keep on climbing.

Ultimately, you reach a point where you discover that you are circling the pinnacle and can go no higher by climbing. The peak is now in clear view, and you discover that the only way you can reach it is by dropping everything, shedding your clothes, letting go—even of your desire to reach the top, and floating upwards. Nothing in your journey until now has prepared you for such a move, but you let go, discovering as you do that the mountain is actually inside you, and that you can reach the top any time you want, even within the confines of the city, simply by being who you already are.

# CHAPTER 7

# USING HEARTFELT COMMUNICATION AND CONFLICT RESOLUTION SYSTEMS DESIGN IN MEDIATING MARITAL, COUPLE, AND FAMILY CONFLICTS

*Family life! The United Nations is child's play compared to the tugs and splits and need to understand and forgive in any family.*

~ May Sarton ~

*The greatest tragedy of the family is the unlived lives of the parents.*

~ Carl Jung ~

*The beauty of the world has two edges, one of laughter, one of anguish, cutting the heart asunder.*

~ Virginia Woolf ~

M EDIATION HAS BEEN USED with great success for several decades in settling and resolving marital, couple, and family conflicts. Yet we have not developed the methods, processes and approaches needed for us to respond preventatively and proactively—not merely to individual disputes—but to the chronic and systemic sources of conflict within these relationships, by imagining what could be done creatively to avert them altogether or make them easier to handle.

Far more importantly, we have not adequately appreciated the role that conflicts play in the relationships between family members and couples, or acknowledged their ability to pinpoint precisely the places where those relationships are cracked and need mending. Every conflict within every family, marriage, civil union, and couple represents a crisis that can lead either to disruption and a severing of the relationship, or to profound learning, deeper levels of intimacy, and improved communications and relationships.

Conflicts in intimate relationships are often accidental, occasional, and unique; yet they are also systemic, repetitive, and alike in both form and content to previous conflicts that may have occurred countless times in the past and may occur over and over again in the future until they are resolved. Why? Because they are initiated, organized, and brought to fruition by deep, important, unresolved issues that are systemic and fundamental to the relationship.

These systemic issues are difficult and sometimes dangerous to approach because they lie at the heart of what holds the relationship together. Therefore, simply discussing, let alone negotiating or resolving them, will always contain the possibility of even greater divergence, separation, or loss, and with them, the experience of grief and pain. Yet also contained within these issues is the possibility of deeper understanding, renewal, recommitment, and transcendence, and with them, the experience of joy, love, and freedom.

We have all experienced marital, couple, and family conflicts that are cyclical, chronic, and systemic. What we have not adequately recognized is that for this very reason, they are amenable to systemic analysis and inhibition through an examination of their chronic sources, and by applying the preventative methodologies of conflict resolution systems design.

The central difficulty, however, with ordinary forms of systemic analysis, including conflict resolution systems design, is that they do not begin by prioritizing the emotional and affective significance of conflict within the relationship, are not grounded in the heart, and are not able to work with the intimate, relational aspects of marital, couple, and family conflicts These are deeply sensitive, yet highly complex emotional relationships that require an approach to conflict resolution systems design that is informed by the heart.

## THE DANGERS IN HEART-BASED INTERVENTIONS

The emergence of chronic conflict is a sign that a system is unable to reform or repair itself, and has decided to erect makeshift lines of denial, defense, and counter-attack, resulting in over- and under-compensation in order to protect itself against any resolution that might trigger fundamental changes in the core elements of the system.

As these defenses and imbalanced responses aggregate, they produce growing insecurities, fears that the whole structure might collapse, and heightened resistance even to minor modifications that could trigger an avalanche. As the fear of systemic meltdown increases, even those who favor change often retreat and seek to preserve or roll back the status quo, or deflect the change by focusing on less serious issues, blaming others, or opting for settlement rather than resolution. At this point, simply discussing the issues becomes dangerous.

When the relational systems that drive relationships in marriages, couples, and families begin to sense the possibility of a general breakdown or possibility of rupture, every open, honest, heartfelt conversation can be seen as making change possible, and therefore leading into "dangerous," uncharted territory. In these interactions and exchanges, traditional analytical conflict resolution techniques will be of little use, and may even cause emotions to escalate and resistance to harden. Whenever we seek to avoid emotional or heartfelt communications in discussing our conflicts, it is a clue that deep-seated and systemic issues are at stake.

## SOME VARIETIES OF DANGER

Among the many dangers for mediators in initiating open, honest, heartfelt communications between family members and couples in relational conflict, most fall roughly into two categories: 1) those that are readily apparent and could result from any effort to resolve the conflict; and, 2) those that are more elusive and stem from efforts to generate deeper, subtler, more profound understandings that are potentially transformational in scope. The readily apparent dangers include:

- The danger that we could escalate the conflict further;
- The danger that there could be physical violence;
- The danger that we could be subjected to other people's intense emotions;
- The danger that we could have to revisit our own emotionally painful experiences;
- The danger that we could do or say things we do not mean, or become someone we do not like;
- The danger that we could increase resistance and make resolution less likely.

The deeper, subtler, and more profound dangers include:

- The danger that we could discover we are wrong and feel compelled to change our minds and behaviors as a result;
- The danger that we could never resolve the underlying issues for our conflict and be condemned to repeat it;
- The danger that we could continue lying to ourselves about what we have done;
- The danger that we could not tell the truth to someone whose life might change as a result;
- The danger that we could be required to change our own lives and suffer consequences we are not prepared to accept;
- The danger that nothing will ever change;
- The danger of not ever finding out who the other person is;
- The danger of not ever waking up to who we really are;
- The danger that we could have to forgive our enemies, or

worse, ourselves;

- The danger that the conflict will cease, and we will stop growing because there is no more danger and no one asking us to improve.

Openhearted communications are especially dangerous in these latter ways, each of which defines a moment when playing it safe becomes more dangerous than taking the risk of being honest and opening heartfelt conversations. When we take these risks in conflict, we wake up, face our fears, pay attention to details, drop our egos, become more humble, operate out of the center of who we are, connect more authentically with others, and think creatively. All of these strengthen authentic relationships and deepen intimacy and heartfelt connection. Yet by doing so, we transform our conflicts, acquire skills that allow us to transcend what got us stuck in the first place, and no longer face the same kind of danger. [For more on this topic, see *Mediating Dangerously: The Frontiers of Conflict Resolution*.]

To encourage dangerous, transcendent, system-breaking, heartfelt conflict communications, we need to navigate a middle passage that simultaneously avoids the twin traps of well intentioned, hypersensitive, mindlessly sentimental, pop-psychological, superficial, endless emotional processing; and manipulative, insensitive, hardheaded, dispassionate, emotionally disconnected legal and logical systemic analysis. This "deeper" or "higher" synergistic middle way requires us to communicate, plan, mediate, and design conflict resolution systems not merely from the mind, or even the emotions, but from the heart as well.

## HEART-TO-HEART COMMUNICATIONS

Communicating from the heart is highly intuitive, holistic, sensuous, and circular, and cannot be accessed using techniques or attitudes that are excessively emotional, chaotic, abstract, and sentimental; or those that are excessively rational, reductive, linear, and insensitive. To avoid these pitfalls, we need to be clear not only about what we want to communicate, and when, how, and to whom, but most importantly, *why* we want to communicate it, because the answer to this question, in moments of conflict or crisis, commonly comes from the heart.

The goal of heart-to-heart communications in conflict resolution is to encourage profound, poignant, authentic, intimate connections that dissipate conflict at its deepest locations inside each person, i.e., in their "hearts." Heart-based communications in conflict resolution are often, in the beginning, less about professing love or caring for one another than about recognizing the other person's pain, releasing them from the burden of their own false expectations, and helping them learn skills that will allow them to transcend what got them into the conflict in the first place. For this reason, the deepest dangers in heartfelt conflict communications lie not in what people say outwardly to their opposites, but what they realize inwardly and sometimes do not dare to say to themselves.

In marital, couple, and family mediations, the underlying issues that people worry most deeply about and most want to communicate to each other do end up being about love and caring, and these also have external and internal aspects. These underlying issues commonly fall into two emotionally sensitive categories:

1. Does the other person love or care for me?
2. Am I unlovable; do I deserve to be loved and cared for?

As an illustration, consider a family member who complains that some other family members don't pick up their dirty clothes or wash their dishes. If asked why that is important to them, they may respond, "Because it is irresponsible/disrespectful/unclean." And when asked why *that* is important and pressed for a deeper answer, they may say, "It shows they don't respect me and what I want." And when asked what it means to them that the other person doesn't respect you and what you want, and probes even deeper, they will often say, "It means they don't love me."

And now, finally, after all the accusations, counter-accusations, defenses and justifications, we can see that their deepest conflict is not about the dirty clothes or dishes at all, but about whether they feel loved and believe themselves to be lovable. The object of conflict resolution systems design *ought* to be to identify the questions that allow people to realize and communicate these deeper reasons for their conflicts and resolve them at that level.

## SOME HEARTFELT QUESTIONS FOR MEDIATORS

In ordinary mediations, and in conversations between family members and couples, it is possible to address a variety of minuscule, seemingly minor yet heartfelt issues that indirectly but profoundly influence their conflict. This can be done by asking questions that emanate from a place of loving or caring; that are profound or poignant; and that invite people into a heart-space and ask them to answer.

Here are some questions that can be asked by mediators in marital, couple, and family conflicts that can move their conversations gradually but inexorably into a sensitive and intimate danger zone, while seeking to surround it with the safety of a genuine heartfelt response:

- Before we begin, can you tell me a little about yourselves?
- What do you hope will happen as a result of this conversation? Why is that important to you?
- Why are you here? Why do you care? What did it take for you to be willing to come here today? What gave you hope that this conversation might prove useful?
- What kind of relationship would you most like to have with each other? Why?
- What is one thing you love/like/respect about each other? Can you give an example? Another?
- How does it feel to hear the other person say these things? What would happen if he/she said them more often?
- Is there anything you have in common? Any values you share?
- What life experiences have you had that have led you to feel so strongly about this issue?
- What role have you played in this conflict, either through action or inaction?
- If you had 20/20 hindsight, what would you do differently?
- Is there anything you would like to apologize for?
- On a scale of one to 10, how would each of you rank that apology? What could you do to make it a 10? Are you willing to try right now?
- What is one thing you would like him to acknowledge you for? What is one thing you are willing to acknowledge him for?
- What do you think she was trying to say in that apology/ acknowledgment? [To her] Is that accurate? [If not] Would you like to know what is accurate for her? Why don't you ask her?

- How would you evaluate the effectiveness of what you just said in reaching her? How could you make it more effective? Would you like some feedback? Why don't you ask her?

- Is this conversation working? Would you like it to work? Why would you like it to work? What is one thing she can do that would make it to work for you? [To her] Are you willing to do that? Would you be willing to start the conversation over and do those things now?

- What is the crossroads you are at right now in your conflict?

- Will you ever convince him you are right? [If not] When will you stop trying?

- What would you most like to hear her say to you right now?

- What would you have wanted him to have said instead?

- What does that mean to you? What other meanings might it have? What do you think it meant to her? Would you like to find out? Why don't you ask her?

- Can you imagine what happened to him also happening to you? What would it feel like? Would you like to know what it felt like to him? Why don't you ask?

- Would you be willing to take a moment of silence right now to think about that?

- Has anything like this happened to you before? Who? When?

- What are you not talking about that you still need to discuss?

- What issues are you holding on to that the other person still doesn't know about?

- What price have you paid for this conflict? What has it cost you? How much longer are you going to continue paying that price?

- What would it take for you to give this conflict up, let go of what happened, and move on with your life?

- Do you really want this in your life? What would it take for you to let it go?

- What would change in your life if you reached an agreement?

- If this were the last conversation you were going to have with each other, what would you want to say?

The object of these questions, and countless others like them, is to define a choice point, a place where things can shift on the basis of intention and caring. Fundamentally, for mediators, our goal is not to skew, manipulate, or predetermine what others choose, which belongs solely to them, but simply to present them with an authentic choice by asking questions that invite a heartfelt response. It is, in other words, to draw the parties into a crossroads that has been created by their conflict, a place where their lives could change as a result of what they decide (or not decide), and ask them then to choose. In the moment of an authentic choice, our task is complete, and we need to respect their decision, whatever it may be.

## SOME CROSSROADS IN FAMILY, MARITAL, AND COUPLES CONFLICTS

Most conflicts in marriages, couples, and families appear on the surface to be entirely personal in nature, and are sometimes described as "personality clashes." Yet as these conflicts accumulate, what initially seems unique and entirely personal may suddenly emerge as general, widespread, chronic and omnipresent, or as the byproducts of a dysfunctional family system. Yet these larger issues often remain hidden beneath the issues marriages, couples, and families are fighting over, even when they happen hundreds of times.

Together, they create a crossroads, a choice point where every decision, including no decision, takes the participants in a different direction. Here are some of the crossroads we encounter in every one of our conflicts, until we transcend it and move on to a higher crossroads:

- Whether to participate in the conflict and behave badly, or calm down and try to discuss it;
- Whether to acknowledge the other person's truth or deny it, remain rooted in our own story, and slip into biased or delusional thinking;
- Whether to experience intense negative emotions and feelings, or to repress and sublimate them;
- Whether to aggressively assert and hold tight to our position, or search for solutions that satisfy both sides' interests;
- Whether to experience our opponent as an equal human being

entitled to respect, or demonize him or her and victimize ourselves;

- Whether to acknowledge and grieve our losses and let them go, or hold on to our pain as something precious and continue reliving it;
- Whether to learn from our opponent and the conflict so as to transcend it, or hold on to our grievances and being right, leaving it bottled up inside;
- Whether to try and correct the person or the system we have both been operating in;
- Whether to forgive and re-integrate with our opponent, or remain isolated and wounded deep inside;
- Whether to open our hearts again to the other person, and reach true reconciliation.

[For more on this topic, see *The Crossroads of Conflict: A Journey into the Heart of Dispute Resolution*.]

Each of these crossroads requires a higher, more complex set of skills to resolve, transform, and transcend, and with each new set of skills we are able to evolve to a higher order of conflict, and so on. This idea, that our conflicts evolve over the course of our lifetimes, offering us countless opportunities to learn new skills and confront new conflicts, needs to be integrated into the conflict resolution systems design process, so that it does not become static and circular.

Each of us also evolves in the larger crossroads we face in life, as we learn to form intimate relationships, date, become a couple, enter committed relationships, and have families. Each of these requires a successively higher level of skill in being able to work through our conflicts, and if we do not have these skills we will find it difficult to form lasting, satisfying, intimate relationships with another person and may separate when we might have been able to create a better relationship by developing higher order skills in problem solving, negotiation, and conflict resolution.

## MARRIAGES, CIVIL UNIONS, COUPLES, AND CONFLICT

*In Marriage: A History*, Stephanie Coontz brilliantly chronicles the transition from marriage as coerced and women as property or slaves, to the rise of romantic love and equal partnerships. This early history led

Ambrose Bierce, writing in the 1920s, to cleverly define marriage as "A friendship recognized by the police."

While weakening many unsatisfying relationships, the transition to choice made it possible for love and partnership to grow in marriage, family, and for couples to make their relationships more satisfying, intimate, and lasting, partly because the removal of force and coercion creates a choice in each person regarding whether to be in the relationship or not, and when chosen, ceases to generate resistance.

So what are marriages, and how are they, along with civil unions and lifetime couples, different from other relationships in ways that matter when they engage in conflict? In the first place, marriages, civil unions, and long-term couples are committed relationships, and because both parties are free to choose whether to be together, their relationships are almost entirely acts of the heart. This means that conflict prevention and resolution procedures that are designed to work in marriages, civil unions, and other voluntary committed relationships, in order to be successful, must also touch the heart. But how exactly do we do this as mediators?

In the beginning in every intimate relationship, there is attraction. Later, this becomes, for example, "the story of how we met"—allowing us to regard marriages, couples and families as defined partly by the stories people tell others and themselves—stories of serendipity, romance, and true love. But stories are not always factually accurate, and there are ways that even romantic stories can distance people from each other, diminish their problem solving capacity, and reduce their authenticity. For most couples, the experience of conflict results in an entirely different set of stories, ones that need to be analyzed, resolved, transformed, and reconciled with their earlier stories in order to make sense of their relationship.

Marriages, couples, civil unions and families are also rituals that have extraordinary transformational power, created partly by the couple themselves and partly by their relatives and friends, who invest these ceremonies with a particular meaning. There are also thousands of little rituals couples engage in every day, reassuring sacraments that recreate their connectedness, including even rituals surrounding polarization, individuation, and conflict. By examining a couple's conflict rituals, it is possible to gain deep insight into their relationship, and even transform them from negative to positive, simply by shifting them in small ways or investing them with a different set of meanings.

Couples can also be defined by their experience of regular emotional, personal, and sexual intimacy, the immense power of which we still do not fully comprehend, in which two become one, and each becomes as vulnerable as it is possible for them to be. The cessation of sexual relations is often the result of a withdrawal of emotional vulnerability and personal intimacy, and a byproduct of injured feelings and distrust that are generated by chronic unresolved conflicts. Yet we know little about how to mediate these issues, in spite of the fact that they are often the driving force in extra-marital affairs and can inflate the impact and significance of even the smallest disappointments and disagreements. Discovering ways of reversing this coldness, sulking, and distancing should also be an integral part of the systems design process for marital, couple, and family conflicts.

Marriages, couples and families can alternatively be viewed as a set of expectations arising from the families of origin of each partner, together with a set of inherited approaches to solving problems, negotiating and resolving conflicts, and a set of attitudes toward disagreements, disapprovals, and disparities that need to be transformed and transcended for the marriage to evolve and rise or fall on its own merits. These often involve unmet expectations, unresolved issues from the past, and attitudes toward money, intimacy, cleanliness, and similar problems. Initiating an open and honest discussion of these issues and a negotiation of expectations can have a transformative impact on marital, couple, and family relationships.

Marriages, couples and families can also be thought of as a sum of spoken and unspoken conversations in which implicit expectations are communicated and accepted, rejected, or negotiated; in which hopes and dreams, fears and anxieties, wishes and requests are telegraphed, with varying rates of success; in which people connect beneath the literal meaning of their words, or fail to do so and retreat into silence, criticism, tears, and yelling. It is the frustrating failure of these circular, ineffective conversations that often end a marriage or dissolve a family, and finally exhaust their ability to love each other.

Marriages, couples and families can also be considered as objects, or rather, as the investment of ordinary objects with emotional meaning, transforming them from things into fetishes. Ordinary household objects can become comforting and reassuring, and are somehow able to contain the intimacy and connectedness of the couple. This attribution of meaning carries over into conflict, especially in divorce, in which objects, times, and places, including the family home, become infused with negative energy from memories of conflict. As a result, these objects may require a kind of exorcism in which they are dis-invested of meaning or de-fetishized after the conflict is over.

Marriages, couples and families, moreover, generally consist of a division of labor, in which each person becomes primarily responsible for carrying out a different set of tasks and responsibilities. Each then becomes somewhat specialized, with their own set of misunderstood, unappreciated tasks, and increasingly dependent on the other. In divorce and separation, this dependency is broken, triggering primal fears in each that they will not be able to function without the other person's contributions: i.e., in those who have not earned as high an income, whether they will be able to make it financially; or in those who have not cared as much for the children, whether they will be able to create the relationships they want.

Marriages, couples, and families, in addition, are economic units in which money and property are amalgamated, power and status are shared, and purchases and sales, including the sale or barter of each person's labor power, are negotiated or consented to; where resources are allocated, expenditures and investments are decided upon, and money is earned and spent. These also can become sources of chronic conflict in families and couples, as it often happens that individuals differ in their financial orientation and style, their willingness to incur debt or live beyond their means, their desire to save, and in the meaning money has for them.

Marriages, couples and families are thus a set of express and implied negotiated agreements on how to live together, raise children, spend time and energy, visit friends, eat and sleep, grow sick and heal. In short, they are vast, complex, multi-faceted, multi-dimensional systems in which each contributes and from which each receives something special and different. These reciprocal relationships can be jointly defined, negotiated collaboratively, and agreed to by consensus, or they can be autocratically imposed, negotiated competitively, and coerced.

This yin/yang inter-relationship of marriages, couples, and families creates a *system* that is self-reinforcing and resists change, yet needs to evolve and adapt to constantly changing conditions in the overall environment, as well as in each person, which also creates an on-going source of conflicts. Marital, couple, and family conflicts also take place within a larger environment or context that is influenced by cultural, social, political, and economic issues that impact couples directly, but are rarely noticed, discussed or addressed.

Each of these ways of understanding families and couples, whether in marriages, civil unions, families, or other committed relationships, needs to form a major part of our efforts, via conflict resolution systems design, to prevent conflicts from destroying caring relationships, as each aids us in identifying systemic sources of conflict within the relationship. Each, in turn, needs to be recognized as lying beyond traditional conflict resolution systems design processes, and incorporated into any successful, strategic, comprehensive conflict prevention and resolution program for couples and families. Moreover, each needs to be regarded not as fixed, but evolving over time as the couple ages and their conflicts change as they move through various life stages.

## CONFLICT EVOLUTION AND ERIKSON'S LIFE STAGES

Both our conflicts and our approaches to resolution evolve as we achieve higher orders of skill and graduate to higher levels of conflict. These closely follow and can be matched with the life stages identified by Erik Erikson, which, together with his sense of their primary associated conflicts, are:

- Infancy: trust versus mistrust;
- Early childhood: autonomy versus shame and doubt;
- Preschool: initiative versus guilt;
- School age: industry versus inferiority;
- Puberty: identity versus identity confusion;
- Young adulthood: intimacy versus isolation;
- Middle adulthood: generativity versus stagnation;
- Late adulthood: integrity versus despair.

These stages might be redefined from a mediation perspective and the conflicts given a somewhat different focus, but what is critically important that does not appear from a casual reading of this list is how the resolution of each core conflict that arises in each life stage creates a platform for the resolution of the next, higher order of conflicts, and how these translate into specific, typical marital and family conflicts.

If we consider, for example, classic teenage/parent conflicts over curfew, we can see that, beneath the surface of the dispute, an evolution is taking place, allowing the dispute to be addressed on the following levels, each with its own higher order or level of skill:

1. Simply exchanging insults or accusations that lead nowhere except impasse;

2. One parent "laying down the law" and insisting on a time to return home, leaving the teenager with three options: blind obedience, passive-aggressive acting out behavior, or open rebellion and consequent punishment;

3. Both sides negotiating adversarially over curfew, ending in a compromise based on their relative power;

4. Each side clarifying the interests that underlie their positions, with the parent arguing for safety (while minimizing or denying the importance of independence, fun and being with a peer group), and the teenager arguing for independence, fun and being with a peer group (while minimizing or denying the need for safety), and negotiating collaboratively in an effort to achieve mutual gain, or "win/win" outcomes;

5. Both parties speaking openly about their emotions, acknowledging each other's feelings, and telling stories about the experiences that produced them, resulting in increased empathy and understanding;

6. Recognizing that the family as they have known it is about to end, since the teenager is getting ready to leave home forever, and openly discussing sensitive, heartfelt questions, such as:
   • Who will they be without each other?
   • How will they continue to express their love for each other?
   • How will they learn to function without each other?
   • How can they increase their ability to accept and trust each other?

- What can each of them do to improve their relationship and keep the family together?

7. These largely unspoken, heartfelt questions will surreptitiously yet profoundly affect their conflict over curfew and allow them to evolve—not only to higher levels of communication, negotiation, relationship, and decision-making, but to higher orders of conflict and resolution as well.

8. Discovering ways to improve their family "conflict culture," and redesigning now-outmoded family conflict resolution systems and expectations to accommodate their joint transition from childhood to adult relationships, and allow for different outcomes at different agreed upon stages.

These levels of communication and conflict resolution, starting with impasse, can be diagrammed succinctly and practically as follows:

| Focus | Parent | Teenager |
|---|---|---|
| Insults & Accusations: | "Irresponsible" | "Bossy" |
| Parent's Position: | 10 PM | Obey or be Punished |
| Both Positions: | 10 PM | 2 AM |
| Interests | Safety | Freedom |
| Emotions | Fear, Guilt, Loss | Shame, Anger, Loss |
| Spiritual Reality | Death of the Family | Loss of Security/ Support |
| Heartfelt Desire | Love, Acceptance | Love, Acceptance |
| Family System | Prevention, Redesign | Supportive Relationship |

In the end, through this analysis, we can see that there are actually only two goals for family members in any conflict over curfew:

1. To transfer responsibility for safety from the parent to the teenager consistent with freedom;

2. To transition from a family system based on autocratic parental control to one based on democratic, consensual, adult relationships grounded in familial love.

These goals only *begin* to become possible at level three, yet many families never get beyond level two. Nonetheless, we can see in retrospect that this is precisely what their conflict took place in order to teach them. We can also see that each transition to a higher level of conflict requires higher order resolution skills, and can be triggered by a few relatively simple questions. For example, a mediator might ask each of the parties the following simple questions:

- What do you want;
- Why do you want it;
- What are you feeling;
- What deeper issues and realities are you about to face;
- What kind of relationship do you want to have with each other;
- What do you think you might do to make your family system and conflict styles more satisfying and effective in the future?

Underlying much of the resistance to using these techniques and evolving as a family is that family members often recognize subconsciously that doing so will require them to surrender their ability to deny that change is taking place and they are about to lose their old relationship, that they finally need to genuinely transfer power to the teenager, and that they need to transform the way their conflicts are resolved in ways that reflect an evolutionary shift from power and rights to interests, with no guarantees in the end that they will be wanted or have the relationship they desire.

As members of marriages, couples and families proceed through these stages in their individual lives, three alternatives always emerge as options.

1. Their relationships may change as a result of what they decide and how they choose to resolve their conflicts;
2. Or, they may decide to leave those relationships if others no longer meet their needs;
3. Or, they may decide to remain in unsatisfying, or autocratic relationships, but these will become increasingly dysfunctional and keep them from evolving to higher orders of conflict and resolution.

Family, couple and family conflicts are often a result simply of people moving through different life stages at different speeds, creating contradictory needs and expectations and competing demands for attention. These constitute an important source of dysfunction in many family and marital systems, and another element that needs to be added to our systems design toolkit when working with families and couples. Let us now examine conflict resolution systems design principles more closely to see how they might be applied in marital, couple and family conflicts.

## WHAT IS CONFLICT RESOLUTION SYSTEMS DESIGN?

Conflict resolution systems design techniques were initially conceived and used primarily in organizations and workplaces, but with a little modification and some tweaking, they can also be applied in marriages, couples, and families to develop inexpensive and effective ways of preventing and reducing their levels of chronic conflict, increasing the capacity for collaboration and teamwork, improving morale and revitalizing relationships.

Conflict resolution systems design was originally conceived and developed by William Ury, Steven Goldberg, and Jeanne Brett in their book, *Getting Disputes Resolved*. Their core idea was to design a comprehensive set of conflict resolution mechanisms that would encourage prevention, informal problem-solving, early intervention, loopbacks to collaborative negotiation, on-going feedback, evaluation, monitoring, and de-escalation throughout the life of the conflict.

This systemic approach to conflict resolution supports varied and diverse methodologies that can incorporate multiple and divergent perspectives, employ widely varying processes and techniques, produce synergistic results, be ranked from low to high cost, and encourage feedback, learning and self-improvement. Comprehensive approaches can be designed that prevent conflicts before they happen; support problem solving, negotiation, dialogue and coaching as they escalate; and mediation, arbitration and other forms of resolution after they have become intractable or reached impasse.

Systems design procedures can be used to encourage people in marriages, couples, and families to regard their conflicts as parts of an interlocking, interdependent whole that they can address in multiple, assorted ways. It therefore allows for the development of a variety of integrated dispute resolution mechanisms, rather than isolated, disconnected procedures, and focuses attention directly on the sources of chronic conflict within the relationship. Conflict resolution systems design prioritizes interest-based approaches, such as direct, informal problem solving, marital mediation, family circles, couples counseling and collaborative negotiation.

By retooling and modifying organizational processes and experiences, designing interest-based conflict resolution systems for marriages, couples, and families might include:

- Conducting a "conflict audit" to assess the chronic sources of conflict within the couple or family system, identify their causes and assign a cost, both financial and relational, to unresolved disputes;
- Analyzing the sources of conflict, including their connections to marital and family systems, hierarchical structures, couple or family conflict cultures, ineffective forms of communications, decision-making processes, family goals and strategies, recent and impending changes, shared values, individual morale, conflict styles, etc.;
- Identifying core elements of the conflict cultures in their parents families of origin and developing alternative approaches, reinforce informal mechanisms already in place for resolving disputes, and how these might be supplemented with enriched alternatives;
- Focusing on interests, rather than on power- or rights-based solutions;
- Emphasizing prevention and systemic solutions;
- Expanding the numbers and kinds of resolution alternatives available internally within the family or couple, and externally within their friends and community;
- Arranging resolution procedures from low to high cost;
- Including a full range of options from minor communication and process changes to mediation and arbitration, with low-cost rights and power backups;
- Building in "loopbacks" to informal problem-solving and collaborative negotiation;
- Incorporating consultation, facilitation, coaching, dialogue, circles, mentoring, feedback and evaluation, and similar processes;
- Rewarding people for prevention and using resolution procedures;
- Providing training, motivation, skills, support, and resources

to make sure these procedures work and evolve;

• Continuing to improve understanding within the family or couple of how these efforts succeed and fail, increase skills, and augment the overall design.

In addition to these, mediators can offer questions, assign homework, and design mechanisms that allow marriages, couples, and families to affirm and acknowledge each other, reach forgiveness and reconciliation in their conflicts, and openly state their love and affection for one another.

The core goals of the systems design process, as applied to families and couples, would then be to match conflict resolution mechanisms with specific family or couple needs, prevent and resolve interpersonal and chronic conflicts at their source or inception, achieve higher levels of resolution than whatever the current system allows, and promote insight, change, improved relationships, heartfelt communications, intimacy and learning, so that conflicts can be transformed and transcended, rather than merely settled or forgotten and chronically repeated.

The most commonly used procedures in the typical systems design toolkit for organizations include informal problem-solving, peer counseling, coaching, mentoring, feedback, team and relationship building, public dialogue and open forums, peer and professional mediation, supportive confrontation, ombudsman offices and processes, internal appeals and organizational review boards, binding and non-binding arbitration, and similar processes. Some of these can easily be applied to couples and families, while others will prove less useful.

As marriages, couples, and families evolve or change, their conflicts naturally accumulate along the fault lines that lie hidden within their systems. These conflicts point directly to what is not working in their relationship, while their resolution often reveals some new processes, principles or kinds of relationship that are waiting to be born. In this way, family and marital conflicts can be seen simply as the sound made by the cracks in their system, the first indication of the birth of a new paradigm, a warning light signaling imminent breakdown, a path to improvement, and an evolution to a higher order of conflicts.

## DESIGNING CONFLICT RESOLUTION SYSTEMS
## FOR FAMILIES AND COUPLES

Few families or couples have designed or implemented adequate systems for resolving conflicts, and most do not use the systems they have until after unacceptable damage has occurred. When this happens, the conflict is generally pigeonholed as someone else's problem, or beyond the reach of conversation and mediation, or not within the expertise of family members or couples to resolve. As a result, whatever solution they come up with often does not reach deep enough into underlying attitudes and expectations, and comes back later to create new difficulties. If this goes on for long, people grow exhausted, become cynical and defensive, and begin to give up on the relationship.

What is needed, then, are complex, collaborative, self-correcting conflict resolution systems, with early intervention procedures that are designed to prevent disputes before they arise, nip them in the bud, get people back into constructive communication, resolve whatever disputes may arise, and create a rich array of alternatives leading to resolution, learning and improved relationships.

If we imagine how we might design an ideal approach to conflict prevention, it would certainly begin by educating children at the earliest ages in conflict resolution. But even if we decide to be less visionary and scale back our expectations, it would be useful to begin by offering new couples and those who are planning to live together, marry, or start a family, ways of designing their responses to the future conflicts they will experience, including how they want to prevent, engage in, and resolve them. Here are a few options they can consider in doing so:

1. Conflict Coaching: One clear entry point for systems design might be the decision to live together, or the marriage ceremony, either of which could entail a conflict coaching session or a meeting with a systems design practitioner, in which the couple can discuss how they want to minimize the destructive impact of their future conflicts and are offered resources and options that can help them throughout their relationship and life stages.

2. Mediated Prenuptial Agreements: Another entry point might arise by redesigning the ways parties negotiate prenuptial

agreements and mediating their differences. Ordinarily, these conversations take place in the presence of attorneys who can make the process unnecessarily adversarial by negotiating the terms of their divorce before they've even been married! An alternative would be to mediate these agreements so as to create a heartfelt context for their negotiations and transform their discussion of the prenuptial agreement into a conflict resolution systems design process. For example, a mediator might ask the following questions of a couple seeking to negotiate a prenuptial agreement:

- Does this feel strange to you, discussing your divorce before you are even married?
- What do you hope to achieve through this conversation that might strengthen your marriage rather than weaken it?
- How did you meet?
- What attracted you to each other? What do you love about each other?
- What made you decide to get married?
- Why are you interested in reaching a prenuptial agreement?
- Do you have any fears, anxieties, or concerns about talking to each other regarding these issues and negotiating a prenuptial agreement? What are they?
- What can we do in this conversation to reduce those fears, anxieties, or concerns?
- Have you had any arguments or conflicts in your relationship so far? What happens when you argue that you wish would happen differently?
- What is one thing the other person could do or say that would help you communicate better when you have a disagreement?
- What are some of the patterns you get into when you argue that you would like to break?
- Are there any ground rules you would like to propose for your future conflicts and disagreements with each other?

- What words or phrases would you use to describe the kind of relationship you most want to have with each other?
- What are the patterns in your family of origin regarding conflict? Regarding money? Regarding intimacy? Regarding time or space?
- How did people fight in your family? Over what issues? How did they resolve or overcome their differences? What would you like to do the same or differently?
- What does the word "wife" mean to you? The word "husband"? The word "marriage"? The word "conflict"?
- Why do you think it is important to clarify your intentions and agreements regarding the legal, monetary, or property issues in your marriage?
- What does money or property mean to you? Why do you want it? What are you afraid will happen if you don't reach an agreement about it?
- What would you like to have happen, once you are married, with respect to these issues, or any others you want to add:
- Property or investments you acquired before you were married?
- Property or investments you will acquire after you are married?
- Financial, emotional, and other contributions either of you may make to your life together in the future?
- Income either of you will earn?
- Debts you acquired before you were married?
- Debts you will acquire after you are married?
- How will you pay for your joint living expenses?
- How will you take care of children you already have, or may have in the future?
- How will you take care of family members who may need your assistance?
- How would you like to handle illness, old age, and retirement?
- Other issues you would like to resolve?

- What would you like to happen in the event that either of you dies or is seriously injured while you are married?
- What would you like to happen if you decide, may you never have to consider it, to separate or divorce? What would you most like to avoid? How would you like to feel about each other and the process?
- Would you want to place any pre-conditions on the payment of spousal support, or the distribution of property and debts, if you were to separate at some point in the future?
- If you are not able to agree on issues that arise in the future, how would you like to resolve your differences? What methods of resolution would you like to use? Would you like to know what the options are and how they each work?
- If you decide to use coaching, mediation, or arbitration, who would you like to use as a coach, mediator, or arbitrator?
- What other issues would you like to discuss in advance of your marriage?
- If you were to write a "Marital Constitution," what would you want to include? What would the Preamble say? The Bill of Rights? How would you like to make decisions regarding different issues? Would you each be willing to write a draft of a "Marital Constitution" and read it to each other at our next meeting?
- What do you want to do or say, and not do or say to each other about your future life together?
- What questions would you most like to ask each other that you haven't yet had a chance to ask?
- What issues, concerns or fears are you holding on to that you still haven't mentioned?
- What questions would you most like to be asked by each other?
- What would you like to say to each other as reassurance that, in spite of having separate interests and negotiating

these difficult issues, you really do love each other and still want to be married?

3. Analysis of Family and Marital Conflicts: It is also possible, either separately or as part of the negotiation of a prenuptial agreement, to undertake a deeper analysis of the principal issues that are likely to arise within the family or couple and how they might be handled more positively in the future; or to facilitate a discussion, analysis and brainstorming session on how their disputes might be prevented. Here are some examples, in the form of a checklist the parties can complete and share with each other:

# Common Issues in Marital, Couple, and Family Conflicts

- Power
- Intimacy
- Career
- Cleanliness
- Control
- Identity
- Monogamy
- Age
- Holidays

- Money
- Children
- Commitment
- Privacy
- Alcohol/Drugs
- Expectations
- Religion
- Communication
- Negotiation Styles

- Sex
- Love
- Responsibilities
- Friends
- Personal Space
- Blended Families
- Values
- Culture
- Goals

## Common Ways of Handling Them

- Arguing
- Leaving
- Silence
- Shopping
- Sarcasm
- Illness/Injury
- Denial
- Medication
- TV

- Screaming
- Talking
- Insults
- Eating
- Sex/Affairs
- Move
- Avoidance
- Focus on Children
- Become a Workaholic

- Physical Violence
- Hiding
- Crying
- Punishing
- Alcohol/Drugs
- Remodel
- Depression
- Call Parents/Friends
- Separation/Divorce

## A Few Ways of Handling Them More Positively

- Time-Outs
- Family Meetings
- Gifts
- Counseling
- Marital Mediation
- Family Councils
- Giving Thanks

- Apologizing
- Vacations or Retreats
- Sex / Cuddling
- Individual Therapy
- Marital Encounters
- Circles / Dialogues
- Asking Questions

- Setting Times to Talk
- Take Turns Speaking
- Going on Dates
- Family Interventions
- Couple Coaching
- Skill Building
- Acknowledgements

4. Adjunct processes: Here are some additional methods and processes that may be useful for marriages, couples, and families to consider and select from in designing their own unique mix of preventive measures and responses to conflict:

- Schedule pre-marital discussions on topics such as:
  - Shared values for their relationship;
  - Unspoken assumptions and expectations;
  - Breaking patterns regarding to how conflicts were handled in their families of origin.
- Agree on specific ways conflicts will be handled, including things both partners agree they will not do or say the next time they argue.
- Improve motivation by rewarding positive behaviors.
- Receive joint training in communication, anger management, and other interpersonal skills.
- Receive joint training in problem solving, collaborative negotiation and conflict resolution skills.
- Schedule "dates," surprises, family gatherings and vacations to repair their relationship.
- Periodically go on facilitated "marital retreats" or "encounters."
- Make time for periodic reviews, evaluations and feedback on how the relationship is working.
- Ask each other, "What is one thing I could do differently that might improve our relationship?"
- Select a couple's coach, life coach, or conflict coach, and agree to get coaching at the other person's request.
- Schedule regular "family/marriage check-ins" and "tune ups."
- Create and maintain a joint list of resources with a rich variety of support systems including friends, relatives, and professional services for various kinds of problems and conflicts.
- Use hybrid approaches that emphasize the responsibility of both partners for the success of the marriage.
- When stuck, agree in advance to go to couples' counseling

if the other person requests it.

- Agree in advance to go to individual therapy if the other person requests it.
- Agree in advance to go to marital mediation on request, preferably before the argument becomes destructive.
- Pick a mediator or therapist to represent the interests of minor children in difficult family mediations.
- Identify for each other the things each person needs to do or say or let go of in common arguments, or to open their hearts and reach forgiveness and reconciliation.
- Celebrate successes and design rituals of reconciliation.

5. Creative Relational Exercises: In addition to these, mediators can design creative exercises that draw people into deeper awareness of what is actually at stake in their conflicts and help them find heartfelt ways of deepening and improving their relationships. Among these exercises might be the following:

- Write a celebratory speech or eulogy in advance for your family, marriage, or relationship and share it with each other, explaining what you value in it, or what you want to preserve and why.
- Write a detailed description of the other members of your family or relationship, including their favorite likes and dislikes, from food to entertainment and behaviors, then share it with them and see how accurate you were.
- Say three to five positive, acknowledging, complimentary things about the other person each day for a week, then evaluate and decide whether to continue.
- Discuss what you would most like the other person to do for you when you are feeling sick or down, and agree to do at least one of them.
- Discuss and plan in detail in advance how each person would like to be addressed or spoken to when there are problems to be solved or conflicts to be discussed.
- Discuss various options for family decision-making, including announcement, consultation, delegation,

voting, consensus and unanimity, and decide which ones you want to use for each major variety of decision you are likely to face.

- Identify and share what you feel most strongly about and are unwilling to give up or compromise on, and what you feel less strongly about and are willing to modify or give up if it is important to the other person.
- Clarify your dreams, wishes, fears, expectations, and assumptions with each other by writing them down and sharing them.
- Jointly design rituals that both people agree to engage in every day.

6. Exercises After Reaching Impasse: Beyond these, consider the following exercises that can be used to improve intimate relationships after conflicts have occurred or become destructive, and threaten the continuation of the relationship:

- Love Story: What drew you to the other person in the first place? What did you like about him/her? What did it feel like to be together?
- Tragedy: What went wrong? When? Why?
- Sour Grapes Inventory: Make a list of all the things that are wrong with the other person and what they did.
- Poison Pen letter: Write a letter to the other person giving expression to all your intense wounded, enraged, and angry feelings. Then put it aside and decide later whether to send it.
- Letter of Confession: Make a list of all the things that are wrong with you and what you did.
- Balance Sheet: Next prepare a balanced list with a more realistic accounting of what you each might have done better.
- Apology: Write a sincere apology to the other person listing all your crimes and faults. Make it as honest as you would like them to be in return.
- Letter of Forgiveness: List all the expectations you had of them that they did not meet, then choose to forgive them

for not meeting them.

- Letter of Self-Forgiveness: Write a letter that starts "Dear Me ...," listing all the expectations you had of yourself, and forgiving yourself for not meeting them.

- List of Costs:  If you can't forgive them or yourself, write down what it will cost you to hold on to each expectation.

- Letter of Gratitude:  Write a sincere letter of thanks for all the lessons you have learned and received from them.

- Wish List: Write a list of all the things the other person could do that would make you happy.

- Promises: Write a list of all the things you could do to make the other person happy.

- Redefining the Relationship: List all the negative words you have used to characterize the other person. Then write a new list of positive words that create the definition you would like to have of them going forward.

- Defining a New Frontier: What can you continue to learn from the other person? How can you make sure you will carry this lesson with you and not lose it? What is the next challenge in your relationship? [Drawn from Daphne Rose Kingma, *Coming Apart: Why Relationships End & How to Live Through the Ending of Yours*]

These are only a few of the innumerable ways of using conflict resolution systems design in heartfelt ways to deepen and repair relationships and help marriages, couples, and families prevent and resolve destructive adversarial conflicts. Other methods can be developed by deepening our understanding of the systems design process, and applying a set of design standards, or algorithms, to measure their present system against.

## AN ALGORITHM FOR SYSTEMS DESIGN PROCESSES

When we examine systems design processes as a whole, regardless of whether they are used in public or private sector organizations or in families or couples, it is apparent that they follow certain rules or patterns and express a set of shared values, and it is possible for these to be expressed directly in the form of design criteria, or as an algorithm or procedure that works through a series of steps to produce a result.

Here are some of the design criteria, values, principles, standards, or elements that might be used to guide the systems design process in general, or to evaluate a current conflict resolution system to see whether it meets them:

- All interested parties are included and invited to participate fully in designing and implementing content, process, and relationships;
- Decisions are made by consensus wherever possible, and nothing is considered final until everyone is in agreement;
- Diversity and honest differences are viewed as sources of dialogue, leading to better ideas, healthier relationships, and greater unity;
- Stereotypes, prejudices, assumptions of innate superiority, and ideas of intrinsic correctness are considered divisive and discounted as one-sided descriptions of more complex, multi-sided, paradoxical realities;
- Openness, authenticity, appreciation, and empathy are regarded as better foundations for communication and decision-making than secrecy, rhetoric, insult, and demonization;
- Dialogue and open-ended questions are deemed more useful than debate and cross-examination;
- Force, violence, coercion, aggression, humiliation, and domination are rejected, both as methods and as outcomes;
- Cooperation and collaboration are ranked as primary, while competition and aggression are considered secondary;
- Everyone's interests are accepted as legitimate, acknowledged, and satisfied wherever possible, consistent with others' interests;
- Processes and relationships are considered at least as important as content, if not more so;
- Attention is paid to emotions, subjectivity, and feelings, as well as to logic, objectivity, and facts;
- Everyone is regarded as responsible for participating in improving content, processes, and relationships, and searching for synergies and transformations;

- People are invited into heartfelt communications and self-awareness, and encouraged to reach resolution, forgiveness, and reconciliation;
- Chronic conflicts are traced to their systemic sources, where they can be prevented and redesigned to discourage repetition;
- Victory is regarded as obtainable by everyone, and redirected toward collaborating to solve common problems, so that no one feels defeated;
- As people are encouraged to learn from their conflicts and prevent them from recurring, they are transformed and transcended.

In these ways, it is possible for mediators to significantly alter the course of chronic conflicts in families, marriages, and couples by inviting them to speak to each other directly—not just about their recollections of facts and opinions, or about their angers and fears—but about their love for each other and what they care most deeply about. It then becomes possible for mediators to design conflict resolution systems that can genuinely turn conflicts into learning experiences and heartfelt opportunities for deeper and more satisfying relationships. Doing so takes considerable ingenuity and skill, but these are exactly the skills needed to keep love alive in any family or couple, and worthwhile practicing whatever effort it takes.

# CHAPTER 8

# CONFLICT, CLIMATE CHANGE, AND ENVIRONMENTAL CATASTROPHE

## How Mediators Can Help Save the Planet

*Human history becomes more and more a race
between education and catastrophe.*

~ H. G. Wells ~

THE OIL SPILL BY British Petroleum in the Gulf of Mexico several years ago highlights an escalating set of difficulties in our responses to environmental catastrophes, with echoes that resonate and reverberate with experiences responding to Hurricane Katrina in New Orleans, earthquakes in Haiti and Peru, firestorms in Russia, flooding in Pakistan, tsunamis in Indonesia and Japan, and others.

As population, technology, and globalization continue to expand, so undoubtedly will environmental deterioration, including global warming, allowing us to reasonably anticipate, and perhaps predict the following outcomes:

1. That environmental disasters will become more widespread, severe, impactful, costly, and common;
2. That conflicts will be triggered by these events, and escalate as more individuals, groups, nations and eco-systems are impacted;
3. That these conflicts will accumulate around the failures in local, national, and global emergency response systems;
4. That the ability to resolve these conflicts quickly and effectively will have a direct impact on the degree of damage they create;
5. That mediation, collaborative negotiation, and allied conflict resolution methodologies will increasingly be used to address and resolve disputes that result from climate change and environmental disasters.

## THE LOGICAL CHAIN

There is a more detailed chain of logic that can be offered to support these ideas, which proceeds as follows: As human populations have grown more numerous and technologically advanced, we have naturally had a greater ecological impact on the planet. Simply by not paying attention to these impacts for centuries and seeking to maximize our separate competitive short-term advantage as nations, corporations, and separated communities, we have wasted exhaustible resources, despoiled and desecrated our environment, and created the preconditions for mass extinctions and global catastrophe.

As a consequence, it is no longer possible to pursue non-sustainable approaches to survival, particularly those that aggravate the problems we already face. Instead, these problems demand not only the collective attention of everyone, but respectful, collaborative, democratic ways of communicating; complex, creative, paradoxical ways of solving problems; and interest-based methods for negotiating, discussing, and resolving conflicts over how to address them. Without these shifts, it is likely that many people around the planet will not survive.

How do we know that this is true? A number of far-reaching environmental changes have been taking place on a global scale for some time, and increasing in their pace, momentum, and potential to inflict disastrous consequences on human societies internationally. Perhaps the most important of these changes is that the rate of change is itself changing, in an exponential direction.

Changes in the natural world can, of course, take place incrementally and piece by piece or exponentially and with increasing rapidity. Exponential changes look something like this:

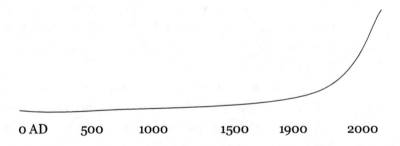

o AD        500        1000        1500      1900        2000

Many of the most serious problems we face today reveal rates of change that can arguably be plotted along this curve. These include, but are by no means limited to, the following:

- The size and density of human population;

- $CO_2$ and methane emissions that increase global warming;
- Species extinctions;
- Loss of bio-diversity;
- Loss of tropical rainforest and woodland;
- Desertification, erosion, and loss of arable land;
- Decreasing genetic diversity in agricultural commodities;
- Loss of potable water;
- Loss of fish stocks;
- Resistance to antibiotics;
- Pollution, loss of bio-degradability, and use of toxic chemicals;
- Vulnerability to pandemics;
- Rising cost of medical care;
- Disruption of weather patterns;
- Increasing severity of natural catastrophes and weather conditions;
- The global effect of local, relatively minor environmental decisions.

In addition to these, we are facing worldwide problems in other areas that can easily trigger severe environmental consequences, escalate conflicts, and make it more difficult for us to solve these problems, including:

- The increasing destructive power and availability of military technology;
- Nuclear proliferation;
- Willingness to use war and resort to violence;
- Intentional targeting of civilians in warfare;
- Terrorism and unending cycles of revenge and retaliation;
- Acceptability of the use of torture and cruelty in response;
- Global financial crises;
- Financial cutbacks in government services, especially in education, corporate regulation, and science and technology;
- Unregulated economic transactions;
- Increasing poverty, social inequality, and economic inequity;
- Destabilization due to political autocracy and dictatorship;
- Rise in prejudice and intolerance;
- Hostility to immigrants, refugees, minorities, and outsiders;

- Genocidal policies and "ethnic cleansing";
- Growth of the drug trade, sexual trafficking, and organized crime.

In Collapse, Jared Diamond argues from somewhat different premises that we are presently facing 12 sources of ecological and social collapse, each of which is growing steadily and has to be solved correctly in order to avoid catastrophic consequences.

1. Deforestation and habitat destruction
2. Soil problems (erosion, salinization, and soil fertility losses)
3. Water management problems
4. Overhunting
5. Overfishing
6. Effects of introduced species on native species
7. Human population growth
8. Increased per-capita impact of people
9. Human-caused climate change
10. Buildup of toxic chemicals in the environment
11. Energy shortages
12. Full human utilization of the Earth's photosynthetic capacity

In Diamond's well-researched account, it was rare for earlier societies to face more than one of these crises at a time, or for them to spread beyond local environmental limits, yet all seem to be occurring today, and no place on the planet is safe. Moreover, globalization has introduced a synergistic element into the feedback loop, allowing each of these crises to deepen and aggravate the others, speeding the rate of collapse and spreading it around the world.

Diamond also provides a framework for assessing the likelihood of environmental collapse, which includes a quantitative and qualitative assessment of the following criteria:

1. Environmental damage
2. Climate change
3. Hostile neighbors
4. Friendly trade partners
5. Society's responses to its environmental problems

Diamond does not explicitly cite funding for education, science and technology, or support for the use of a rich array of conflict resolution methods, yet the willingness to use mediation, collaboration negotiation, public dialogue, group facilitation, conflict resolution systems design, and similar conflict resolution techniques needs to be included in any realistic assessment of the likelihood of eventual ecological collapse. This is extremely important for our purposes, as we will see, since it places mediation at the very center of international efforts to prevent and respond to environmental disasters.

In a different, calmer, and therefore more shocking analysis, a number of scientific experts in different fields were asked in 2013 by Scientific American to estimate the limits on growth, citing preindustrial levels, current levels, and their best estimate of the boundary beyond which more serious consequences might occur. Their results were as follows:

1.  Climate Change:

    Preindustrial $CO^2$ = 280 ppm

    Current = 387

    Boundary = 350

2.  Ocean Acidification:

    Preindustrial Aragonite saturation = 3.44 Omega units

    Current = 2.90

    Boundary = 2.75

3.  Stratospheric Ozone Depletion:

    Preindustrial value = 290 Dobson units

    Current = 283

    Boundary = 276

4.  Nitrogen Removal:

    Preindustrial value = 0 tons/year nitrogen removal from atmosphere

    Current = 133

    Boundary = 39

5.  Phosphorous Cycle:

    Preindustrial value = 1 ton/year flow into oceans

    Current = 10

    Boundary = 12

6.  Freshwater Use:

    Preindustrial value = 415 cubic kilometers/year

    Current = 2,600

Boundary = 4,000

7. Land Use:

Preindustrial value = Negligible conversion to cropland

Current = 11.7 percent

Boundary = 15 percent

8. Biodiversity Loss:

Preindustrial value = 0.1 to 1.0 species per year

Current = 100

Boundary = 10

9. Aerosol Loading:

Preindustrial value = Negligible particulate concentration in atmosphere

Current = Undetermined

Boundary = Undetermined

10. 10. Chemical Pollution:

Preindustrial value = Negligible amount emitted to or concentrated in the environment

Current = Undetermined

Boundary = Undetermined

[Boundaries for a Healthy Planet, *Scientific American*, April 2010]

In most of these cases, there is a growing scientific consensus that we are well beyond the boundary conditions that permit environmental sustainability. A wide range of scientific reports from around the world confirm the existence of these problems, the urgent need for solutions, and the devastating consequences of failing to address them. In addition, a number of these problems are synergistically related to others, so that deterioration in one will likely cause increased deterioration in others.

How is it possible for any of us to read this information calmly and do nothing about it? We have buried our heads in the sand for far too long and ignored escalating evidence that we are tilting our world in an unsustainable direction that will predictably result in environmental catastrophes.

Narrowing our focus to the issue of climate change, even conservative scientific studies document the following significant shifts in recent years, with each appearing to increase irregularly on an annual basis, but significantly over decades. To demonstrate that global warming is happening, the following statistics for the 20th century were presented in scientific papers circulated at the United Nations Copenhagen Climate Change Conference in 2009, which I attended with a team from Mediators Beyond Borders:

- Global-average surface temperature has increased by about 0.6 degrees Celsius over the 20th century.
- The 1990s were the warmest decade and 1998 warmest year in last 1000 years in Northern Hemisphere, exceeded only by the decade that followed it.
- Over the last 50 years, nighttime minimum temperatures have increased by about 0.2 degrees Celsius per decade.
- There has been a 10 percent reduction in snow cover ice since late 1960s.
- There has been a reduction of about two weeks in the annual duration of lake and river ice over the 20th century.
- There has been a widespread retreat of mountain glaciers during 20th century.
- Northern Hemisphere spring and summer sea-ice extent decreased by 10–15 percent since 1950s.
- There has been a 40 percent decline in late summer Arctic sea-ice thickness in recent decades.
- Global-average sea level has increased by 10–20 cm during 20th century.
- There has been a 0.5–1 percent per decade increase in Northern Hemisphere mid-latitude precipitation during 20th century.
- There has been a 2–4 percent increase in frequency of heavy precipitation events in Northern Hemisphere mid- and high-latitudes over latter half of 20th century.

More recent studies have developed forecasts for the future impact of climate change that conservatively, to my mind, include the following projections:

- Global-average surface temperature is expected to increase by from 1.4 degrees Celsius to 5.8 degrees Celsius by 2100, a rate of warming that is unprecedented in the last 10,000 years.

- Land areas will warm more than the global average.
- Global average precipitation will increase over the 21st century, with more intense precipitation events and irregular precipitation in areas that have become accustomed to stable rainfall.
- Snow cover and sea-ice are projected to decrease dramatically.
- Glaciers and icecaps are projected to continue their widespread retreat.
- Global mean sea-level is projected to increase by nine to 88 cm or more by 2100, and in some reports, by as much as two to five meters.
- There will be a loss of agricultural stability as crops requiring temperate weather such as cereals move steadily north.

The list of evidence continues, but somehow exceeds our ability to grasp. One reason may be that we are surrounded with so many other, more immediate and palpable catastrophes. Another may be that the news media make so much of catastrophe in order to attract customers to secure the advertising that pays their way, and does not want to cover anything that might be bad for business or advertising revenues. A third reason may be that while many of these changes are taking place rapidly, and in some cases exponentially, several interdependent yet equally critical changes are taking place only gradually, allowing us to feel that something is in fact being done about them.

Moreover, responding to global environmental disasters and climate change will require a dramatic increase in our ability to mount a sustained, energetic, collaborative global response, which will inevitably *have* to include finding solutions for a much broader range of social, economic and political problems, such as:

- Implementation of solutions to poverty and hunger;
- Reductions in bigotry and prejudice;
- Fewer assertions of territoriality;
- Decreased willingness to use warfare, torture, and threats of force;
- Reduced vulnerability of civilian populations to terror;
- Increased effectiveness of national and international regulatory institutions;

- Less openness of political institutions, including in the U.S., to corporate influence, bribery, and control;
- Regulation of currency speculators, hedge funds, and multinational corporations;
- Increasing life expectancy and reducing child mortality;
- Responses to amplified vulnerability to infectious diseases;
- Reducing the rising cost of medical care;
- Elimination of illiteracy;
- Improvements in the treatment of women and children;
- More rapid government responses to ecological problems;
- Improved methods of international cooperation;
- Greater acceptance, expanded training, and widespread institutionalization of conflict resolution;
- Far greater awareness of the extent, seriousness and exponential increase in many environmental and climate change indicators.

The last item deserves a more detailed explanation. One of the main difficulties in responding to exponential changes is that our awareness and understanding are not equipped to recognize it, and inevitably lag behind even the hardest scientific evidence. As Albert Einstein ominously wrote following the explosion of atomic bombs over Hiroshima and Nagasaki, "Everything has changed, except the way we think." Yet the way we think is perhaps the largest part of the problem, reminding us that, as Einstein also famously observed, "The significant problems we face cannot be solved at the same level of thinking we were at when we created them."

There is a wonderful story told by science writer K. C. Cole that illustrates the difference between exponential and incremental change and highlights our difficulty in assessing its importance: Assume for a moment that two bacteria are living inside a bottle, and that they reproduce and double in number once each minute, allowing us to predict that at the end of one hour they will completely fill the bottle. How much advance warning will they have that they are about to do so?

The answer is nearly none, since at 58 minutes before the hour, with only two minutes remaining, the bottle is only a quarter full. At 59 minutes, with one minute remaining, the bottle is still only half full. In another minute the bottle will be filled, and in another, the bacteria will fill an entire second bottle. It is unfortunate, yet entirely possible, that we are now just a minute or two from irreversible environmental collapse.

A similar example comes from an ancient story of a king who offered a mathematician who performed an important service anything he wanted in return. Seeing a chessboard nearby, the mathematician asked for a single grain of rice, which would be placed on the first square, two on the second, four on the third, etc. The king agreed, not realizing that before reaching the 64th square, he would be giving away more grains of rice than there are grains of sand on Earth.

## GLOBAL INTERDEPENDENCY

We know from the scientific study of chaos and complexity that the flapping of a butterfly's wings in the Amazonian rainforest can trigger a tornado in Texas. Is it not equally possible for the killing an unarmed civilian by a U.S. soldier in Baghdad to spark a hurricane of political anger that results in the death of equally unarmed civilians in an unrelated city elsewhere on the planet? Or for a small mistake in the hierarchical transmission of safety information at BP to devastate an entire ecosystem?

The scientific definition of chaos is "sensitive dependence on initial conditions." As any system approaches criticality and begins to undergo a "phase transition," its previously stable systemic make-up becomes increasingly unstable and dependent on minor fluctuations in its environment. This scientific metaphor suggests that instability in the social, economic, political, and environmental conditions in one region can dramatic impact people in other regions.

The science of ecology reveals that the loss of even a single important species can rapidly turn catastrophic for others, triggering a cascade of consequences vastly greater than anything we might have imagined beforehand. The same can be said of seemingly isolated events, such as those that followed the elimination of apartheid in South Africa, the collapse of Enron, or the assassination of Archduke Ferdinand prior to World War I.

If we consider, for example, avian influenza, or bird flu, it is clear that extreme poverty and a consequent reliance on domestic poultry for survival anywhere in the world will create favorable conditions for the H5N1 virus to mutate into a form transmissible by air between human beings. The ease of international travel, panic, and a desire to escape infection could then spread the virus rapidly to other countries, creating a platform for global pandemic.

Similarly, with regard to global warming, without a coordinated international response, scientists are nearly unanimous that significant temperature increases will occur before the end of the current century, leading to rising sea levels that will inundate many of the world's urban centers, triggering mass migrations, heightened competition for scarce resources, militaristic responses, and political polarizations that will make environmental problems more difficult to solve.

As we become more interdependent, a disaster in one part of the planet can easily turn into a catastrophe elsewhere, making it clear that global problems require global solutions. As climate is naturally chaotic and unpredictable, even small, seemingly insignificant changes can produce vastly larger ones later.

## THE PROBLEM WITH EXISTING SOLUTIONS

To solve any of the problems I have mentioned, and others we will inevitably confront as we develop and expand, all the disparate nations races, religions, cultures, societies, organizations, and institutions on the planet will need to learn how to work together to solve their common problems. To do so, we need better ways of communicating with each other, expanded skills in open and honest dialogue, and better techniques for solving problems, negotiating collaboratively, and resolving disputes without warfare, coercion, and other adversarial methods.

This may sound simplistic, even idealistic. Clearly, our history of working together to solve pressing social, economic, political, and ecological problems offers few reasons for unabashed confidence. Instead, it reveals an astonishing record of avoidable disasters, pointless miseries and needless deaths. For centuries, we have gotten away with murder, and no longer have resources to waste.

What is worse, these escalating problems cannot be solved completely or in time by nation states, or by large groups of countries, or by the use of military, legalistic, bureaucratic, or autocratic methods. Indeed, none of the following well-established, centuries-old problem solving mechanisms by themselves can succeed in solving these problems:

- Military force;
- Negotiated treaties and international agreements;
- Legal interventions, litigation, and the rule of law;
- Administrative rules and regulations or policies and procedures;
- Power-based diplomatic negotiations;
- National political leaders and institutions;
- Capitalism and market principles;
- The United Nations, as presently constituted.

So what is left? The answer is, we are, we as citizens and we as mediators. While it sounds ridiculous, when it comes to solving global problems, mediation can make a difference. The good news is that as our problems have multiplied, so has our social and technological ability to solve them. We have vastly increased our scientific and technological capabilities in recent years, and have also enormously improved our understanding and skills in effective communication, group facilitation, creative problem solving, public dialogue, conflict coaching, collaborative negotiation, prejudice reduction and bias awareness, mediation, conflict resolution system design, and similar methods. And it is precisely these skills that we now need in order to "save the planet."

If we consider the BP gulf oil spill as an example, there were numerous well-recognized long-term problems that led to that environmental disaster, or contributed to making it worse. In my mind, these include:

- Dependence on fossil fuels;
- Powerful oil and gas companies with assets and sales larger than the gross domestic products of all but a handful of nations;
- Inadequate market mechanisms to dampen the lust for quick profits, creating an incentive to cut corners on costs, including safety;
- Regulatory agencies that are led, managed and lobbied by people who pay greater attention to corporate influence than public safety and environmental sustainability;
- Disputes over how to manage the off-shore platform that were resolved hierarchically, bureaucratically, and autocratically, leaving those with direct experience of the problem without

the power or authority to solve it;

- Concentrating the problem solving authority in the hands of those who were more concerned with company profits than safety or environmental damage.

In the BP spill, as in the Exxon Valdez spill before it, there was a concerted effort in political circles and the media to find someone to blame for what happened. Yet a secondary effect of blaming individuals is that the systems that permitted, caused, or encouraged the mistake are ignored and let off the hook, increasing the likelihood that there will be fresh occurrences in the future.

As described above, it is likely that environmental catastrophes are increasing in frequency, reach and cost, and in the process, are generating conflicts around the world, including arguments over causation, responsibility, and competition for scarce aid resources. Without mediation, open dialogue, collaborative negotiation, and a common approach to implementing solutions to these problems, improving aid and recovery, and systemic preventative approach to future disasters, relief will be less effective, and delayed by years, if not decades.

In responding to BP and similar disasters, and in efforts to negotiate climate change issues at Copenhagen, where I was present, and similar international problem solving endeavors, political leaders, envoys and delegates continue to rely on classic international diplomatic processes, which are, for the most part, adversarial, distributive and power-based, and tend to have the following characteristics:

- Complex rules, protocols, policies, and procedures that make the process arduous, bureaucratic and confusing, and discourage conversation, participation and informal problem solving;
- Large, formal, highly structured meetings with processes that are influenced by political agendas, that attempt to consider multiple wide-ranging proposals to modify the language of proposed legal agreements;
- Limited opportunities for small, informal, unstructured conversations with open agendas, collaborative dialogues, and creative processes designed to satisfy common interests;
- Public declarations, official statements and pronouncements

in which positions are elaborated without engaging in genuine exchanges, admitting mistakes, or stopping to discuss important questions, critiques and alternative approaches;

- Traditional behind the scenes "hardball" negotiations, with arm-twisting, hidden agendas and adversarial, competitive bargaining tactics in which the largest, most powerful and wealthiest parties "win," while others "lose" and leave feeling excluded, disempowered and disrespected;

- Disagreements over diverse approaches and proposals that escalate into hardened positions and avoidable conflicts that result in impasse because there are no conflict resolution processes or professionals available who are empowered to assist in clarifying communications, brainstorming options, facilitating dialogue, and mediating solutions.

Mediators, facilitators, ombudsmen, and other conflict resolution professionals have had considerable experience designing effective problem solving, communication, negotiation, and conflict resolution processes over several decades, and would agree that there are much better ways of reaching agreements and that unsuccessful outcomes are not inevitable. It would be possible, for example, for the United Nations, without significant financial investments, to measurably improve the quality of its meetings and negotiations at important climate change events in at least the following 20 ways, by:

1. Conducting an in-depth, broadly inclusive, collaborative evaluation of the process used in Copenhagen and other climate change meetings to identify what worked and what could be improved;

2. Consulting widely with diverse public and private sector organizations and individuals who have experience designing dispute resolution systems and can provide ways of improving the entire negotiation process;

3. Developing a comprehensive set of process recommendations for future talks and securing agreement to implement them prior to the session, and brief delegates on them before they arrive;

4. Creating international negotiation and conflict resolution

protocols, model mediation language, and annexes to existing agreements that encourage a broad range of collaborative interest-based dispute resolution processes, including mediation, ombudsmen, facilitated dialogue, and similar methods;

5.  Asking each delegation to future talks to include among their members one or more trained mediators, collaborative negotiators, ombudsmen, or small group facilitators who can assist in bridging differences as they occur;

6.  Assigning one or more UN mediators or ombudsmen to every delegation, and to each small group and problem solving meeting;

7.  Sending experienced negotiators, facilitators, ombudsmen, and mediators to meet with the parties in advance of conferences and negotiating sessions to help set targets and timetables and encourage compromises that could lead to better and quicker agreements;

8.  Drastically simplifying and reducing the rigidity and formality of protocols, rules and official processes, especially as they effect the negotiation and agreement writing process;

9.  Shortening large meetings and breaking participants up into small, diverse, informal teams to brainstorm alternatives, agree on common goals or shared values, and reach consensus recommendations on specific problems, led by facilitators and mediators;

10. Offering free trainings throughout the process for individual delegations and teams in collaborative negotiation, group facilitation, and conflict resolution;

11. Reaching agreement on a variety of next steps that can be taken when consensus is not reached, including dialogue, informal problem solving, collaborative negotiation and mediation;

12. Appointing fast-forming, diverse problem solving teams with experts representing all nations, regions, groups, types of alternatives and ranges of opinion, with professional facilitators and recorders to aid them in their work;

13. Facilitating meetings of climate change experts and scientists to develop consensus-based recommendations, including them on problem solving teams, and convening meetings of diverse specialists to advise delegates on specific topics;

14. Conducting frequent open dialogue sessions on critical topics without attempting to reach agreement and providing multiple opportunities for free-ranging small group discussions, and open recommendations for ways of reaching consensus;

15. Appointing facilitators, ombudsmen, and mediators in advance for every meeting and asking them to recommend ways of improving the meeting;

16. Focusing not only on reaching a single comprehensive agreement, but also on smaller, specialized, limited, tentative, provisional, national, regional and bloc agreements as well, then work to accumulate and amalgamate them into a single draft;

17. Periodically conducting process checks to make sure everything is on track and making improvements as needed;

18. Allowing facilitators to stop the process if it isn't working, discuss it openly, invite suggestions, and propose ways of improving it;

19. Considering the entire multi-year agreement drafting process as a conflict system and using conflict resolution systems design principles to develop better ways of responding to obstacles, impasses and conflicts as they occur;

20. Continuing to search for preventative measures that can be adopted by all parties and UN organizations, that will help reduce the severity of future problems.

In these ways, it is possible for professional mediators, collaborative negotiators, ombudsmen, group facilitators, and conflict resolution systems designers to contribute to making climate change and other UN meetings more effective and collaborative. Mediation and conflict resolution can also be used to resolve conflicts that arise after agreements have been reached, and a culture of conflict resolution can be systematically reinforced throughout the community of nation states.

A great deal is riding on the success of these negotiations and the world's most experienced conflict resolution professionals, if asked, would be honored and pleased to work together to create a more thoughtful and acceptable set of recommendations for action. Thus, there is little to lose and much to gain from asking for their help, analyzing new approaches, and beginning to experiment with them.

This does not mean it will be easy to move away from existing processes or alter methods that are familiar and understood, even when they prove in practice to be ineffective, inefficient, and time-consuming. But mediators and conflict resolvers have faced similar difficulties before, and with the right approach, have experience convincing conflicted parties to try new ways of achieving their goals and designing more successful agreements.

## WHAT NEEDS TO BE DONE

Our ability to act in harmony with ecological limits is also reduced by our dependence for social status on luxuries and material possessions, our unrelenting economic expansion and competitive pursuit of profits, and our division into hostile, un-democratic nation-states, adversarial political parties and factions, and intolerant religious orthodoxies. Each of these sources of chronic conflict reduces our ability to think and act globally.

A revealing report by an official British commission on global warming chaired by Sir Nicholas Stern reported that climate change "is the greatest and widest-ranging market failure ever seen." And former head of the U.S. Fish and Wildlife Service, Mollie Beattie, wrote, "In the long term, the economy and the environment are the same thing. If it's unenvironmental, it is uneconomical. That is the rule of nature."

Still, the U.S., China, and other governments continue to act in isolation, using aggressive and hostile bargaining techniques, competitive market principles, power diplomacy, and threats of economic sanction or military force to achieve their goals, all of which increase resistance and reduce the likelihood of solving environmental problems.

If we are to solve environmental problems internationally and sustainably over a period of decades, if not centuries, it is becoming increasingly clear that we will not be able to do so without helping people in less developed countries improve the quality of their lives, or enforce the changes we want by military force or coercive adversarial negotiations. Instead, we will require honest communication, egalitarian financing, genuine collaboration, democratic decision-making, and a massive infusion of interest-based processes, conflict resolution initiatives, and interest-based interventions on all levels.

As a result, we will not be able to require problem-solving methods that allow the wealthiest countries to predetermine outcomes and processes in advance, or that pursue selfish economic policies, or that stack the deck in favor of wealthy nations that are already technologically advanced. If we do, others will dig in, drag their feet, and change efforts will falter. Instead, we require a collaborative attitude that encourages participatory problem solving, greater use of consensus, and a shift from relying on power or rights to trying to satisfy everyone's interests.

Over the last several decades, we have developed a powerful, complex set of methods and techniques that enhance collaboration and conflict resolution. These have proven highly successful, even with committed adversaries. While our skills have improved substantially, we have yet to fully acknowledge the need to adapt them to reducing environmental conflicts, or assuaging the chronic social, economic, and political hostilities that fuel them; or the need to implement them globally in a large-scale, organized, and coherent way.

At the moment, we are not even close to being able to respond sensibly or successfully to global disasters, let alone accept responsibility for solving the far more arduous problem of becoming ecologically sustainable and halting global warming in the long run. What is worse, the skills we need to leverage these changes are widely regarded as optional, too expensive, "touchy-feely," and threatening to the social, economic, and political status quo. How, then, do we overcome these obstacles?

## SAVING ALL SENTIENT BEINGS

There is an ancient Buddhist command that directs each of us to personally save all sentient or conscious beings. I have always thought this meant that no matter how difficult or seemingly impossible the task, it is important to extend compassion to others, focus on what blocks our growth and commitment, be mindful of our impact on others, and dismantle the pessimistic attitude that assumes it can't be done.

Changing times, however, require fresh interpretations, and I now believe this command needs to be taken quite literally. I believe it is uniquely the task of this generation to harness the power of conflict resolution and associated techniques and contribute to actually saving as many sentient beings as possible, principally by bringing conflict resolution to bear on environmental problems, building preventative global systems, and working to transform and transcend conflicts at their internal and external sources.

There is a famous story about two people walking along a beach that is strewn with thousands of dying starfish washed up from a storm. As one of them began tossing the starfish back into the ocean, the other remarked, "What difference can that make?" The first person answered, "It made a difference to that one," and they both began throwing them back. More deeply, the Dalai Lama wrote, "'We' and 'they' no longer exist. This planet is just us. The destruction of one area is the destruction of yourself. That is the new reality."

Just as our personal development reaches a limit in our capacity for affection and compassion, which is revealed in our external relationships with those who differ from us, our ability to make heartfelt connections with others rests on our internal capacity for affection and compassion. We cannot save ourselves without saving the world, or the world without saving ourselves.

In this way, the original paradoxical meaning of the command endures. In order to save others and ourselves, we need to become more aware of the environment and the impact we are personally having on it. This leads to the profound realization that we and the environment are not one. We will only finally succeed in dismantling selfishness, apathy, prejudice, greed, and brutality *both* by becoming aware of their sources internally within ourselves, and by redesigning the social, economic, and political systems that sustain them, transforming and transcending them in each of their locations.

As science and technology revolutionize our understanding of natural phenomena, they exponentially expand our capacity to manipulate and change the world. But our compassion, open-heartedness, and wisdom have not grown at the same pace. And in the past, when science has outstripped wisdom, we have discovered that a lot of knowledge and very little heart can be an extremely dangerous thing.

# THE WAY FORWARD

So how do we help save the planet? I believe we start by educating ourselves regarding global problems and accepting responsibility for improving them, including ourselves. Next, we realize that neither we nor any group or nation can succeed in isolation, and that the depth, seriousness, and reach of our problems require international collaboration. Finally, we recognize that our capacity for collaboration will remain limited in the absence of a:

- Profound appreciation for the value and importance of diversity as a basis for unity;
- Strategic insight into the chronic sources of social, economic, and political conflict;
- Willingness to apply advanced communication, negotiation, and conflict resolution skills to the ways we interact socially, economically, and politically;
- Concerted efforts to develop more skillful approaches to resolving conflicts before they result in intolerable, irreversible damage;
- Readiness to redesign our social, economic, and political institutions and practices from a conflict resolution perspective.

It is possible that we will not succeed. But are these not worthwhile goals in any event? Might they not lead to significant improvements in the quality of our communications and relationships, regardless of their eventual outcome? And do not our very lives, and those of our environmentally inseparable cousins among other species increasingly depend on our doing so?

As the brilliant anthropologist Margaret Mead presciently wrote, "We are continually faced with great opportunities which are brilliantly disguised as unsolvable problems." The unsolvable problems we now face offer immense opportunities for improving our condition and rethinking our social, economic, political, and ecological relationships. Doing so will develop our capacity to prevent, resolve, transform, and transcend conflicts at their chronic sources, and allow us to see that the solutions to our problems are already imaginable and being lived every day. As historian Howard Zinn wrote:

We don't have to wait for some grand utopian future. The
future is an infinite succession of presents, and to live
now as we think human beings should live, in defiance
of all that is bad around us, is itself a marvelous victory.

Mostly what is lacking is our realization that we can indeed make a
difference. The world is waiting. As the surrealist artist Andre Breton
wrote, "What are we waiting for? A woman? Two trees? Three flags?
Nothing. What are we waiting for?" [Portions of this chapter were
excerpted from *Conflict Revolution*.]

# CHAPTER 9

# LET'S TALK POLITICS

## An Analysis of Political Conflicts and a Guide to Designing, Organizing, and Conducting Dialogues on Difficult, Dangerous, and Controversial Issues

*"So tell me, sir, for whom are you spying today?"*
*"I've given up spying," said Ka. "These days I'm a mediator."*
*"That's even worse. Spies traffic in snippets of information that aren't much use to anyone, and mostly they do it for the money. Mediators, on the other hand—we'll, they're just smart alecks who think they can stick their noses into private business on the pretense of being impartial."*

~ Orhan Pamuk ~

*We ask only that men think it over carefully and then decide whether they will add to the misery of the world to achieve vague and distant goals, and whether they will accept a world crowded with weapons where brother kills brother; or whether, on the contrary, they will avoid as much bloodshed as possible in order to give future generations—who will be even better armed than ourselves—a chance for survival .... What we must fight is fear and silence, and with them the spiritual isolation they involve. What we must defend is dialogue and the universal communication of men. Slavery, injustice, and lies are the plagues that destroy this dialogue and forbid this communication, and that is why we must reject them.*

~ Albert Camus ~

A S WARS, GENOCIDES, AND bitter political battles rage daily around the globe causing devastating human losses, inspiring enduring enmities and hatreds, undermining national and international relationships, compromising environmental sustainability, and generating chronic conflicts, conflict resolvers have largely remained silent.

Perhaps this is because we feel we lack the skills to tackle such deeply divisive issues, or do not possess the commitment and dedication needed to work through difficult and dangerous political issues, or are afraid we will get drawn into polarizing political arguments ourselves and be consumed by them. Perhaps we are worried that we will be overwhelmed with insatiable demands for help, or are waiting to be invited to offer assistance, or are not clear enough about what we would do even if we were invited.

We have all watched political conversations that were ostensibly oriented to issues, values, vision, and direction degenerate into angry quarrels between deeply wounded, frightened, adversarial people; then deteriorate into brutal personal attacks and antagonistic power contests; only to sink into screaming matches, shaming and blaming, and personal viciousness, eventually descending into pushing and shoving, senseless violence, and appalling acts of brutality.

Successful political decision-making and conflict resolution require not silence or rage but dialogue, not aggression but collaboration, not accommodation but courageous, constructive, creative contention. Silence in the face of critical issues is not merely the absence of speech, but also of integrity, and therefore of self, values, citizenship, and community. As Dr. Martin Luther King, Jr. presciently said, "Our lives begin to end the day we become silent about things that matter."

Whatever our reasons for remaining silent, our ability to avoid addressing the complex, all-consuming, immensely challenging issues that characterize modern political conflicts are rapidly diminishing. As our world shrinks, these conflicts impact us in increasingly significant ways, allowing distant social, economic, and political decisions, environmental choices, and technological innovations to directly and acutely affect our lives.

Indeed, it is arguable that in the absence of improved conflict resolution skills it will prove difficult, if not impossible, for us to survive as a species. Political conflicts have grown so costly, destructive, and global that there is really no alternative, either as citizens or as conflict resolution professionals, than to summon our courage, evaluate what we can contribute, and do what we can to ease the world's suffering. Nor is it utopian or presumptuous to imagine that we can expand and evolve dialogue techniques in ways that will allow us to discuss and resolve contentious political issues without resorting to violence or coercion.

## CONFLICT AND POLITICAL SPEECH

If the goals of politics are, as Aristotle and Socrates believed, to maximize social justice, ethical self-improvement, and the common good, the role of political speech ought to be to achieve these outcomes by convincing others through honest dialogue and rational discourse, rather than by silencing those who disagree with violence, verbal manipulation, coercion, personal intimidation, and economic retribution.

In the first place, violence, manipulation, coercion, intimidation, and retribution merely polarize the opposition, driving it to more desperate measures in an effort to communicate its legitimate interests and points of view. In the second, as with all conflicts, it is easy to be seduced by false polarizations and come up with convincing rationalizations, sentimental platitudes and justifications for anything. None of these forms of speech, however, bring us any closer to social justice, ethical self-improvement, or the common good.

The essayist Isaiah Berlin argued that political communications and ideas are "inherently un-philosophical," in the sense that they are based on values over which people naturally disagree because they are based on dissimilar orientations and experiences. Political communications should therefore be regarded as unscientific, leading to different truths and representing unique experiences, each of which is regarded by others as valid.

This is the essence of interest-based approaches to conflict resolution. More interestingly, from a conflict resolution perspective, Berlin asked, "In what kind of world is political philosophy—the kind of discussion and argument in which it consists—in principle possible?" He answered, "Only in a world where ends collide." Thus, political speech *is* conflict speech. For this reason, the answer to the question "What should be done?" is inherently undiscoverable as a complete and exclusive answer. Berlin writes:

> Not because it is beyond our powers to find the answer, but because the question is not one of fact at all, the solution lies not in discovering something which is what it is, whether it is discovered or not—a proposition or formula, an objective good, a principle, a system of values objective or subjective, a relationship between a mind and something non-mental—but resides in action: something which cannot be found, only invented—an act of will or faith or creation obedient to no pre-existing rules or laws or facts.

From this fundamental circumstance, Berlin concludes that no political argument powerful enough to convince large numbers of people can be entirely wrong. Thus, every powerful political idea represents, and continues to represent, some important piece of political truth, based on a genuine social experience. In an insightful passage, he wrote:

> The social contract is a model which to this day helps to explain something of what it is that men feel to be wrong when a politician pronounces an entire class of the population ... to be outside the community—not entitled to the benefits conferred by the State or its laws. So too, Lenin's image of the factory which needs no supervision by coercive policemen after the State has withered away; Maistre's image of the executioner and his victims as the cornerstone of all authority ... Locke's analogy of

government with trusteeship; ... all these illuminate some
types of social experience.

Political philosophies are therefore not scientifically provable, but
poetic, metaphoric truths about the human desire for freedom from
tyranny, domination, and oppression and alternative ideas about how to
end it. What is important, therefore, in analyzing political argumentation,
is that we probe beneath the formal, factual arguments people offer, and
elucidate the metaphors and analogies, syntax and grammar, interests
and emotions, stories and experiences that give rise to them.

To do so, as in all conflict resolution, it is necessary to surrender the
idea that there is a single political truth, which is ours, and recognize
instead that every political argument is an effort to establish the truth and
validity, even the value and importance, of a particular personal and social
experience. This implies that politics, despite its linguistic assumptions
and orientation to power, need not be a zero-sum game in which one side
is right and all others are wrong, but an effort to acknowledge, investigate
and integrate multiple, diverse, contradictory interests and truths in the
course of formulating a common policy and direction.

This is precisely what conflict resolution, at its core, represents: a way
of resolving disputes based on diverse interests using consensus building,
power-balancing and similar techniques, in which no single group is
allowed to dominate. Thus, mediation possesses a hidden political
dimension that is inherently democratic, egalitarian, and collaborative
because it allows a variety of interests and truths to contend and seek
synergistic combination. It defeats prejudice and hatred not with opposing
prejudices and hatreds, but by combining, averaging, undermining,
and canceling them, then searching beneath their hostile veneer for the
hidden, unsatisfied, heartfelt stories about experiences and interests that
have been fueling them, and reframing them in ways that make them
understandable to all.

## CONFLICT, POLITICS, AND THE STATE

From the outset, politics and conflict seem intertwined and inseparable.
Indeed, political conflicts have historically been used to strengthen and
define the state, and to provide it with a sense of unifying meaning. As

FDR's Assistant Attorney General Thurman Arnold put it, "No nation, no social institution ever acquired coherence without some sort of fight. Out of the fight come its myths and its heroes."

These myths and heroes, however, generally take the form of adversarial stories about others that define political identity and meaning, but do so negatively and antagonistically. As a result, politics and the state are initially defined through opposition, competition, adversity, conflict, and hostility toward others, producing a political culture that is grounded in aggression, suspicion, distrust of differences, and power- or rights-based solutions to conflict. This history raises a critical question: Is it possible for nations to acquire coherence, identity, and meaning positively through collaboration, participation, and interest-based solutions, without the destructive, dehumanizing consequences that flow from fighting? And if so, how?

## THE STATE AS MEDIATOR

Politics and the state are mechanisms not only for avoiding and suppressing conflicts, but also for managing and settling them, principally by means of military force, legal coercion, and bureaucratic regulation. These methods, however, fall far short of what is now possible using interest-based processes like mediation and dialogue, which can also lead to prevention, resolution, transformation, and transcendence, and seek to end conflicts at their chronic, systemic sources by enhancing learning, problem solving, collaboration, heartfelt communication, and openness to consensus-based systemic change.

What is worse, the state is itself a source of chronic, systemic conflict, and often unwilling or unable to reach deeper, general levels of resolution. These chronic conflicts stem historically from competition for power, wealth and status, and struggles for dominance between masters and slaves, lords and serfs, capitalists and workers, whites and blacks, men and women, haves and have-nots, citizens and foreigners, manufacturers and consumers, and countless others.

The state has not often been neutral in these conflicts, but more commonly sided with those who were already powerful and dominant against those with less power, wealth, and status. The more equal the balance of power, wealth, and status between competing groups, the more the state has been forced to defend itself by equivocating, retreating from open partisanship, adopting the language of neutrality, focusing on legal enforcement, obeying the logic of election returns, and transforming itself into a relatively pluralistic, bureaucratic, and apolitical institution.

In this way, the economic transition from feudalism to capitalism was accompanied by a political transition from power-based hereditary monarchies to rights-based electoral democracies. For the early American colonies to gain independence from colonial domination and the constraints imposed by English commercial and monarchical power, it became necessary to advance the idea of a right to life, liberty, and the pursuit of happiness. These values implied, reinforced, and increasingly required political self-determination, national independence, democratic government, popular elections, and rights-based conflict resolution processes like litigation.

Yet from the beginning, rights-based politics and processes manifested themselves in contradictory, conflict generating ways. On one hand, the U.S. Bill of Rights and Constitution enormously expanded democratic rights over what had been available in England and Europe. On the other, slavery was supported and only white male property owners were permitted to vote. On one hand, everyone had an inalienable right to life, liberty, and the pursuit of happiness, implying self-determination. On the other, these rights were systematically denied to native nations and tribes that already inhabited the country.

Nonetheless, the appeal of these democratic principles proved more powerful and lasting than efforts to constrain them within narrow bounds, and as they increased in popularity, the willingness of governments to oppose the rights of those who could vote them out of office has steadily declined. This process has expanded over the course of centuries in the direction of increased openness, collaboration and democracy, but always within a context of bureaucratic constraint.

More importantly, the evolution of power-based hereditary monarchies into rights-based electoral democracies required the emergence of new forms of politics, a new kind of state and a new set of political processes, including debate. This raises the following question: what shifts in politics and the state would be likely to occur if we were to evolve further and adopt interest-based processes and relationships?

If power-based political institutions require hierarchy, operate by command, and result in obedience; and if rights-based institutions require bureaucracy, operate by control, and result in compliance, what would interest-based institutions require? How would they operate? And what would they result in?

## NEUTRALITY, BUREAUCRACY, AND THE STATE

Historically, neutrality can be seen as a consequence of inequality, domination, and the inequitable distribution of status, wealth, and power. The state had to support the ideas and attitudes of the dominant groups that funded and operated it, yet it also had to preserve its own legitimacy, authority, and persuasiveness. The second of these goals, as populations coalesced into national groups, could not be achieved as effectively using power-based options such as dictatorship and military force, which are unfavorable in the long run for commerce and political stability, as it can through rights-based options which promise rights and a possibility of gaining power to those who feel excluded.

This is because rights are essentially *limitations* on the exercise of power, and are based on formal neutrality, including legal forms of coercion, bureaucratic regulation, abstractly worded legislation, impartial judges, due process of law, administrative agencies that are somewhat removed from the political process, and professional police who administer and enforce the laws. These measures still generate chronic conflicts, but are more popularly acceptable, and therefore less likely to encourage open hostility, rebellion, revolution, and civil war than power-based systems.

As a result, a self-reinforcing set of ostensibly neutral rights-based processes emerged over the course of several centuries that reduced the need to resort to power-based contests and curtailed its worst abuses, while simultaneously reinforcing inequality and generating less adversarial chronic conflicts. These conflicts could now be avoided, suppressed, managed, and settled by being channeled through formally neutral legal and bureaucratic systems that would sidetrack and co-opt collective acts of rebellion, ameliorate political antagonisms, and deflect proposals that might result in large-scale alterations of the system.

Paradoxically, as the state became more neutral it also grew less political and more capable of responding humanely, empathetically, and flexibly. But as it became more bureaucratic, it grew less sensitive to the needs, feelings, desires, and suffering of others. Its ability to recognize human differences and subjective variations became increasingly inconsistent with its formality and orientation to rules and technical details, thereby increasing its callousness, subtle corruption, distance, hypocrisy, and need to appear neutral.

As rights-based democratic republics altered their leadership and policies through popular elections they became more vulnerable to shifts in public opinion and required the development of bureaucracies, which are more insulated against dissent, apolitical, and stable. There may be a rough democracy practiced within the ranks of elected officials, but there is little in the civil service. Most bureaucracies aspire to be run like corporations, but lack corporate efficiency, entrepreneurship, leadership, and incentives, while at the same time possessing all the lethargy, cynicism, and disinterest that characterize the worst hierarchies and autocracies.

On the one hand, bureaucracies reflect the evolution of political states from power-based arbitrary exercises of absolutist dictatorial will, to rights-based, rational exercises of abstract logical decision-making. On the other, their rules are rational, orderly, and equal, regardless of how irrational, disorderly, and unequal human life is. Bureaucracy is thus both an enormous step away from tyranny and despotism, and an enormous step removed from authentic popular democracy.

Bureaucracies, as rights-based social institutions, are designed to placate irate citizens who have been denied fairness, channel dissent into isolated backwaters where it can boil ineffectively without contaminating the whole, grudgingly provide social services to those they secretly look down on, mitigate the effects of otherwise uncontrollable greed, monitor public spending, and enforce arcane, Kafkaesque rules and regulations. Novelist J. M. Coetzee writes:

> ... you must at every moment remind yourself of what it is like to come face to face with the state—the democratic state or any other —in the person of the state official. Then ask yourself: Who serves whom? Who is the servant, who the master?"

Honoré de Balzac, in his novel *The Bureaucrats*, described it this way:

> Made up entirely of petty minds, the bureaucracy has stood as an obstacle to the prosperity of the nation, has delayed for seven years by its machinery a canal project that would have stimulated the production of a province, is afraid of everything, prolongs procrastination, and perpetuates the abuses which in turn perpetuate and consolidate its very existence. The bureaucracy holds everything in its control: even the minister is in its web; finally, it stifles men of talent who are bold enough to be independent of it or to expose its follies ... Bureaucracy, a gigantic power set in motion by dwarfs, is thus born.

The consummate chronicler of bureaucracy, however, was novelist Franz Kafka, whose descriptions, especially in *The Trial* and *The Castle*, of politeness combined with cruelty, proximity with distance, rationality with insanity, dedication with irresponsibility, and efficiency with waste, reveal its twisted sensibility and the inherent limitations of trying to fit round human objects into square, bureaucratically engineered holes.

We can trace the sources of rights-based ideas and language to the essential characteristics of bureaucracy, described in detail by German sociologist Max Weber. Today, these can be altered and amended to include a number of traits that disrupt political discourse, including the following:

- Precise, formal separations that make communications problematic;
- Distinct jurisdictional areas defined by regulation that interrupt the natural flow of work;
- Over-centralization of functions, leading to inflexibility, waste, and reduced innovation and motivation;
- Impersonal hierarchies of titles, offices, powers, and privileges that reinforce relationships based on superior and inferior status;
- Fixed rules and consequences that reduce creativity, authenticity, and individuality;
- Recruitment and promotion based on technical skills,

degrees, and formal, objective qualifications, masking informal, subjective bias and favoritism;

- Government positions as the private property of officials
- Goals, processes, rules, and policies that are determined by others, disempowering those who do the work;
- Separation of official from unofficial truth, resulting in rumors and gossip to fill in the blanks;
- Division of what is personal and private from what is official and public, while simultaneously confusing them;
- Loyalty to regulations and positions, rather than ideas or people;
- Systems, structures, and rules are regarded as superior to values, processes, and relationships;
- Facts, reality, details, and evidence are given great respect, while emotions, art, abstract thinking, and intuition are discounted;
- Stability, tradition, conformity, and experience are valued over change, innovation, criticism, and insight;
- Personalized blame and impersonalized responsibility;
- Secrecy and "need to know" are used to withhold information and augment personal status and power;
- Avoidance, aggression, and accommodation take precedence over listening, dialogue, and collaboration.

The values of bureaucracy are those of control, conformity, formality, diffused responsibility, discouragement of initiative and impersonal compliance. For these reasons, German sociologist Robert Michels argued that bureaucracy is inextricably linked with "the iron law of oligarchy," since increasing complexity and bureaucratization cause power to be concentrated in the hands of elites that are then able to make decisions autocratically, even within political states and parties that profess to value democracy and the rule of law.

Hannah Arendt described bureaucracy as "the rule of Nobody," and the most formidable form of domination:

> If, in accord with traditional political thought, we identify tyranny as government that is not held to give account of itself, rule by Nobody is clearly the most tyrannical of

all, since there is no one left who would even be asked
to answer for what is being done... In a fully developed
bureaucracy there is nobody left with whom one could
argue, to whom one could present grievances, on whom
the pressures of power could be exerted. Bureaucracy is
the form of government in which everybody is deprived
of political freedom, of the power to act; for the rule by
Nobody is not no-rule, and where all are equally powerless
we have a tyranny without a tyrant.

Bureaucracy concentrates access to communication hierarchically
at the top and suppresses it at the bottom, reinforcing isolation, apathy,
passive aggressive behavior, and cynicism. This concentration forces those
in the middle to manipulate information, control formal communication
networks, and consolidate their power. It also encourages them to use
their positions to acquire unique, secret knowledge and skills that make
them difficult to replace, ossifying leadership and alienating the public.

These dynamics led French political philosopher Maurice Merleau-
Ponty to begin his analysis of political conflicts in the 1920s with the
assertion that bureaucratic language and abstract politics are a kind of
crime against individuality:

Before the [First World] war, politics seemed to us
unthinkable because it is a statistical treatment of men
... [I]t makes no sense, we thought, to treat these singular
beings ... as if they were a collection of substitutable
objects.

The experience of World War I completely altered Merleau-Ponty's
view of the necessity of politics and convinced him that there was little
or no connection between the ordinary language of everyday life and the
power-infected language of bureaucracy and politics. Several decades
later, the English critic John Berger reached a similar conclusion:

Between the experience of living a normal life at this
moment on the planet and the public narratives being
offered to give a sense to that life, the empty space, the
gap, is enormous.

For Merleau-Ponty and others of his generation, the most elementary forces influencing political life were those of social inequality, economic inequity, and political autocracy. These suggested the necessity, even the inevitability, of adversarial conflicts, bureaucratic relationships, and the inhuman use of violence and coercion against others. Merleau-Ponty wrote, "Political problems come from the fact that we are all subjects and yet look upon other people and treat them as objects." He considered this double standard in how we regard ourselves versus how we treat others as a "fundamental condition of politics" that is distorted because it "unfold[s] in the realm of appearance." While employing coercion and violence as tools, democratic politics nonetheless requires the tacit consent of the governed. Consent is therefore manufactured by creating an appearance of legitimacy, neutrality, necessity, civilization, and even morality, so as to justify actions such as executions that might otherwise seem illegitimate, unnecessary, uncivilized and immoral.

In a similar way, the apparently innocent clichés of "civilizing morality" and the "white man's burden" under colonialism translated directly into the violent, brutalizing oppression of dark-skinned peoples, overturning ordinary precepts of private, interpersonal morality and causing politics to violate Kant's categorical imperative that we should act only in ways that we would accept if they were to become universal law.

Indeed, the mere existence of prejudice, exploitation, domination, and oppression fundamentally distort political discourse, either by implicitly justifying what is unjustifiable in principle, suppressing the voices of those who seek to end it, or encouraging people to remain silent, knowing of its presence. These acts cause politics to violate a second principle of Kantian morality, that one should "So act as to treat humanity, whether in your own person or in another, always as an end, and never as only a means."

In these respects, moral violations and reversals are subtly reflected in nearly all varieties of official, bureaucratic, power- and rights-based political communications. We can spot them in the ways disingenuous politicians abstract general principles from individual cases to create an appearance of breadth and statesmanship while avoiding troublesome details, and in the ways they personalize abstract principles by referring to specific individual instances so as to avoid ethical difficulties while creating an appearance or "image" of morality and integrity.

Thus, in power- and rights-based political language we experience repeated references in noble, stentorian tones, to "our country," or "the people;" crass manipulations of maudlin sentimentality, particularly regarding children, struggling families, religious figures, and recently departed political leaders; facades of personal outrage and affront; loud protestations and harsh denunciations of moral transgressions by others; and simplistic claims of uncompromising toughness or unyielding principles regarding complex, multilayered problems. Each of these undermines political discourse and makes dialogue more difficult.

These twists of political language become more common during elections and wars. As journalist H. L. Mencken wrote, "The whole aim of practical politics is to keep the populace in a continual state of alarm (and hence clamorous to be led to safety) by menacing them with an endless series of hobgoblins, all of them imaginary." Every so often, the imaginary nature of these hobgoblins becomes known and the magnificence of the patriotic illusion disappears, exposing a reality of social snobbery, economic greed, and political self-aggrandizement.

In these ways, political language can be turned into a weapon of domination, intimidation and coercion, as when it is used to indict internal opponents as traitors who offer aid and comfort to enemies, or when it adopts a syntax of demagogic exhortation through calls for immediate uncompromising action and does nothing, or when it claims victory or responsibility for changes it did little to bring about. Political speech can also be a perfect cover for naked greed, prompting Mencken to comment acidly, "When you hear a man speak of his love for his country, it is a sign that he expects to be paid for it."

The language, syntax, metaphors, and narrative assumptions common to power- and rights-based political speech make it difficult to avoid or de-escalate violence, transform debates into dialogues, or come to grips with the difficult, often painful issues that inform our most important political choices. Thus, it is common in politics, as in personal conflicts, to construct false absolutes regarding our opponents in order to justify our own unconscionable behaviors. Is it possible, then, to bring a more nuanced, mediative sensibility to conflicts triggered by political speech and turn hostile denunciations and debates into appreciative disagreements and dialogues?

According to neutral, bureaucratic, rights-based thinking, no matter how disastrously people have been treated, laws and public policies must be the same for everyone, subjecting victims and perpetrators to identical rules. Yet as William Blake wrote, "The same law for the lion and the ox is oppression." While rights are clearly a step forward from the openly subjective power of monarchies and dictatorships, they fall short of accepting human strengths and weaknesses, responding uniquely to individual needs, acknowledging emotions and heartfelt subjectivity, and satisfying diverse human interests in diverse ways.

While neutrality, bureaucracy, and rights have moderated the impact of persistent political conflicts, they have made it nearly impossible to address the deeper dissensions and antagonisms generated by inequality, inequity, and autocracy. Rights distort and to some extent camouflage the nature of these conflicts by resorting to abstract rule-making, remaining formally neutral in the presence of prejudice, channeling disagreements through bureaucratic agencies and coercive legal institutions that are required to support the status quo, and confining results to win/lose outcomes.

## THE WIN/LOSE NATURE OF POLITICAL POWER

The principal *human* goal of politics is to create a public space within which every group can satisfy its unique interests, establish its way of life, and orient institutions to meet its members' needs. Democracy and its underlying demands for equality, equity, and freedom are thus symbols whose deeper meaning is the ability to live personally and socially as oneself, rather than in the shadow, image, or self-interests of others.

Power-based politics is seen by some simply as a means of living as oneself, but exclusively and anti-socially, exercising domination over others and preventing them from doing the same. Rights, on the other hand, permit everyone to live formally as themselves, but thwart them in doing so by requiring them to exercise their rights in competitive, adversarial, bureaucratic ways. Rights are small slices of freedom from tyranny for those who otherwise lack status, wealth, and power. They are provisional concessions, small chunks of freedom, and piecemeal guarantees, for anyone with the will and strength to enforce them.

Consequently, power- and rights-based politics are fundamentally competitive, win/lose, adversarial processes, suggesting that any gains in equality, equity, or freedom by one group must require its withdrawal from others. For this reason, power-based political conflicts turn into fierce power contests and efforts to seize complete control over state institutions from insiders, while rights-based conflicts turn into legal battles to enforce rights and efforts to share power by regulating it, or subdividing it with outsiders.

Yet once a group of outsiders gains access to power, they commonly use it to satisfy their own exclusive interests over and against those of others, and thereby become new insiders. They then find it necessary to defend their power and rights by force and coercion, giving rise to a new group of dissidents who demand rights and access to power.

Interest-based approaches, on the other hand, do not require these win/lose outcomes, and are able to increase social equality, economic equity, and political democracy for multiple constituencies simultaneously. They dismantle domination in both large and small ways, aiming at its source, and for that reason, are methods by which it becomes possible to redesign political dialogue, including its language, processes, and relationships.

When people shift from exercising power or recognizing rights to satisfying interests, even on a small scale, equality is no longer seen as a threat to the social status of existing elites, but as a source of immense richness, creative problem solving, and collaborative relationships. Economic equity ceases to be regarded as stripping wealth from the rich, but as a way of reducing insecurity, implementing social justice, and improving everyone's quality of life. Political democracy is no longer perceived as mob rule, anarchy, or electoral charade, but as the best way of collaboratively discussing, analyzing, and solving common global problems.

In other words, political history can be seen as a progression from the use of power, to rights, to interests, and thus, as successive stages in the resolution of social, economic, and political conflicts leading to higher, more cooperative, democratic, and human forms of political organization. When the state is organized around the satisfaction of interests, it is increasingly influenced by, transformed into, and made identical with civil society, thereby transforming the character of its communications, processes, and relationships.

## MEDIATING POLITICAL SPEECH

The fundamental orientation of politics to power and rights, as opposed to interests, automatically reinforces the assumption that there is a single truth or correct outcome, and more bizarrely, that it is morally acceptable to lie and kill in pursuit of it. This leads directly to verbal chicanery, character assassination, prejudicial statements, demagoguery, and pursuit of victory at any price.

During the last few decades, interest-based methods, processes, and techniques have developed that allow us to transform not only ordinary adversarial interpersonal speech, but unnecessarily divisive political rhetoric as well, and to do so in ways that reveal human interests, deepen empathy, and invite a collaborative search for higher, intersecting, synergistic solutions to common problems.

It is possible, for example, even with hardened political adversaries, to identify ground rules, forms of communication, and process agreements that allow them to constructively address their problems. It is possible to separate highly adversarial groups and ask them to identify what kind of relationship they would like to have with their opponents, then list the obstacles preventing them from achieving it, or the behaviors their side engaged in during previous negotiations that made trust more difficult. They can then present these lists to their opponents and discover how accurate they were, shifting their communications in a new direction.

In addition, large meetings and assemblies can be divided into small, randomly selected, politically diverse teams, allowing structured, facilitated conversations to take place face-to-face. Each team can then be asked to list, analyze, and prioritize the problems they are experiencing and brainstorm possible solutions, without necessarily agreeing on them. It is also possible to ask each person some profound internalizing questions that stimulate reflection, such as these, which are sometimes used in mediation:

- Why did you decide to join this group? What attracted you to it?
- Why do you care what happens here? What about it touches your passion?
- What have you done that has contributed to this conflict?

How have you, by action or inaction, fueled or allowed it to continue?

- What has this conflict cost you? What price have you paid for it? How much longer are you prepared to continue paying that price?
- Do you believe your communication has been effective in creating understanding in the other side? What might you do to improve it?
- What is one thing you would be willing to do to improve communication with the other side?
- What request would you most like to make to the other side? What promise are you willing to make in response?
- What most needs improving in your relationship?
- What is one thing the other side could do to restore your trust?
- What is one thing you have learned from, or appreciate about the other side?
- With 20/20 hindsight? Is there anything you wish you had done differently? What are you willing to do differently in the future?
- Is there anything for which you would like to apologize? Are you willing to do so now?
- If you had one wish for what we might achieve in this session, what would it be?
- What changes would need to take place for you to act differently in the future? What support would you need from others? How could they encourage or support you?
- What might the either side do that would undermine or sabotage the progress you've made?
- What is likely to happen if nothing changes and the conflict continues? Is that what you want? If not, why not?

Conflict resolution has demonstrated in countless instances that people are able to stop accusing and start listening to each other, not as a result of political argumentation, which is nearly always experienced as confrontational and disrespectful, but through authentic interpersonal dialogue. This may take the form of stories, empathetic questions, open-minded discussions, emotionally vulnerable admissions, acknowledgements, apologies, confessions, informal problem-solving conversations, collaborative negotiations, personal requests, sincere promises, honest disagreements, heartfelt declarations, or discussions of mutually important issues.

The unspoken assumption behind most political communications is that there is a single truth and one correct outcome. This illusion is partly a consequence of the natural orientation of political speech to decision-making and a need to select one out of many diverging paths, competing options, and alternative views of the future. Yet intelligent political decisions emerge more easily, naturally, and successfully from an appreciation of the complexity and multiplicity of truths, rather than an assumption that other truths are inferior or do not exist. The shift from single to multiple truths happens automatically when we alter the form of political discourse by transforming debates into dialogues, and ask questions that do not produce a single correct answer. Even simple algebraic equations can produce more than one correct answer, so that the square root of 16, for example, is both four and negative four.

## TRANSFORMING DEBATES INTO DIALOGUES

Once populations reach a certain size, political participation and direct democracy become more complex, vulnerable to conflict, and time consuming, allowing representative democracy and bureaucratic political institutions to rise and take their place. Yet these less direct forms of political representation encourage a variety of adversarial, rights-based forms of communication, including debate.

Clearly, population density and urban sprawl reduce the likelihood that people will behave toward one another as if they were members of the same family, tribe, or species. Yet large groups can be reorganized into small groups and teams that work collaboratively or in parallel to make political decisions more democratically without significant reductions in efficiency or effectiveness.

If we define democracy as "government of, by, and for the people," what would government "of, by and for" all the people actually look like? How might it be done? Democracy, of course, has two distinct and entirely different meanings. First, it can be thought of as a form of state or system of government in which leaders are elected and decisions are made by majority rule. Alternatively, it can be thought of as a problem solving process that is free, equal, open, and participatory, in which power is shared and decisions are made collaboratively. These two definitions sometimes conflict, since elected governments and majority rule do not always entail equality, openness, and participation, yet dialogue can work for both.

Naturally democratic, interest-based processes encourage the second form of democracy, and include group facilitation, public dialogue, informal problem-solving, strategic planning, public policy mediation, even large group computer conferencing. These methods make it possible for large numbers of people to discuss difficult issues and reach consensus on common approaches, in spite of significant differences in beliefs, size, and diversity. They make it possible to bridge the gap between ordinary language and political discourse by shifting communication from debates over who is right to dialogues over what is possible, using stories and life experiences to explain why they care about these issues.

Conversations about difficult, dangerous and controversial issues are minefields, full of hidden traps and camouflaged dangers. As a result, most people assume it is better not to talk about them at all, rather than enter conversations that could blow up. Yet silence in the face of difficult problems simply guarantees their continuation. Is it possible for us to design processes that take account of these difficulties and avoid, reduce or overcome them? Can we design dialogues in which people talk about difficult, even dangerous topics in ways that are safe and effective, yet directly address the issues and allow people to discover solutions? If so, how do we begin?

## DIALOGUE VS. MONOLOGUE

First, it is useful to distinguish dialogue from other forms of communication and identify the principal elements that make it effective. Dialogues are different from monologues, which can take place even when more than one person is speaking. Here are some important distinctions between them:

- Monologue is one way. Dialogue is two ways.
- Monologue is an assertion. Dialogue is a responsive conversation.
- Monologue is talking at each other. Dialogue is talking with

each other.

- Monologue assumes there is a single truth. Dialogue assumes there are multiple truths.
- Monologue is announcing "The Answer." Dialogue is asking respectful questions and exploring diverse answers.
- Monologue is preaching to the choir. Dialogue is talking with people who are different about their similarities and differences.
- Monologue is about me. Dialogue is about us.
- Monologue is about power. Dialogue is about interests, which are the reasons why people want to accumulate power.
- Monologue moves toward opposition. Dialogue moves toward relationship.

Monologues tend to advance narrow, self-centered truths that divide us from one another because they are too small, inflexible, and simplistic; because they cannot encompass the greatness and complexity of all the possibilities that reside in the problem. Dialogues, on the other hand, are broader, collaborative searches for synergistic truths that unite us, that are large, flexible and complex enough to include everyone, yet not make problems simpler than they actually are. Dialogues allow us to cross the divide of our differences and discover what we have in common. They encourage us to communicate and thereby overcome the isolation of individual experience and learn from other points of view.

## DIALOGUE VS. DEBATE

We can also distinguish dialogues from debates, which are simply two successive monologues pretending to be a dialogue. Debate defines issues and solutions adversarially, in ways that make them automatically unacceptable to the other side. Dialogue, on the other hand, as defined by physicist David Bohm, is "a stream of meaning flowing among, through, and between us." Dialogue defines issues and solutions collaboratively and searches for ways of making them acceptable to all parties.

Debate is a circular process, in which opponents argue and disagree with each other and are more interested in demonstrating that they are right than that they are in discovering the truth. In dialogue, truths emerge not from one side winning and the other losing, but from both sides explaining their different perspectives, identifying the meaning of their disagreements, and searching for solutions that satisfy their underlying interests. Bohm explained how dialogue achieves these results:

> In ... a dialogue, when one person says something, the other person does not, in general, respond with exactly the same meaning as that seen by the first person. Rather, the meanings are only similar and not identical. Thus, when the 2nd person replies, the 1st person sees a difference between what he meant to say and what the other person understood. On considering this difference, he may then be able to see something new, which is relevant both to his own views and to those of the other person. And so it can go back and forth, with the continual emergence of a new content that is common to both participants. Thus, in a dialogue, each person does not attempt to make common certain ideas or items of information that are already known to him. Rather, it may be said that two people are making something in common, i.e., creating something new together.

Here are some distinctions between debate and dialogue, developed largely by Bohm and the Dialogue Group for the Boston Chapter of Educators for Social Responsibility:

| **DEBATE** | **DIALOGUE** |
| --- | --- |
| 1. Debate is oppositional: two sides are opposed and attempt to prove each other wrong. | 1. Dialogue is collaborative: two or more sides work together to develop a common understanding. |
| 2. In debate, the goal is to be the only one to win. | 2. In dialogue, the goal is to find common ground and to find better solutions. |

| | |
|---|---|
| 3. In debate, one listens in order to find flaws and refute arguments. | 3. In dialogue, one listens in order to learn and find commonalities. |
| 4. Debate affirms each side's own point of view. | 4. Dialogue enlarges and transforms both side's points of view. |
| 5. Debate rarely questions assumptions but defends them against criticism. | 5. Dialogue questions assumptions and discusses and re-evaluates them. |
| 6. Debate rarely results in open apology or introspection. | 6. Dialogue encourages apology and introspection, and openly shares them. |
| 7. Debate defends one's own position as the best solution and excludes the other side's positions and solutions. | 7. Dialogue elicits interests rather than positions and reaches better solutions by creatively combining them. |
| 8. Debate produces closed minds and hearts, a determination to be right, and resistance to change. | 8. Dialogue produces open minds and hearts, a willingness to be proven wrong, and participation in change. |
| 9. Debate results in the solidification and entrenchment of beliefs. | 9. Dialogue results in the modification and re-examination of beliefs. |

| | |
|---|---|
| 10. In debate, one searches for disagreements, mistakes, and difficulties. | 10. In dialogue, one searches for agreements, opportunities, and potential synergies. |
| 11. In debate, one searches for flaws and weaknesses in other's positions. | 11. In dialogue, one searches for strengths and commonalities in other's positions. |
| 12. Debate involves opposing the other side without recognizing feelings or relationships, and belittling or deprecating the other person. | 12. Dialogue involves genuine concern for the other person, acknowledges feelings and relationships, and empathizes with, and supports the other side. |
| 13. Debate assumes there is a single truth or correct answer, only one side has possession of it, and that combining them only weakens them. | 13. Dialogue assumes there are many correct answers, many people have pieces of it, and that combining them creates much more satisfying and effective solutions. |
| 14. Debate implies an end or conclusion. | 14. Dialogue is open-ended and on-going. |
| 15. Debate assumes that conflict is only resolvable when one side wins. | 15. Dialogue assumes that conflict is resolvable by both sides winning. |

In his book *On Dialogue*, Bohm explains why we need to pay attention to the process of dialogue and design ways of making it more effective:

> Dialogue is really aimed at going into the whole thought process and changing the way the thought process occurs collectively. We haven't really paid much attention to thought as a process. We have ENGAGED in thoughts, but we have only paid attention to the content, not to the process. Why does thought require attention? Everything requires attention, really. If we ran machines without paying attention to them, they would break down. Our thought, too, is a process, and it requires attention, otherwise it's going to go wrong.

Another way of thinking of dialogue is to regard it as a learning process in which participants with diverse ideas, backgrounds, and experiences try to understand not only what the other thinks that is different, but more importantly why they think that way, and what events and experiences led them to do so. Part of the power of dialogue is its encouragement of personal stories, life experiences, and the lessons people draw from them. These induce empathy in the listener and invite deeper levels of listening.

For this reason, it is often useful to open a dialogue by asking people to say something about who they are in relation to the issue. For example, in a dialogue conducted by Mediators Beyond Borders in Los Angeles about conflicts in the Middle East that was attended by more than hundred people on both sides of the issue, small groups began conversations with a facilitator asking each participant to briefly introduce themselves and say what personal experiences or connections they have with the Middle East. People were invited to tell stories about their experiences and encouraged to express empathy with them.

In another dialogue conducted by members of Mediators Beyond Borders in Athens on problems associated with immigration, small groups with immigrants and Greek citizens began by answering one of the following questions:

- What is your name? Does it have a meaning in your family or culture? If so, what is its meaning?
- What is your personal experience with immigration? Your

family's experience?

- Have you ever come into a new family, neighborhood, school or workplace and felt like an outsider? Have you ever experienced an outsider come into your family, neighborhood, school or workplace and felt disrupted?
- What stories do you or your friends and family tell about their experience getting here, or living here and interacting with immigrants?
- What has it been like for you being an immigrant, or being a citizen of a country that others have immigrated to?
- What is one thing you would most like others in the group to know about you before we begin?
- What is one wish or hope you have for our dialogue today?

## SOME FORMS AND STAGES OF DIALOGUE

It is possible to conduct dialogues between two people, dozens, hundreds, or entire communities and nations, as occurred informally in the days following September 11, 2001. The main difficulty with two-person dialogues is that no one is present to facilitate the conversation if it starts to go off-track. The main difficulty with larger dialogues is that people tend to "grand-stand," give speeches, and become so distant from one another that they fail to listen empathetically to what is being said, especially by dissenters, opponents, outsiders, and critics.

For this reason, the most effective dialogues, in my experience, are those that take place in small, diverse groups of about five to ten people, led either by a trained facilitator or a volunteer from the group, with a recorder to capture everyone's ideas and discourage repetition, a presenter to report to the large group on what they did, and a "process observer" who can reflect on what worked or went wrong in the conversation and how to get it back on track.

William Isaacs, CEO of Dialogos and author of Dialogue, distinguishes four unique stages of dialogue based on Bohm's ideas. He describes, for example:

1. "Shared Monologues," in which group members get used to talking to each other;
2. "Skillful Discussion," in which people learn the skills of

dialogue;

3. "Reflective Dialogue," in which people engage in genuine dialogue;

4. "Generative Dialogue," in which "creative" dialogue is used to generate new ideas.

As Isaacs sees it, participants in dialogue pass through a number of stages in their ability to listen, process, and interact with each other. Dialogue is therefore an evolutionary process in which people adapt their ideas and beliefs based on what they are able to learn from each other. This suggests that what is useful and important at one stage may not work when people move to a different stage, which requires considerable presence, awareness, sensitivity, and understanding on the part of the facilitator.

## HOW TO ORGANIZE A DIALOGUE

To organize a dialogue regarding divisive political issues in a community or organization, it is helpful to break the process down into 15 core steps or elements, and examine each separately:

1. Designing the process
2. Training facilitators
3. Convening participants
4. Setting the stage
5. Agreeing on ground rules
6. Introducing participants
7. Asking questions to encourage dialogue
8. Listening in a committed way
9. Summarizing important and useful points
10. Intervening to encourage listening and resolve conflicts when necessary
11. Breaking into small groups
12. Listening to small group reports
13. Inviting feedback
14. Reaching closure
15. Evaluating the process

Here are a few suggestions on how to go about designing a dialogue using these steps. [Some portions excerpted from *Conflict Revolution: Mediating Evil, War, Injustice, and Terrorism*.]

# 15 Steps in Designing a Dialogue

1. *Designing the Process*

Every dialogue will attract a different mix of participants and cultures, occur in different locations and times, and therefore require different designs to be effective. The steps in organizing a dialogue will vary, depending on the nature and size of the group, the needs of the parties, the character of the issues, the timing of the process, cultural expectations, and other considerations. While fine-tuning the process is important, in my experience, the principal elements in the dialogue remain the same, and can be said to consist of these steps, unless more difficult exchanges occur, in which case mediation may be necessary.

The design process should take account of the beliefs, culture, and experience of all the people who are expected to participate, their personal backgrounds, anticipated moods and attitudes, degrees of expressed open hostility, recent events, willingness to talk to the other side, and similar factors. It is equally important to be flexible and ready to modify the design if it is not working.

2. *Training Facilitators*

It is important to prepare facilitators in advance, including those who will be guiding small group sessions, and make sure they have read and understand the training materials and feel ready to lead the process. It is often useful to have one or two mediators who can "float," listen in to small group sessions, watch for warning signs like raised voices, and be prepared to intervene and help out as needed.

3. *Convening Participants*

The first step is to identify the main parties who will participate in the dialogue, who should include:

- The primary parties to the dispute;
- Affected groups in industry, labor, government, and community;
- Recognized experts and scholars;
- Leaders of local community organizations;
- Concerned individuals, such as students, teachers and officials;
- Anyone who can contribute to the success of the dialogue or undermine it.

Next, interview key participants in person in advance of the session to discover their issues and interests, build trust in the process, uncover hidden obstacles to moving forward, gather information to assist small-group facilitators, fine-tune a design for the process, and communicate these to encourage openness and buy-in.

4. *Setting the Stage*

Arrange the setting in a friendly, open location and manner. If possible, have chairs arranged in small circles so people can talk to each other. Have flip charts, marking pens, masking tape for hanging them on the wall, paper, and pens for note taking, tissues, and refreshments available if possible.

In addition, it is useful to meet in advance with small group facilitators to prepare them for what they are about to do. Here are some sample instructions that can be used to assist small group facilitators:

## Suggestions for Dialogue Facilitators

Facilitators perform the following functions, or ask group members to do so:

- Moderate the discussion, if necessary, to keep it on topic.
- Record key points, preferably on flip chart paper.
- Keep track of time.
- Observe and give feedback on the process.

Facilitators should also:

- Ideally arrange chairs in a circle or semi-circle so that each person has eye contact with you and with each other. This seating arrangement encourages interaction and sharing so no one is left out.
- Use each person's name. Nametags or tents are useful to help you remember and make them feel welcome.
- Do not discount, dismiss or minimize participants' ideas or feelings. Stop the process or reframe comments if others do so.
- Be aware of everyone's differences and encourage them to do so as well. Each comes with a different family system, culture, religion, political beliefs, and experience that influences our views.

- Respect requests for confidentiality.
- Show respect, friendliness, and interest. Use humor (especially about yourself) whenever appropriate.
- Be fair when you present information or respond to comments or remarks.
- Be less concerned about securing agreement over content and more concerned with reaching agreements over process.
- Focus on positive qualities, and reframe negative ones.
- Discourage individuals from monopolizing the conversation. This helps those who withdraw or refrain from participating who may need encouragement.
- Be a good listener. It is helpful to paraphrase or summarize comments to show that you are listening. It also gives you an opportunity to clarify what was said.
- Be flexible. Go with what is happening.
- Observe how the participants interact and where they seat themselves.
- Listen for words of welcome or hostility, watch for eye contact, observe body language, and especially notice withdrawal and hostility.
- Note the effect on participants of words or actions by others, both positive and negative and consider giving feedback on these at the end.
- Take written notes of statements to come back to, group interactions, specific suggestions for follow-up, and suggestions for improvement of the process.
- Phrase suggestions for improvement positively, so as to encourage continued improvement.
- Ask participants questions such as:
  - "How did it make you feel when s/he said that?"
  - "Why did you want to come here today?"
  - "Where are you heading with that question?"
  - "What are you feeling right now?"
  - "How could this dialogue be improved?"
  - "What are some other questions you might ask?"
- The facilitator should allow the group time to perform

exercises before intervening and not try to manipulate or control the group process.

- If a particular group is not working well, try switching groups so a different person is facilitator, or stop and ask why the conversation is not working.
- If a group is getting sidetracked, ask a question about the original topic.
- Take some time at the end of the session to ask each person what they thought of the discussion, or what they learned from it, or what they will do differently. Encourage participants to report on their experiences and suggestions on how to improve the process.
- Compliment participants on their work.
- Thank everyone for sharing their feelings, experiences, and information with the group.

5. *Agreeing on Ground Rules*

Invite participants to discuss and agree on ground rules for the dialogue. Here are some common ground rules, principles or process agreements that can encourage constructive attitudes and help create a trusting environment in which dialogue over difficult issues can be useful:

## Some Common Ground Rules

- We agree to be present voluntarily and that no one will be coerced into attending or speaking.
- We agree that everything we say to each other will be confidential and will not repeated to others, unless we expressly agree otherwise. [Or: We agree that all statements made during the dialogue are not for individual attribution, unless we decide otherwise.]
- We agree that the process will be completely transparent and open.
- We agree that no group decisions will be made until we have finished discussing the issues.
- We agree to participate in a spirit of learning and open communication.
- We agree to be honest and not withhold our differences or

disagreements.

- We agree to communicate respectfully and not engage in personal insults.
- We agree to act with courtesy and not engage in violent or disruptive behavior.
- We agree that we will jointly investigate factual discrepancies.
- We agree that we will not retaliate for anything anyone says or does during the dialogue.
- We agree to publicly support the group's consensus, if there is one.
- We agree that all public announcements, press releases, global emails, bulletins, and disclosures issued during these dialogue sessions will be presented in a spirit of collaboration and improving relationships.
- We agree to mediate any disputes we can't resolve ourselves.

6. *Introducing Participants*

As they convene, welcome the participants and invite them to be present in a spirit of inquiry, learning, and discovery. Tell them you will review the ground rules, give an overview of the design for the process, and present a list of issues to be discussed that has been drawn from the interviews.

You may want to invite people to introduce themselves, either in the large group, or if there are too many, in the small groups they will belong to, as the first or second item on their agenda. If you use self-introductions, asks each participant to state their name, perhaps where they are from, and answer a question that will introduce the dialogue, such as:

- One reason why you decided to be present;
- One reason you want to see this issue discussed or resolved;
- One thing that, in your life, has led you to feel strongly about this issue;
- One outcome you want to achieve;
- One thing you believe both sides have in common;
- One success you had last year and one thing you are working on this year;
- One wish you have for the group or the discussion;
- One mistake you made in the past in discussing the issue;

- One prejudice or source of hostility you would like to overcome;
- One thing that, thinking about the conversation afterwards, you will wish you had said or done.

7. *Asking Questions to Encourage Dialogue*

Thousands of dialogue sessions have been facilitated or mediated over the last three decades between conflicted parties, including communities, political organizations, governments, and national minorities. The Public Conversations Project, Dialogos, Common Ground, Mediators Beyond Borders, and similar organizations have developed a rich array of methods for opening lines of communication. Here are a few questions that can be used to begin a political dialogue:

- What life experiences have you had that have led you to feel so deeply and passionately about this issue?
- What is at the heart of this issue, for you as an individual?
- Why were you willing to participate in this dialogue?
- Why do you care so much about this issue? What does it mean to you?
- Do you see any gray areas in the issue we are discussing, or ideas you find it difficult to define?
- Do you have any mixed feelings, uncertainties, or discomforts regarding this issue that you would be willing to share?
- Is there any part of this issue that you are not 100 percent certain of, or would be willing to discuss and talk about?
- Even though you hold widely differing views, are there any concerns or ideas you think you may have in common?
- What underlying values or ethical beliefs have led you to your current political beliefs? What values or ethical beliefs do you have in common?
- Do the differences between your positions reveal any riddles, paradoxes, contradictions, or enigmas regarding this issue?
- Is it possible to view your differences as two sides of the same coin? If so, what unites them? What is the coin?
- What is beneath that idea for you? Why does it matter?
- Can you separate the issues from the people you disagree with? What will happen if you can't?

- Is there anything positive or acknowledging you would be willing to say about the people on the other side of this issue?
- What processes or ground rules would help you disagree more constructively?
- Instead of focusing on the past, what would you like to see happen in the future? Why?
- Are you disagreeing about fundamental values, or about how to achieve them?
- Is there a way that both of you might be right? How?
- What criteria could you use to decide what works best?
- Would it be possible to test your ideas in practice and see which work best? How might you do that?
- Would you be willing to jointly investigate your conflicting factual assertions?
- What could be done to improve each side's ideas?
- Could any of the other side's ideas be incorporated into yours? How?
- Is there any aspect of this issue that either of you have left out? Are there any other perspectives you haven't described?
- Are there any other ways you can think of to say that?
- Do you think it would be useful to continue this conversation, in order to learn more about each other and what you each believe to be true?
- How could you make your dialogue more ongoing or effective?
- What could you do to improve the ways you disagree with each other in the future? For encouraging future dialogue?
- Would you be willing to do that together?

The purpose of these questions is not to eliminate or discourage disagreements, but to place them in a context of common humanity and allow genuine disagreements to surface and be discussed openly and in depth. These questions reveal that political conversations need not be pointlessly adversarial, but can be transformed into authentic engagements by allowing opposing sides to come to grips with difficult, complex, divisive issues without being hostile or abusive.

These questions also demonstrate that it is possible, even in small ways, to strengthen dialogue, encourage learning and change, and return to the original purposes of politics. The mere possibility that we might do so is sufficient to encourage us to consider how we might redesign political processes and activities so as to draw people together—not over and against others, but with and for them, so as to maximize political clarity, ethical self-improvement, and the common good. As Supreme Court Justice Robert Jackson wrote, "It is not the function of government to keep the citizen from falling into error; it is the function of the citizen to keep the government from falling into error." Only an active, collaborative, democratic citizenry can make this happen.

8.　*Listening in a Committed Way*

It is important to begin the dialogue process by listening. Here is what Brenda Ueland says about the importance of listening:

> I want to write about the great and powerful thing that listening is. And how we forget it. And how we don't listen to our children, or those we love. And least of all— which is so important too—to those we do not love. But we should. Because listening is a magnetic and strange thing, a creative force. ... This is the reason: When we are listened to, it creates us, makes us unfold and expand. Ideas actually begin to grow within us and come to life. ... Who are the people, for example, to whom you go for advice? Not to the hard, practical ones who can tell you exactly what to do, but to the listeners; that is, the kindest, least censorious, least bossy people you know. It is because by pouring out your problem to them you then know what to do about it yourself. ... So try listening. Listen to your wife, your children, your friends; to those who love you and those who don't; to those who bore you; to your enemies. It will work a small miracle—and perhaps a great one.

So listen to those you disagree with, even to those you find abhorrent. We are human beings first, before we are left or right, Black or White, or however you define yourself. By listening in a committed way to each other, we create pathways and connections that hold us together and do not allow us to imagine we are so completely different from one another that we could harm each other without feeling guilty or ashamed. The Chilean journalist Ariel Dorfman, who was tortured by the military junta under General Pinochet, wrote, "How easy it is to kill someone you don't have to mourn because you never dared to imagine him alive."

Committed listening is listening as though your life could change as a result of what you are about to hear. We get there by discussing things that matter in small conversations, by having facilitators to keep us on track and recorders to make sure our voices are heard, by agreeing to take turns, by coming to grips with the difficult things people want to say, by searching for practical things we can say to make a difference.

9. *Summarizing Important and Useful Points*

It is useful for facilitators to summarize people's points—not everything that is said, but the most important and useful points, as a way of making people feel heard and reducing repetition. This can be done on a flip chart, by a recorder, or orally. It can also be done by asking each side to see if they can summarize the other sides' views. Summarization should not be simply verbatim repetition, but capturing its essence and repeating it using different words.

10. *Intervening to Encourage Listening and Resolve Conflicts* when Necessary

Sometimes, the dialogue process goes off track. What do we do then? To begin, try these interventions:

- Draw participants into responsive conversations, defuse tensions, acknowledge divergent points of view, summarize agreements, and record "points of consensus and disagreement" on flip charts.
- Ask each side to present its position, offer back-up information, detailed explanations, and provide ample opportunity for questions and dialogue from all points of view.
- Shift the focus from positions to interests, past to future, personalities to issues, and prescriptions to options. Ask why people want what they want and probe for underlying concerns.
- Caucus periodically with each side to encourage them to trust and speak freely with you, and to bring their interests and hidden issues to the table.

- Ask representatives of opposing positions to meet in "side-bar" negotiations to come to consensus on recommendations to the larger group. Select the strongest advocates so others will not question their recommendations.
- Transition into small group problem solving and collaborative negotiation, identify areas of agreement, disagreement, mutual interest, and consensus. Re-focus attention on relationships and qualities the parties have in common.
- Summarize points of agreement regularly, to build confidence in the process and limit the range of disagreement.
- As the parties reach full and final agreements, review each point of agreement to ensure consensus.
- If they have not reached full and final agreement, confirm interim agreements, agree to limit the use of destructive methods between meetings and encourage continued dialogue.
- List outstanding disagreements to work on at the next session. Elicit recommendations and agendas for following sessions.
- Hold repeated sessions, picking up where you left off and distribute summaries of the last session before the next one.
- Draw each separate session to a close, not a conclusion. Thank participants, assign homework and encourage continued dialogue over open issues.
- Confirm agreements to meet until the conflict is resolved and to forge a genuine resolution.
- Reach for closure, acknowledge participants and celebrate successes. Make the process transparent throughout, explaining what you are doing and why, while you are doing it, so everyone can learn skills to resolve conflicts in the future.

David Bohm wrote that the main problem people offer in refusing or rejecting dialogue is that the other side is prejudiced and unwilling to listen.

> After all, it is easy for each one of us to see that other people are 'blocked' about certain questions, so that without being aware of it, they are avoiding the confrontation of

contradictions in certain ideas that may be extremely dear to them. The very nature of such a 'block' is, however, that it is a kind of insensitivity or 'anesthesia' about one's own contradictions. Evidently then, what is crucial is to be aware of the nature of one's own 'blocks'. If one is alert and attentive, he can see for example that whenever certain questions arise, there are fleeting sensations of fear, which push him away from consideration of those questions, and of pleasure, which attract his thoughts and cause them to be occupied with other questions. So, one is able to keep away from whatever it is that he thinks may disturb him. And as a result, he can be subtle at defending his own ideas, when he supposes that he is really listening to what other people have to say. When we come together to talk, or otherwise to act in common, can each one of us be aware of the subtle fear and pleasure sensations that 'block' the ability to listen freely?

Here are some process interventions that can be used by facilitators to help each side become aware of the ways they are blocking listening, keep the conversation on track and encourage respectful communication:

- Transparency: "What just happened in the conversation we were having?"
- Inquiring: "What do you think should be done? Why do you think so?"
- Supporting: "I appreciate your willingness to speak up and express your opinions. Here is an example that supports your point."
- Acknowledging: "You took a risk in making that apology/ concession."
- Refereeing: "What ground rules do we need so everyone can feel we are behaving fairly? "
- Concretizing: "Can you give a specific example?"
- Exploring: "Can you say more about why you feel so strongly about this issue?"
- Summarizing: "Is this what you are trying to say ... ?"

- Challenging: "Is that consistent with the ground rules/what the group has already decided?"
- Coaching: "Is there a way you could respond less defensively?"
- Connecting: "That point connects directly with what was said earlier ... "
- Re-orienting: "I think we're lost. Can we get back on track? Are we talking about the real issue?"
- Problem Solving: "What do you see as some possible solutions?"
- Uniting: "What can we agree on here?"
- Contextualizing: "Why have we come together to discuss this issue?"

If these do not work, consider taking a break and ask those involved to meet separately with a mediator to see if they can resolve their issues.

11. *Breaking into Small Groups*

It is always useful to break large groups into smaller ones to give everyone a chance to participate and reduce the tendency to grandstand and use adversarial styles of speech that trigger conflicts in large groups. Each small group should have a facilitator, and if possible, a recorder to take notes, a process observer to reflect back to the group how they did and intervene with process suggestions if the conversation becomes too heated, and a timekeeper to stay on track.

12. *Listening to Small Group Reports*

Ask each small group to select someone who will present the results of their conversation, elicit comments from the large group, draw people into dialogue about possible disagreements, and applaud each small group for its work.

13. *Inviting Feedback*

At the end, ask if anyone would like to offer oral feedback on how the process went for them, and whether they have any suggestions on how it could be improved next time. Thank them for their comments, make sure someone records them and draw the meeting to a close. Instead, or together with oral comments, it is possible to hand out an evaluation form, as suggested below.

14. *Reaching Closure*

At the end, ask people to reflect on their experience in the dialogue, what they learned or will do differently as a result, or how they felt about the process. Try to end on a positive note that looks toward common action and continued dialogue.

15. *Evaluating the Process*

Sometimes it will be best to ask the participants to complete a written evaluation. More people will participate and the confidentiality of their comments will produce different feedback. Here is a sample dialogue evaluation form you can modify or ask people to fill in at the end. The most important element is that you take every suggestion seriously and consider what can be done next time to make the process work better.

## Sample Dialogue Evaluation Form

*Please add your comments for the benefit of the facilitators and future participants.*

1. On a scale of 1 to 5, 5 being highest, how would you evaluate the usefulness of your dialogue?
2. 1   2        3        4        5
3. What was the most useful and enjoyable part of the dialogue for you?
4. What was the least useful or enjoyable?
5. What could be done to improve future dialogues?
6. What is the most important thing you learned this evening? Is there anything you intend to do differently as a result?
7. Is there anything you are willing to do to help?
8. Other suggestions and comments:

[Excerpted partly from *Mediating Dangerously: The Frontiers of Conflict Resolution*.]

# CONFRONTING PREJUDICE, BIAS, AND STEREOTYPING

Prejudice is complex and operates on many levels. It can be found not only in insults and judgments, caricatures and stereotypes, but refusals to listen and communicate, stories of demonization and victimization, inability to experience empathy with others, and small, infinitesimal denials of humanity. It is reflected in personal selfishness and hostile relationships, bullying and aggressive behaviors, and ego compensations based on poor self-esteem. It is expressed through contempt, disregard, and domination, as well as through low status, inequitable pay, and autocratic power. It is endemic to power- and rights-based politics, and a barrier to dialogue.

Prejudice commonly operates by stereotyping. People form stereotypes, in my experience, in eight easy steps:

1. Pick a characteristic.
2. Blow it out of proportion.
3. Collapse the person into the characteristic.
4. Ignore individual differences and variations.
5. Disregard subtleties and complexities.
6. Overlook commonalities.
7. Match it to your own worst fears.
8. Make it cruel.

If these steps routinely produce prejudice, it is possible to undo them, for example, by making people more complex than their stereotype permits, or distinguishing unique individuals within a group, or recognizing commonalities between people. It helps, in doing so, to acknowledge that everyone is equal, unique and interesting; that everyone forms prejudices; that everyone can learn to overcome them through awareness, empathy and communication; and that everyone can become more skillful in communicating across stereotypes and lines of separation created by fear.

It is common for people, when accused of prejudice, to respond defensively, yet confront other people's prejudices aggressively, leveling accusations and instilling shame. These responses may initially succeed in suppressing the expression of prejudicial attitudes and undermining social permission for hate speech and the cultures of discrimination that allow it to continue. But to root out the deep-seated biases that keep prejudice alive, it is necessary to dismantle it at a much deeper level, in people's hearts and minds.

Our principal goals in responding to prejudice are therefore not to castigate, blame, or point fingers at those who exhibit prejudicial attitudes, as shaming and blaming merely trigger defensiveness and counterattack. Instead, they are to defuse prejudice by assisting those in its grip (including ourselves) to:

- Develop a knowledgeable, confident self-identity, and appreciate who they are without needing to feel superior to others;

- Experience comfortable, empathetic interactions with diverse people and ideas;
- Be curious and unafraid of learning about differences and commonalities;
- Feel comfortable collaboratively solving problems and negotiating differences;
- Be aware of biases, stereotypes, and discrimination when they occur;
- Stand up for themselves and others in the face of prejudice, without becoming biased in turn;
- Experience diverse affectionate relationships that grow stronger as a result of differences.

There are many ways of confronting prejudice, bias, and discrimination that allow us to alter not simply the overt prejudicial statements and behaviors that express it, but the covert places in people's hearts and minds where it lies buried. To begin with, we can each acknowledge and speak openly about our own prejudices, how we have struggled to overcome them, and how it feels when others act prejudicially toward us. When confronting other people's prejudicial statements, we can:

- Bring awareness to our emotional responses and calm ourselves before speaking;
- Assume their good intentions;
- Try to understand where their prejudice came from;
- Discuss their statement one-on-one, privately, in a non-threatening way;
- Request permission to offer feedback;
- Be low-key and non-aggressive;
- Don't shame, blame, attack, or accuse;
- Be friendly and accepting, yet assertive and clear;
- Be hard on the problem and soft on the person;
- Ask if the effect they created was the one they intended;
- Ask if they ever felt discriminated against or harassed for any reason, and get details;
- Indicate what it feels like to experience prejudice, using "I" statements;
- Tell a story about prejudice to help them listen and learn;

- Try to assess the cost of prejudice, offering examples from personal experience;
- Suggest alternative phraseology, approaches, or perspectives;
- State your disagreements openly and honestly;
- Bring in a third party to mediate differences;
- Ask for feedback on your feedback.

In addition, here are a number of questions facilitators can use to address issues of bias or prejudice proactively, before it arises:

- What has your experience been with prejudice, bias, discrimination or stereotyping?
- Have you ever felt discriminated against for any reason?
- Have you had any stereotypes or beliefs about other people in the past that you later discovered to be false?
- How did you overcome them?
- Do you have any prejudices or biases now that you would like to overcome? What are you doing to overcome them?
- What do you believe are the main reasons for prejudice, or sources of hostility that need to be overcome?
- What are some ways of responding to prejudice, bias, discrimination or stereotyping that you think might be successful?
- What can each of us do as individuals in response to prejudice?

Here are some follow-up questions in case the issue has already begun to dominate group discussion or the proactive questions haven't worked:

- What has your personal experience been with the people you describe?
- Are there any ways you think your experiences are different from theirs?
- Are there any ways you think your experiences of a native Greek are similar to theirs?
- What worries you most about your ability to communicate with them?
- What do you think you are most afraid of regarding them?
- What do you think they are most afraid of about you?
- If you met the person you describe and had some time to talk, what would you be curious about? What questions would you

want to ask?

- What would you want him or her to know about you?
- What would you want him or her to think about you?
- What changes in behaviors would you want to request?
- What advice would you offer? What advice do you think he or she would offer you?
- What kind of life would you wish for him or her? Why?

In some cases, as in the Mediators Beyond Borders dialogues in Athens on immigration, the presence in the community of an active Nazi organization like Golden Dawn that was regularly beating up and even murdering immigrants made it unlikely that either group would agree to engage in dialogue of the other group was invited. Here is what I wrote in response to members of the dialogue facilitation team as proposed points of agreement for moving forward without them:

1. We do not believe in excluding any person or group that wants to participate in dialogue.
2. We require a clear commitment to safety and ground rules from all participants that will allow people to actually talk to each other.
3. We come as capacity builders for Greek mediators, not as people who will run the dialogue ourselves.
4. Given the political philosophy and public statements of Golden Dawn, it is highly unlikely at this point that they would agree to the ground rules and safety concerns required of participants in dialogue.
5. Given the decision by the other political parties that they will not participate if Golden Dawn is invited, we respect their wishes and those of our Greek hosts and will not invite them to attend this dialogue.
6. We envision multiple dialogues of which this is the first, in hopes of laying the groundwork for future dialogues.
7. Given the political situation in Greece, with real attacks being made on immigrants and those who support them, we recognize that work needs to be done to create the conditions in which all parties will be willing to participate in dialogue with each other.

8. One element in creating those conditions is our contribution to the development of capacity and skill among Greek mediators who will gain some experience facilitating less difficult dialogues.

9. One topic we can encourage the Greek team to raise in the dialogues is how to expand it to reach all groups within Greek society.

10. In our trainings, we can present techniques and jointly search for ways of gaining agreement on the ground rules and safety concerns among groups that have publicly rejected them.

Tactically we are required in dialogue to work with what we have, but strategically it is necessary to actively create the skills and conditions for expanded communication. We cannot, in the long run, afford to leave anyone behind. On a larger scale, all nations, political groups, minorities, cultures, classes, races, and individuals seek to satisfy their own self-interests, yet rarely recognize that satisfying the interests of others, including those of their opponents, is essential to satisfying their own. Modern forms of warfare, ecological concerns, revolutions in communication and transportation, and economic globalization no longer permit isolated, short-term understandings of self-interest. The long-term interests of each are now increasingly and directly the interests of all, and vice versa.

## TIPS ON DIALOGUE

Engaging people in dialogue is simple, but it is not easy. It means that people have to actually listen to one another. They have to accept as authentic and valid for that person whatever that person says, even if it contradicts the listeners' perceptions and deeply held beliefs. Here are some final suggestions that may help facilitate political dialogues:

• Consider yourself an ally of other participants. If you set out to learn to engage in dialogue together and broaden your knowledge of others' life experiences you can't fail.

• Assume others are sincere in what they say.

• Listen not only for facts and opinions, but the reasons behind them. How and why did the speaker arrive at his or her conclusions?

- Don't take things too literally. Listen for meanings, not just words.
- Be patient. A question that may be easy for you, e.g. "What is your racial and ethnic identity?" may be hard for others. Give them time to work their way through their resistance and find the words.
- Accept silences as part of the process. Don't rush to fill the space.
- Seek clarification. If something is not clear, or if you want to learn more, ask questions. It helps to restate what you think was said, so that the speaker can feel heard, correct wrong impressions and expand on ideas.
- Ask "why" questions, but not in ways that sound judgmental.
- Avoid questions that can be answered with a simple "yes" or "no." A single-word answer may discourage further conversation.
- Be alert to generalizations, both yours and others. A statement may be true of "some," or maybe "most," but surely not "all."
- Use the identifying terms for people that they use for themselves. There's usually a reason behind their choice of group names.
- Say how an experience or statement affected or is affecting you. Reframe "you" or "they" statements as "I messages."
- Use real-life examples as reference points. Tell stories.
- Be honest, but don't release your own pent-up anger, anxiety, or guilt at the expense of others.
- Try not to be defensive. Few of us are smooth talkers. We inadvertently step on toes. Keep the big picture and goal clearly in mind.
- Watch your body language. Be sure it doesn't say, "I'm bored," "I'm superior," "I don't believe you."
- Do not doubt the authenticity of what you hear. Each person is the highest authority on what she or he feels.
- Support others when they try to say something. They may repeat themselves, stammer, or pause a while as they try to get it out.

- Understand that you're getting only a tiny glimpse into peoples' lives. Dialogue happens at a fast pace, and not many are adept at organizing their thoughts on the spot.
- Refuse to give up on anyone, no matter how unpleasant, opinionated or difficult they are to deal with.
- Accept that you and others may hold opposing views. Resist the temptation to find quick solutions, correct, argue, or counter.
- Be willing to have your biases challenged.
- Don't be impatient to talk about broader issues and problems. If and when the group moves on to analysis and action planning, things will go easier if they know and trust one another.
- Don't dominate the conversation.
- Try to open and close on a note of heartfelt appreciation and unity.

(Based partly on materials from the Los Angeles Commission on Human Relations)

## FINAL ADVICE

The most important advice I can offer about dialogue is to simply try it. The process works, and even when it seems impossible to reach people, or when pain and rage begin to emerge, someone will say something that turns the entire conversation in a positive, constructive direction. If you continue to hold the thought that it is possible and are clear in your collaborative intention and transparent in your process, people will understand and walk away having learned something important.

# CHAPTER 10

# AN INTRODUCTION TO MEDIATING CHRONIC ORGANIZATIONAL CONFLICTS

*No longer a monolith, the successful modern organization is like a Lego set whose parts can be regularly reconfigured as circumstances change. The old paradigm that exalted control, order, and predictability is giving way to a nonhierarchical order in which all employees' contributions are solicited and acknowledged and in which creativity is valued over blind loyalty. Sheer self-interest motivates the change. Organizations that encourage broad participation, even dissent, make better decisions.*

~ Warren Bennis and Phillip Slater ~

E VERY WORKPLACE GENERATES CHRONIC conflicts, yet few organizations have rethought the way they work, or used conflict resolution skills and ideas to prevent and transform chronic conflicts at their sources, or examined their organizational communications and "conflict cultures" to discover how these conflicts are generated and reduce their reoccurrence.

Fewer still have integrated conflict resolution and coaching, trained leaders as mediators, used conflict resolution principles to inform their change processes, conducted "conflict audits" to reveal where these streams of conflict originate, or designed complex, multi-layered, self-correcting systems to improve their capacity for conflict prevention, resolution, and transformation.

These ideas provide a framework for people who would like to use their rapidly expanding skills and methods of conflict resolution to resolve the deep sources of organizational conflict. It is possible, for example, using these skills, to learn ways of adapting mediation skills to improve organizational communications, coaching, team building, leadership, change management, and systems design. Indeed, these skills can help organizations rethink every aspect of the way they work from a conflict resolution perspective and use systems design principles to construct more collaborative, democratic, self-managing organizations, and institutions.

To do so, it will be necessary to build new skills in organizational dialogue, leadership, teamwork, and collaborative processes, and to identify the organizational theories and techniques that will help us shape a context of values, ethics and integrity; form living, evolving webs of association; develop ubiquitous, linking leadership; build innovative self managing teams; implement streamlined, open, collaborative processes; create complex self-correcting systems; integrate strategically, and change the way we change.

# The Nature and Sources of Chronic Conflict

Here is what we know at present about the systemic nature of conflict:

- Every conflict takes place not only between individuals, but within a context, culture, and environment; surrounded by social, economic, and political forces; inside organizational systems, structures, and technological settings; among a diverse community of people; at a particular moment in time and history; on a stage, milieu, or backdrop.

- None of these elements is conflict-neutral. Each contributes—sometimes in veiled and unspoken, yet profound ways—to the nature, intensity, duration, impact, and meaning of our conflicts.

- Each profoundly affects the quality of our work lives, our personal capacity for joy and compassion, and our ability to collaborate in solving our problems.

- Like ripples in a pond, every conflict and every resolution in the workplace extends outward, impacting others, and creating a "mediation butterfly effect."

- As a result, we are each responsible as organizational citizens for building conflict resolution capacity in our workplaces.

We also know that organizational systems produce chronic conflicts. In addition to being repetitious and occurring exhaustively over and over again, chronic conflicts can be defined as those that nations, societies, organizations or individuals:

1. Have not fully resolved;
2. Need to resolve in order to grow and evolve;
3. Are capable of resolving;
4. Can only resolve by abandoning old approaches and adopting new ones;
5. Are resistant to resolving because they are frightened, dissatisfied, insecure, uncertain, angry, or unwilling to change.

In practice, chronic conflicts have low levels of resolution. They often reveal an incongruity between high levels of emotion and an apparent triviality of the issues over which people are fighting, and as a result, sometimes appear irrational. At the same time, they reveal underlying similarities. They seem to result from accidental misunderstandings or apparently idiosyncratic causes and circumstances and are commonly mistaken for miscommunications or personality clashes, yet their very repetition suggests these cannot be their cause. What is perhaps worst is that as they repeat, they give rise to a tolerance for disrespectful and adversarial behaviors and a culture of conflict avoidance.

On a societal level, and over the course of centuries, we can easily identify a number of what I regard as "meta-sources" of chronic conflict. The following are my top four:

1. Social inequality
2. Economic inequity
3. Political autocracy
4. Environmental change

Within modern, complex, multinational corporations, it is possible to go significantly further and identify several sources of chronic conflict that flow from the nature and operations of a capitalist global economy, including these twelve:

1. Intense competition for market dominance;
2. Unceasing efforts to maximize sales and profits;
3. Primacy of the financial bottom line;
4. Constant innovations in technology;
5. Dependence of profits on costs of production, especially wages, rents, taxes, and raw materials;
6. Unequal distribution of profits;
7. Hierarchical control over investments, wages, and management;
8. Separation and division of labor;
9. Centralized organization of work processes;
10. Increasing dependence on employee motivation and participation in decision-making;
11. Unending search for inexpensive raw materials, cheap labor, and markets for finished products;
12. Race for the bottom in globalization of production and distribution.

In the U.S. and other countries, many chronic conflicts also occur within organizations as a result of clashes between labor and management over a variety of issues, which can also generate chronic conflicts, including these:

1. Legislation that does not reflect workplace realities;
2. Financing that is not within the parties' control;
3. Political elections that periodically alter attitudes toward labor management relations;
4. Primary responsibility of management for fiscal well-being;
5. Primary responsibility of labor for the well-being of workers;
6. Adversarial styles of negotiation and problem-solving;
7. Power- and rights-based systems, relationships, and processes in labor and management relations;
8. Inability and unwillingness to discuss or negotiate non-mandatory subjects;
9. Unilateral and non-collaborative approaches to decision-making;
10. Conflict avoidance, accommodation, aggression, and compromise.

More difficult to resolve are corporate financial drivers that pit labor against management, reflecting still deeper conflicts between wages and profits. As an illustration, here are ten ways corporations can increase their profits, each of which can be seen as a source of chronic organizational conflict:

1. Directly cut wages or the cost of raw materials (these also can result in wage cuts);
2. Require employees to work longer or harder for the same wage;
3. Increase the price of the product while keeping wages and raw materials costs the same;
4. Reduce the quality of the product while keeping its price the same;
5. Cut or subsidize rents, taxes, health and safety benefits, environmental cleanups, and similar costs;
6. Artificially alter supply and demand ratios through dumping, monopolization, price fixing, government subsidies, etc.;
7. Reduce wages indirectly through increased competition, by unemployment, immigration, racial prejudice, gender pay

differentials, and similar policies that increase the supply of employees willing to work for less, thereby reducing demand;

8. Introduce labor-saving machinery and robotics to reduce the workforce and cut the amount spent on wages;

9. Use speed-up to shorten the time required for investment to return a profit;

10. Decrease costs by transferring them to government, outsourcing, or sending work to countries with lower wages, costs, or taxes.

Clearly, when taken together, these lists suggest that there is a systemic incentive within both capitalism and private sector corporations that encourages management to take actions that will predictably produce chronic labor-management conflicts, even when they do not personally wish to do so. These sources of chronic conflict directly shape organizational structures, systems, processes, and relationships, even in the public and nonprofit sectors.

What is remarkable about each of these very different sources of chronic conflict is that solutions already exist within the field of conflict resolution that are capable of reducing, resolving, and preventing many of them. To see how, we need to consider more carefully what an organization is and how it functions.

## WHAT IS AN ORGANIZATION?

If we consider from a conflict resolution point of view the nature of organizations and workplaces, and think for a moment about what an organization actually is, we can see that there is an array of answers that range from trivial to profound. For example, an organization can be regarded as:

- A place where people work;
- A diverse group of people who are committed to a common goal;
- A system;
- An organism;
- A variety of interlocking activities, roles, responsibilities, and outputs;
- A set of relationships and processes;

- A group of conversations;
- A culture or mind-set;
- A way of diffusing responsibility;
- A compact, agreement, or contract;
- A mix of unspoken expectations and desires;
- An evolving set of values and purposes;
- A method of group learning based on assessment and feedback;
- A figment of our imaginations.

What is most important from the point of view of mediation, however, is that every organization is also importantly a mechanism for resolving conflicts. Every organization is therefore a mediation, though it is not always a skillful or effective one. Every organization brings together diverse individuals whose lives might otherwise collide if the organization did not continually mediate their impulses and activities.

This insight allows conflict resolution professionals to bring a far more advanced and sophisticated set of mediative methods and techniques to every aspect of organizational life; to assist it in preventing, mitigating, resolving, and most importantly, learning from its chronic conflicts. It is this extraordinary opportunity that gives mediation a unique role to play in organizational development, and allows it to adapt highly effective techniques and harness them to the human side of organizational development.

## TEN QUESTIONS ON ORGANIZATIONAL OPERATIONS

As an illustration, here is a list of ten questions that, in large part, define organizational operations, each of which can easily lead to unnecessary and chronic conflict. Rethinking the answers to these questions can allow organizations to save enormous sums by reducing their conflicts—not just by mediating them once they occur, but by preventing their reoccurrence and improving their overall effectiveness. Here are the questions, together with some initial answers informed by mediation revealing how it might be possible to reduce the amount of chronic conflict.

1.   *Who makes the decision to hire?* Hiring has traditionally been a unilateral activity engaged in by managers based on criteria they alone select. Yet better results can be achieved when hiring becomes a collaborative, peer-based responsibility of self-managing teams for these reasons:

- Teams are usually much better qualified to choose coworkers than are managers who do not actually perform the daily work of the team.
- Employees who are hired by a team feel an obligation to support their peers and perform at higher levels than when they work to satisfy a manager.
- Errors are corrected more quickly, and poor performers are disciplined or replaced with less opposition from other employees.

2.   *Who allocates work and assigns tasks?* Self-management and task selection by self-managing teams can dramatically increase productivity by improving motivation, limiting unproductive behavior, and reducing managerial expenses through reverse economies of scale. Teamwork makes assignment flexible and dynamic rather than bureaucratic and static, and oversight becomes a responsibility of everyone on the team, bringing the following benefits:

- Task-oriented self-assigning teams can counter the negative effects of isolation due to the separation and division of labor. Self-assignment can also improve motivation by increasing task and product identity.
- Self-managing teams can allocate work more cheaply, more quickly, with a finer sense of priorities than managers, and an increased ability to change rapidly to meet new demands.
- Teams are more capable of knowing what is required at any given moment in the workday than managers, who are one step removed from problems. Even centralized tasks can be handled more efficiently by team members representing diverse departments.

3.   *How is work evaluated and improved?* Feedback, evaluation, self-correction, learning, and improvement ought to be the responsibility of all team members. Contributions to personal and organizational improvement become far more powerful when feedback is received from everyone affected by the work. The benefits of team-based peer evaluation include:

- 360-degree evaluations based on self, upward, peer,

downward, and client feedback, together with analysis of differences between assessments, encourage more open, honest, meaningful evaluations.

- Quicker, more supportive, and useful feedback can be tailored by teams to help each person learn and change. This means regular, honest, open, timely discussions of difficult issues, starting from the top. The most powerful and effective feedback always emanates from clients, team members, and ourselves.
- For feedback to be effective, judgments need to be separated from evaluation. Feedback in a team environment has only one purpose: improvement. Whatever does not actually improve individual and team performance is either useless or counterproductive and should be eliminated.

4. *Who selects leaders?* Management is a title, a set of involuntary roles assigned to people selected from above; leadership is a voluntary relationship informed by vision and maintained by skill with people who freely choose to follow. To establish a mandate, leaders should be selected, even elected, by those they lead. Leadership requires different skills than management does, for several reasons:

- Leadership is a universal job description for team members, who need to be able to facilitate team meetings, track projects, relate well to customers, solve problems, mediate conflicts, make certain nothing falls through the cracks, and perform countless diverse assignments.
- Leadership on teams is situational and shared, based on whatever task needs to be performed, together with individual skills and desires. Leaders who are chosen by their teams can ask for and receive efforts far beyond what is required.
- Traditional managerial tasks can easily be computerized or rotated among team members, allowing managers to move into roles as facilitators, coordinators, supporters, mentors, mediators, or team members with specialized administrative skills.

5. *Who gets promoted, how, and by what criteria?* In hierarchical organizations, promotions are often based on having done a lower-level job

well, that is, on technical ability; some guessed-at capacity to succeed in meeting a set of abstract, objective criteria; or purely subjective, intuitive feelings about the personality of the candidate. In a team environment, there are alternative ways of promoting:

- Eliminating grandiose titles, enormous wage discrepancies, autocratic power, hierarchical privileges, and compensation based on title or status. Instead, a flexible matrix of skills, contributions, knowledge, seniority, difficulty of assignment, willingness to perform low-status work, voluntary efforts that benefit the team as a whole, and similar criteria might be used. Applying genuine market principles to employment means that those who perform the least desirable tasks might receive the highest wages.
- Rather than promote people out of jobs they do well into managerial positions they do poorly, teams can create a broad array of rewards, including acknowledgment, job rotation, free time for creative projects, and opportunities to develop natural abilities, leading to leadership roles and career development.
- Allowing teams to select and promote their own leaders encourages teamwork and leadership development. Internal career counseling, aptitude testing, attitude surveys, and team selection help eliminate burnout, elitism, tyrannical management and the Peter Principle.

6. *Who gets trained in what?* Training should be organized from the bottom up rather than the top down, and focus on team skills rather than those of individual managers. It should improve practical skills in facilitating, coaching, communicating, negotiating, building ownership, giving honest feedback, building better relationships, resolving interpersonal conflicts, and negotiating collaboratively. Expanding training, education, and development, orienting them to teams, and covering the full range of skills required for self-management can:

- Turn every organization into a university in miniature, providing mandatory and voluntary, free and paid education for all employees.
- Create learning organizations that strongly encourage

employees to teach those with less experience, knowledge, or skill and become lifelong learners. Enormous skills and knowledge can be recaptured by transforming master-employees into mentor-teachers as they develop and before they retire.

- Design a comprehensive team-based internal training, education and development program focused on training team trainers and on leadership, self-management, teamwork, and change.

7. *Who determines and enforces rules?* Every employee in a team environment has a vested interest in increasing productivity and client satisfaction and is capable of setting rules that advance common interests and result in shared responsibility for preventing future violations. Employee-generated rules counteract the dynamic created by externally imposed rules, which lead to blind obedience rather than creativity and result in resistance, unequal enforcement, cynicism, coercion, and duress. Democratically generated rules improve results for a number of reasons:

- Value-based decisions in self-managing organizations are reached by consensus, with regard to how resources are allocated, money is spent, people are paid, and individuals interact with each other. When team members genuinely agree, enforcement and coercion become less necessary.
- Team members who are included in decision making regarding rules and values naturally develop the cognitive and communication skills that allow them to assume increased responsibility for results.
- Fairness, justice, and democracy mean that teams decide what rules they need, the consequences for breaking them, and how to enforce them without becoming responsible for other people's choices.

8. *Who resolves conflicts and how?* Conflicts provide teams with rich opportunities to reveal the inconsistencies between expressed values and actual behaviors. They offer openings for growth, personal improvement, and increased team effectiveness. When teams own their conflicts and become responsible for resolving them, the entire paradigm of conflict shifts from one of avoidance or confrontation to one of learning.

Conflict resolution is far more effective in team-based environments for the following reasons:

- Teams can pinpoint the sources of chronic conflict, design conflict resolution systems, identify early warning signs, create safety nets, develop techniques for prevention and early resolution, and support low-cost procedures such as peer review and coaching as backups.
- Peer mediation can provide a highly effective, voluntary, consensus-based process for resolving conflicts in which team members learn to negotiate differences and resolve conflicts themselves.
- Team-based conflict resolution increases organizational efficiency by improving morale, providing an outlet for emotional venting, reducing resistance, encouraging listening, and making it acceptable to talk openly and honestly about problems. This allows compassion, empathy, forgiveness, transformation, and ethical behavior to moderate differences and the chaos generated by rapid change.

9. *How is compensation determined?* When employees make compensation decisions, productivity increases enormously. Several studies have shown that when employees are permitted to decide what to pay themselves, they not only set aside adequate sums for investment but make their products and services more competitive. Experience in employee-owned firms demonstrates that pay cuts and reductions in benefits are more readily agreed to in employee-owned firms than in hierarchies. Team-based organizations can restructure compensation in several ways:

- Leadership can train employees in accounting principles and budgets, and encourage broad participation in budgetary decision-making, or create an overall budget and let teams decide how to divide it.
- Team members who receive equity or stock, or become partners and co-owners, benefit directly from reduced waste, noninflationary wages, and increased productivity.
- By correlating investments in organizational expansion with future income and reduced investment with lower income,

teams can participate in deciding which path to take and accept the financial consequences for their decisions.

10. *How are profits and losses divided?* As self-managing teams become adept at making strategic financial decisions, dividing profits, covering losses, budgeting, allocating resources, and making investments, they should be permitted to share in the profits and losses that flow from their work. In making decisions regarding profit and loss, teams can be more successful than shareholders and CEOs, for several reasons:

- Changes in employee responsibility and self-management are more successful when compensation is redesigned to reward extra effort, including pay-for-learning, pay-for-skills, bonuses, stock options, gain sharing, and outright employee ownership, which stimulate an ongoing interest in the financial success of the organization.

- The success of employee-owned organizations and cooperatives is based on the long-term interests of employees in sustainable growth and customer service. The greater their responsibility is for profits and losses, the more employees want to make it succeed.

- Employees have a natural long-term interest in sustainable growth, environmental protection, and employee safety, and are likely to be better at making decisions regarding socially responsible investments than shareholders who are focused on quarterly dividends, since their lives depend on their choices.

[Drawn partly from *The End of Management and the Rise of Organizational Democracy.*]

## STRATEGIC INTEGRATION AND ORGANIZATIONAL EVOLUTION

It is increasingly clear that collaboration is critical to the operations of complex organizations and directly affects their ability to compete successfully. As Warren Bennis wrote in *Organizing Genius*:

In a society as complex and technologically sophisticated as ours, the most urgent projects require the coordinated contributions of many talented people. Whether the task

is building a global business or discovering the mysteries
of the human brain, one person can't hope to accomplish
it, however gifted or energetic he or she may be.

Whether public or private, everything organizations do requires collaboration. Yet their structures and processes divide people from one another, isolate them, and encourage them to compete for scarce positions, finances, and resources. In many organizations, departments refuse simply to communicate with each other, let alone coordinate, strategize, or collaborate. Even when they cooperate closely and describe themselves as partners, it is rare that they form an integrated, strategic relationship that maximizes their potential synergies and improves their collaborative advantage.

## FROM INDIVIDUATION TO INTEGRATION, AND SPONTANEITY TO STRATEGY

There are two fundamental conflicts or opposing forces that, in their elaborate combinations and evolutionary patterns, set the direction for much of organizational life. The first of these consist of separation versus unification, or individuation versus integration. These are manifested *structurally*, and can be measured by the degree of interdependence between diverse people and functions. The second set of conflicts or opposing forces consists of chaos versus order, or spontaneity versus strategy. These are manifested *procedurally*, and can be measured by the degree of conscious planning people engage in.

The forces of individuation and integration are largely responsible for determining the degree of individualism and teamwork, centralization and decentralization, competition and collaboration within an organization, and the level of singularity and synergy that are possible in relationships. The forces of spontaneity and strategy are largely responsible for determining the degree of intuition and planning, anarchy and order, complexity and creativity within an organization, and the level of invention and anticipation that are possible in operations, as depicted in the following chart.

| Structural Forces | | Procedural Forces | |
|---|---|---|---|
| Individuation | Integration | Spontaneity | Strategy |
| Individualism | Teamwork | Intuition | Planning |
| Decentralization | Centralization | Anarchy | Order |
| Competition | Collaboration | Creativity | Complexity |
| Singularity | Synergy | Invention | Anticipation |

It is important in understanding these forces that we recognize two additional points:

1. Each conflict can only evolve to a higher level of development through creative and synergistic combination, rather than through competition and isolation from one another. Thus, collaboration and teamwork are improved through strategy and planning.

2. The highest levels of *integration* are achieved through and as a result of individuation, and of *strategy* through and as a result of spontaneity, rather than by means of opposition to them. Thus, it is the synergistic combination of serendipity and planning that produces the most powerful results.

The first set of elements, including individuation, decentralization, spontaneity, anarchy, competition, and creativity, are useful in any organizational design, especially for start-up organizations, but it will prove impossible to achieve higher levels of functioning without adding integration, centralization, strategy, order, collaboration, and complexity.

This second set of elements is equally useful, but organizations can become blocked and unable to develop in the absence of the first set. It is not a question of one or the other but of their creative combination and dynamic interplay that produces the highest results. To achieve these outcomes requires organizations to move from crisis management to strategic integration, which consists of combining these opposing forces and elements into a single, unified operation.

# FROM CRISIS MANAGEMENT
# TO STRATEGIC INTEGRATION

To understand the relationship between strategic integration and other forms of organizational operations, we need to examine the evolution of management over time. Fundamentally, we can identify five forms of management that differ radically in their orientation toward the future, capacity for planning, the complexity of problems they are able to handle, and the degree of collaboration they are able to inspire. These are:

- *Crisis Management*, which is oriented to survival;
- *Administration*, which is oriented to maintaining the status quo;
- *Management by Objectives or Goals*, which is oriented to achieving specific, predetermined results in the near future;
- *Strategic Management*, which is oriented to vision and achieving long-term organizational advantage;
- *Strategic Integration*, which is oriented to value-based leadership, oriented to collaborative relationships, strategic integration, process improvement, and self-management based on responsibility and consensus. For example, see the following chart.

*Form of*
*Organization*
*Degree of*
*Collaboration/*
*Style of*
*Leadership/*
*Complexity of*
*Problem/ Use*
*of Planning/*
*Level of*
*Participation*

Strategic Integration:
(*Organizational Democracy/ Ubiquitous Teamwork and Leadership/Ownership*)

Strategic Planning:
(*Matrixed Organization/Teams and Visionary Leadership/ Participation*)

Management by Goals or Objectives:
(*Managerial Organization/Supervision/Involvement*)

Administration: (*Bureaucracy/Control/Compliance*)

*Time Frame*

Crisis Management:
(*Hierarchy/Command/Obedience*)

Catastrophe: (*Anarchy/Survival/Everyone for Themselves*)

Each of these forms of management naturally gives rise to different organizational structures, relationships, and processes. In the moment of catastrophe or crisis, the dominant form of organization is anarchy, the method of operation is simply survival, and the level of participation during the crisis is one of everyone for themselves.

As the crisis abates, military and police and other power-based institutions engage in crisis management naturally, which predictably and automatically replaces anarchy. Its form of organization is hierarchy and its method of operation is command, as it uses centralized, autocratic, even unilateral decision making and other authoritarian-based processes to respond rapidly to emergencies. The level of participation in crisis management is obedience.

Once the crisis is over, the next task is to maintain the status quo, which requires administration. Administration naturally, predictably, and automatically gives rise to bureaucracy and other rights-based institutions as a form of organization, which uses consultation, delegated decision-making and similar control-based methods of operation to regulate routine on-going operations. The level of participation now is no longer obedience, but compliance.

Together, hierarchy and bureaucracy generate typical command and control-based organizations that do quite well during moments of crises and function effectively day-to-day, but neither focuses much energy on the future, plans strategically, tackles complex issues, or inspires genuine or lasting collaboration or commitment.

To achieve these goals, it is necessary to focus attention not on what has or is happening, but what is intended to happen in the future. This requires setting goals or objectives, which, as Peter Drucker pointed out many years ago, cannot be done as effectively through mechanisms of command and control as through managerial forms of organization and directed processes that aim at the creation of agreed upon goals or objectives. Setting goals or objectives naturally, predictably, and automatically gives rise to management, and employs cooperation, decision-making, and similar processes to bring about incremental organizational improvements. The level of participation is involvement rather than compliance, since employees need to be involved in setting goals, but these are seen as largely the purview of management. But goals and objectives are not the same as strategies, which require strategic planning and an orientation to a yet more distant future, with increased attention to long range planning, greater complexity, and a higher level of collaboration.

Strategic planning naturally, predictably, and automatically gives rise to visionary leadership, as opposed to management, and uses active participation of employees to create collaboration, empowerment, consensus decision-making, and similar interest-oriented processes. Strategies cannot be planned and carried out without everyone participating in the process and gaining their buy-in. For this reason, strategic planning is, to some extent, incompatible with hierarchy, bureaucracy, and management by goals and objectives. Instead of management there is a transition to leadership, because it is not possible, for the following reasons, to successfully manage the elements needed to create a clear and convincing vision.

## WHAT CAN'T BE MANAGED AND MUST BE LED

Management implies that someone other than the person responsible for carrying out a task is in charge of making sure it is done correctly. Certain skills, behaviors, and outcomes can easily be mandated by others, such as attendance ("Be here at 8:00 A.M."), sequential actions ("Do this first and that second"), politeness ("Don't yell"), and repetitive movements ("Tighten this nut"). But, as Joan Goldsmith and I pointed out in *The End of Management and the Rise of Organizational Democracy*, there are certain fundamental skills, behaviors, and outcomes that simply cannot be managed, and an equally fundamental set that lie entirely beyond management's reach and must be led, facilitated, encouraged, supported, mentored, or coached into existence. Here are some critical traits that cannot be managed, but can be led:

| | |
|---|---|
| Trust | Love |
| Caring | Dedication |
| Creativity | Leadership |
| Curiosity | Honesty |
| Insight | Courage |
| Synergy | Empathy |
| Integrity | Compassion |

| | |
|---|---|
| Consensus | Understanding |
| Craftsmanship | Wisdom |
| Values | Passion |
| Perseverance | Forgiveness |
| Initiative | Unity |
| Flow | Trustworthiness |
| Collaboration | Follow-through |

Hierarchy, bureaucracy, and management interfere with every one of these fundamental work requirements. People cannot be ordered to be creative, nor do policies and procedures or management uniformly generate trust. This does not mean creativity and trust cannot be enhanced through leadership. It means they cannot be commanded, controlled, ordered, predicted, mandated, regulated, administered, managed, or required, because they depend on spontaneous, voluntary, unregulated activity, on choice, and on play.

These skills, behaviors, and traits represent the most important elements in every organization. By creating a distinction between what can and cannot be managed, we automatically identify a *human* bottom line of ubiquitous leadership, organizational democracy, and strategic integration, which forms the next highest level of organizational development.

Strategic integration naturally, predictably, and automatically gives rise not just to leadership, but to *ubiquitous leadership*, that exists throughout the organization. It uses not just collaboration, empowerment, and consensus decision-making, but values, webs of association, cross-functional teams, self-correcting systems, and other synergistic processes that go beyond mere participation to create a sense of ownership in employees.

## DEGREES OF ORGANIZATIONAL FREEDOM

The idea of strategic integration can perhaps best be explained by analogy to the idea of a dimension in physics and mathematics, where each dimension is seen to create an added degree of freedom. A point in mathematics has zero dimensions and allows no freedom of movement. A line permits movement in one direction, for example, up and down. A plane grants an additional degree of freedom, allowing one to move horizontally as well as vertically. A cube creates a third dimension, depth. A hypercube permits movement in a hypothetical fourth spatial dimension.

Applying this idea to organizations, we can see that hierarchies encourage vertical movement and discourage horizontal movement across departmental lines. If hierarchy represents one dimension and vertical freedom, cross-functional teams represent a second dimension and the horizontal freedom of employees to work across departmental boundaries. A third dimension or degree of organizational freedom, depth, arises when employees develop shared values and visionary leadership, when teams are linked across professions and disciplines in a strategic direction; and when natural hierarchies of merit replace artificial, fixed hierarchies selected from above. A fourth dimension, *synergy*, occurs when there is a strategic integration that allows diverse departmental functions to combine into a single whole that is greater than the sum of its parts, as in the diagram on the next page.

# Organizational Dimensions

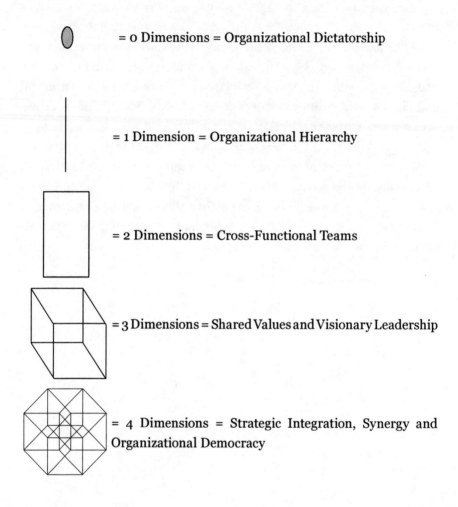

= 0 Dimensions = Organizational Dictatorship

= 1 Dimension = Organizational Hierarchy

= 2 Dimensions = Cross-Functional Teams

= 3 Dimensions = Shared Values and Visionary Leadership

= 4 Dimensions = Strategic Integration, Synergy and Organizational Democracy

Strategic integration produces organizational synergy by crossing the boundaries that divide people. These include vertical boundaries created by hierarchy, power and privilege; horizontal boundaries created by bureaucracy, turf wars, siloed departments, and isolated individuals; depth boundaries created by lack of shared values and ubiquitous, visionary leadership; external boundaries created by competitors, vendors, suppliers, customers, clients, and citizens; internal boundaries created by organizational cultures, resistance to change, competition over power and status, unresolved conflicts, and dysfunctional relationships; spatial boundaries created by static locations, centralized offices, and established domiciles; and temporal boundaries created by assumptions of a fixed past and a predetermined future, and bureaucratic inability to operate in the present. Each of these boundaries hinders employees from moving rapidly and freely within the organization based on need and opportunity.

## STRATEGIC INTEGRATION AND ORGANIZATIONAL DEMOCRACY

Each of these five successive levels of organizational evolution, including strategic integration, involves a shift in the way decisions are made. The greater the degree of planning, complexity, and collaboration, the more organizations need to shift from autocracy and oligarchy to democracy. From this perspective, democracy is a superior means of making decisions in organizations, but like all democracy, it requires a surrender of power on the part of an elite. What is important is to recognize that not only is democracy a way of integrating organizations strategically, but it is also an inevitable consequence of doing so.

Organizational hierarchies concentrate decision making in their top ranks, while most of the problems that require decisions are located in the lower ranks. As a result, not only are the decisions organizational leaders make frequently wrong, but employees in many organizations are required to surrender their right to participate in making decisions that directly impact their work lives, separating other forms of organization from the first principle of democracy, that governance requires the consent of the governed.

When managers make top-down strategic decisions without input from employees, democracy is diminished and hierarchy, bureaucracy and autocracy are enhanced. When abstract rules, policies and procedures are applied to people who are unable to participate in defining or enforcing them, democracy is discouraged and bureaucracy is stabilized.

Moreover, hierarchical, bureaucratic, and rule-driven managerial systems actively distort communications, increase distrust, and exacerbate chronic unresolved conflicts. They block the flow of meaning across their organizations, obstruct teamwork and collaboration, and undermine relationships that sensitively depend on awareness, authenticity, congruence and commitment. They pit managers against employees, block internal connections, generate frustration and result in the deterioration of quality, participation, morale and teamwork. They obstruct learning and encourage people to achieve only minimal levels of competency and commitment, or simply stagnate and wait to retire.

Democracy does not mean putting every decision to a majority vote, but rather that organizational effectiveness requires employees to collaborate and actively lead the organization, which suggests that inalienable rights of life, liberty and the pursuit of happiness deserve recognition not only in government, but in the workplace as well. This means acknowledging the value and importance of freedom of speech, assembly and religion, of due process of law and equal protection guarantees, even in private, non-governmental organizations. Ultimately, it means the right of the governed to govern themselves, as employees as well as citizens. As Abraham Lincoln wrote:

> As I would not be a slave, so I would not be a master. This expresses my idea of democracy. Whatever differs from this, to the extent of the difference, is no democracy.

The relations of master and slave have not entirely disappeared, but are alive and unwell in the workplace, though in a far more civilized form. Yet they continue wherever hierarchy, bureaucracy and autocracy dominate the relationship between managers and employees. By waking either the slave or the master up to the truth of their human equality and collaborative potential, we undermine industrial slavery and strengthen organizational democracy.

The same can be said of the importance of participation and collaborative leadership at work. Every increase in these areas creates an expanded sense of ownership and empowerment on the part of employees and a diminished sense that autocratic managerial elites are required to run organizations. It then becomes clear that democracy is fundamentally an act of *ownership*, whether over government or organizations, and that ownership builds responsibility and fuels learning, motivation, and improvement.

This battle has gone on for centuries. It first established, through the American Revolution, Civil War, World War I, and War in Vietnam, an extension of the franchise to property owners, slaves, women, and eighteen year olds, guaranteeing every adult citizen a right to elect their leaders and agree on the principles by which they will be governed. Only now are we beginning to recognize that there is an equal, commensurate right on the part of employees in organizations to have a voice in selecting *their* leaders and agreeing on the principles by which *they* will be governed. While governments and workplace organizations differ in many important respects, none of them provide a sufficient rationale for upholding democratic principles in one location and not the other. We adhere to democracy not because it is convenient or efficient, but because it is a human right, and it is no less so during working hours and in workplaces than in the halls of government.

## SEVEN STRATEGIES FOR ORGANIZATIONAL TRANSFORMATION

In *The End of Management and the Rise of Organizational Democracy*, Joan Goldsmith and I identified the following seven strategies for transforming organizational hierarchies, bureaucracies, and autocracies into collaborative, self-managing strategically integrated democratic organizations.

### Strategy 1: Shape a Context of Values, Ethics, and Integrity

To support self-management, we require a context of values, ethics, and integrity that is explicit, shared, and embodied in real behaviors that reverberate throughout the organization. Values shape and direct work within the organization and establish its relationship with the outside world. Creating identity, behavior, and culture from a context of shared values and integrity provides a powerful driving force for innovation within the organization that affects each self-managing structure, system, strategy, process, and relationship and integrates them into a sustainable framework.

### Strategy 2: Form Living, Evolving Webs of Association

Self-managing organizations are flexible and renewable. They constantly shift and evolve into shapes and structures that are highly responsive to environmental conditions, revealing changing problems and improved strategies for solving them. These structures spring from seeing organizations as living, evolving organisms and webs of association, in which individuals, partners, teams, networks, and alliances design their own roles, communications, systems, processes, and relationships. Each node of activity in a web of association manages itself and links with others in responding rapidly to ever-changing conditions, problems, and opportunities. Webs of association constantly evolve in purpose, size, shape, structure, process, and direction. They are self-managing, self-directing, and self-referential and operate continually in a learning mode.

## Strategy 3: Develop Ubiquitous, Linking Leadership

A key to success in self-managing organizations is the ability of leaders to link individuals, teams, and webs of association, stimulate energy and commitment, solve problems, build supportive alliances, and learn from experience. Leaders help teams evolve, expand, develop, and stabilize. Organizational opportunities require the development of leadership skills ubiquitously, that is, throughout the organization: character skills that build integrity, relational skills that form interconnections between people, mediation skills that turn conflicts into opportunities, wisdom skills that increase understanding, elicitive skills that motivate people to act, and action skills that marshal forces to achieve results. Leaders in democratic organizations are selected not just by upper management, but by employees as well, together with clients, customers, and shareholders.

## Strategy 4: Build Innovative Self-Managing Teams

At the heart of webs of association are small, flexible, self-managing teams of widely varying sizes, functions, purposes, forms, and life cycles. Teams are responsible for defining and achieving goals, solving problems, and seizing opportunities. The best teams are self-selecting, self-directing, self-managing, and self-sustaining. Their processes include hiring and firing fellow team members, electing leaders, defining roles and tasks, and redesigning organizational parameters from scratch. Networks of teams link up with each other through leadership, information systems, and collaborative processes, which permeate boundaries to build mutual support.

## Strategy 5: Implement Streamlined, Open, Collaborative Processes

A rich variety of collaborative group processes are used to support shared values, build teams and webs of association, and develop ubiquitous, linking leadership in a diverse organizational environment. Customer partnerships are streamlined, individual and team responsibility are promoted, and countless organizational processes are reworked. Communications, meetings, negotiations, and decision-making are redesigned to encourage diversity, collaboration, self-management, and democracy. While unimportant decisions can be announced, consulted on, or delegated and others have to be voted on, the most important require consensus or unanimity. An essential element in self-management is recognizing which decision-making approach to use for what purpose and how to design processes that encourage collaborative relationships.

## Strategy 6: Create Complex, Self-Correcting Systems

Systems for self-correction and self-improvement encourage employees and organizations to learn and continue increasing their capacities. The more complex and multidimensional the organizational tasks and relationships are, the more complex and multidimensional the self-correcting systems needed to keep them on course. These systems include feedback and evaluation, motivation and rewards, discipline and correction, negotiation and conflict resolution, and methods for creating learning organizations or professional communities. Using these devices and techniques, collaborative, self-managing, self-correcting organizations can quickly turn mistakes, problems, conflicts, glitches, and errors into opportunities for improvement.

## Strategy 7: Integrate Strategically, and Change the Way We Change

As organizations implement these strategies, each is simultaneously integrated into a single unified whole, and the methods and change processes used to bring them into existence are transformed. It is not possible to eliminate hierarchy using hierarchical change processes. Democratic changes create multiple opportunities for strategic integration, which adds a new, fourth dimension of organizational freedom, beyond depth. Changing the way we change means turning employees into self-conscious change agents, and conflict revolutionaries.

## IMPLEMENTING STRATEGIC INTEGRATION

For democracy to overcome these obstacles and fully develop in the workplace, it is necessary to bring all these separate and distinct processes and techniques, and the cultures, structures and systems that support them, into a single, cohesive, strategically integrated democratic whole. Integration connects diversity with the unity that always underlies it, drawing people together *across* organizational lines.

Fundamentally, the role of *leaders* in an organizational democracy is to expand the number of degrees of organizational freedom and orchestrate these elements to create learning relationships that link people across artificial boundaries. Organizational separations and divisions that are not integrated produce role confusions, feelings of irresponsibility, misunderstandings, stereotypes, conflicts, and internal dissension, which can be used to justify and rationalize bureaucratic divisions and hierarchical control. Every organizational division is simply a different way of understanding, processing and solving common problems. The task of democratic leaders is to reveal the whole to each of its parts and integrate the concerns of all into a single synergistic, strategically integrated whole.

Collaboration, democracy, and self-management are prerequisites for evolution to higher levels of organizational development based on synergy, community, and strategic integration. Through these processes, it becomes possible to build creative, motivated, high-performance, self-managing teams that harmonize and orchestrate a wide range of organizational skills, strategies, systems, processes, and relationships to produce synergistic results.

Creating fully democratic, collaborative, self-managing organizations requires more than fragmented, step-by-step, tactical reforms. It requires integrated, holistic, strategic transformations that increase diversity, complexity, synergy, and interconnectedness and challenge everyone to operate at their highest levels of effectiveness. In the process, employees need to become owners of the organizations they are changing and of the process by which they are changed.

Hierarchical organizational systems tend to become insular and defensive, walling themselves off from internal and external criticisms in order to preserve the status quo in power and financial rewards, and promote an image of success and self-confidence. Yet in the process, they also wall themselves off from customers, clients, citizens, employees, external competitors, internal departments, government regulators, other professions, and disciplines. Democratic organizations need to dismantle these walls and integrate an increasing variety of strategic, resource, and relational possibilities.

Strategically integrated organizations therefore reduce internal boundaries. They encourage employees to work freely across traditional organizational separations, link isolated departments, and cascade changes in one area to produce changes in others. They support employees in eliminating external boundaries and linking directly with customers, community, environment, and society; producing goods and services that meet human needs; and developing shared values to guide the organization.

This added dimension of organizational freedom also transforms the way they change by making the entire process more strategic and integrated, and therefore more collaborative, democratic, and self-managing. The freedom permitted by organizational depth turns every employee into a leader in some important area, and the change process into an exercise in democracy.

Beyond this lie synergy, innovation, and community, which uniquely require collaboration, democracy, and self-management, as integration allows them to cut across traditional organizational lines. For example, the strategic integration of technology, finance, and management skills can rapidly transform organizational functions, roles, and partnerships, and the context in which they arise. It can create value by offering new ways of doing business and allowing diverse departments, divisions, and business functions to understand each other better and collaborate more effectively. It can build rich information infrastructures, leading to greater organizational flexibility and responsiveness, production planning, data for performance assessment, opportunities for internal partnerships, and recognition of the human side of technological change. It can create entirely new products and services and dramatically increase customer satisfaction. It can give employees instantaneous access to critical organizational data, allow them to communicate with everyone in the organization, and change their personal information and benefit allocations on-line. And in doing these things, it can dramatically reduce chronic conflicts.

In my view, the most important insight mediation offers to organizations is the idea that conflicts are immense sources of learning and improvement. Every conflict represents something that is not working for someone, and if we can stop these conflicts from continuing and not just settle them, but resolve the underlying issues that created them at their deepest chronic and systemic levels, we will learn how to prevent them from re-occurring and evolve to higher orders of conflict and resolution, creating new organizational forms and functions in the process.

# CHAPTER 11

# POLITICS AND VALUES IN MEDIATION

## Reflections on the Chinese Experience

*Contradiction and struggle are universal and absolute, but the methods of resolving contradictions, that is, the forms of struggle, differ according to the differences in the nature of the contradictions. Some contradictions are characterized by open antagonism and others are not. In accordance with the concrete development of things, some contradictions, which were originally non-antagonistic, develop into antagonistic ones, while others which were originally antagonistic develop into non-antagonistic ones.*

~ Mao Tse Tung ~

I N APRIL AND MAY of 1984, I visited China as part of a delegation of 25, including directors of mediation programs, specialists in family, neighborhood, university, and community mediation, together with trade unionists, professors, attorneys, counselors, psychiatrists, and others. The purpose of the trip was to study the Chinese mediation system, and lectures were combined with trips to workers' housing projects, rural communes, factories, a prison, a mental institution, a court trial, and other functions. [See "Politics and Values in Mediation: The Chinese Experience," 17 Mediation Quarterly p. 69 (1987)].

In April of 1988, I returned to China to learn more about mediation, and in particular to study the impact privatization was having on the politics and values used by mediators to resolve marital, neighborhood, and workplace disputes. While China has changed enormously since these trips, it is worthwhile to examine their approach at the time to mediation, which combined ancient traditions and modern political ideas in unique ways.

In ancient China, there was a proverb that expressed a strong source of attraction to mediation: "In death, avoid hell. In life, avoid the law courts." A sharp division was drawn then, and to some extent today, between acceptable emotional ventilation, subject to mediation within the family, the neighborhood, or workplace, most of which was officially ignored, like much of people's private lives that neighbors pretend not to be aware of; versus more serious transgressions against the law, for which punishment was swift, certain, and harsh.

While neighbors in ancient China might have argued violently and threaten, cursed or abused one another, bystanders would nonetheless intervene to prevent blows or informally mediate their differences. Dissent and shades of grey were permissible in mediation, but in law there was only black and white. The expression of anger was regarded as socially acceptable and officially ignored, so long as it remained within well-defined bounds, but even a slight transgression against someone in power required supplication and apology to prevent the triggering of an exponential increase in sanctions. This meant that a great degree of stability was possible, since even the most oppressed and unhappy individuals, families, groups, and classes were permitted, for a wide range of infractions, to discipline and control their own members. As historian Robert van Gulik has shown, the authority of the magistrate in China to torture, imprison, fine, and execute was, for subordinate classes committing serious infractions, practically unlimited for centuries, both in theory and in practice.

Mediation, therefore, from ancient times, was both an instrument of informal justice and social democracy, as it permitted a peer-based dispute resolution process to fashion mutually acceptable results for divergent social classes; and at the same time, it served as a powerful mechanism for social control and self-discipline.

During the civil war between the Communist party and the Koumintang, both sides permitted mediation, but for Mao and the Communists, it took on a special significance, partly because mediation was a traditional form of collective self-government that empowered the masses rather than lawyers and judges who nearly always supported more conservative aristocratic forces. This gave the Communists a way of connecting advanced revolutionary ideas with ancient cultural practices. Also, it was particularly useful in establishing a conflict resolution process in the liberated areas where there were almost no judges or lawyers, and it would have drained precious resources for the Communist party to adjudicate disputes within and between families, neighbors, and workers. It was far more economical to decentralize decision-making and delegate responsibility for general peacekeeping to the people themselves.

It also perfectly expressed the distinction between Chang Kai Shek's army, which raped, pillaged, and looted as it went, and the People's Liberation Army, whose first rule was not to "take even a needle or a piece of bread from the people without paying for it." Using the law with its built-in respect for private property rights, the power of the landowners and capitalists might remain intact, but by empowering and respecting the masses, collective forms of self-rule might gain the strength and legitimacy to succeed them.

In Mao's essays *On Contradiction* and *On the Correct Handling of Contradictions Among the People*, a useful dichotomy was created between "antagonistic" contradictions, as between landowners and peasants or workers and capitalists, for which revolution was the appropriate solution; and "non-antagonistic" contradictions among the people, which should be resolved peacefully and in a spirit of unity. Mediation was exactly such a method.

In Mao's view, mediation meshed nicely with the theory of communism, which looked forward to the "withering away of the state" and its replacement by organs of popular power, or by "civil society." Mediation can therefore be seen as the communist form of the judiciary, or as the "withered away" judicial state already in existence. It can also be regarded as combining the most ancient traditions with the most modern and forward-looking theories.

For these reasons, we were told, mediation became widespread even before liberation. Afterward, Mao wanted, on political grounds, to prevent the rise of lawyers and courts, which Deng Xiao Ping urged as necessary for modernization even in the 1950s. In the 1980s, Deng moved China increasingly in the direction of formal law, with civil codes and law courts, particularly concerned with the resolution of conflicts between economic enterprises, suppression of crime, and the establishment of civil liability for negligent acts.

As a result of these influences China created what was undoubtedly the largest and most comprehensive mediation program of any country in the world. There is some question as to whether all of these practices can properly be called mediation, but there is no question that it was widely available, that it was immediate, that it rapidly deescalated conflict, that it reached successful solutions in an overwhelming number of cases, and that it was widely supported among the population.

One of the primary difficulties in understanding the role of mediation in China is that it was seen not only as a method of resolving disputes, but as a way of reinforcing political and social values, as a source for the creation of ideas about social justice, and as an acceptable normative and political intervention by state and society into the lives of individual citizens.

# SCOPE OF MEDIATION

China, with over a billion people, had only a few thousand lawyers at the time of my first visit, but several million mediators. In 1984, there were some 800,000 neighborhood-mediation committees located in each of China's major cities. In the countryside, there were village mediation committees that had been set up in 1954 as part of the commune system. Factory and mine mediation committees were not formally established until 1972 but were fully operational in millions of workplaces throughout the country.

When I visited Chungquing, a city of nearly 12 million people, there were 11,855 mediation committees with 90,638 mediators: 4,574 neighborhood committees; 61,674 countryside committees; 24,124 committees in factories and mines; and the balance in various institutions and organizations. This city averaged one mediator for every 100 or so residents. In 1983, 130,262 civil disputes were mediated with a 95.7 percent settlement rate. Of these, 31 percent were family disputes (including inheritance), 29 percent involved relations between neighbors, 17 percent were agricultural and rural property disputes, and 23 percent were industrial disputes. The industrial disputes included 2,515 contract disputes between economic enterprises, and of these 97 percent were successfully concluded by mediation. Of the total number of commercial cases, 97.3 percent were mediated, 2.7 percent were arbitrated, and the rest went initially to court. Of those arbitrated, over 80 percent were not appealed.

Of the 13,000 civil suits filed in Chungquing, 80 percent were successfully mediated prior to trial, though my observation of court-directed mediation at a civil trial indicated that the judges, who also acted as mediators at various points throughout the trial, performed the same role they would have in the United States during a mandatory settlement conference, but afterwards went on to decide the merits of the case. There was no regular mediation mechanism for the many private enterprises proliferating under China's new "responsibility" system, which have tended to use courts and arbitration instead.

By contrast, in a relatively small rural "production township" (commune) in Yueyang, consisting of some 10,000 people, 208 cases had been mediated between 1983 and 1984. Of these, 11 were marriage and family disputes; 68 land or property, 15 over houses, one inheritance,

12 over use of forest land or trees, 13 over irrigation, eight over use of collectively owned farm tools or water buffalo, 24 involving family quarrels, l9 between neighbors, and 10 miscellaneous. Of these 28 involved injuries to the person and six eventually went to court. This distribution seemed typical, revealing the extensive role of mediators as "front line" problem solvers, a widespread success rate, and some of the problems typical of Chinese society at the time.

## ELECTION OF MEDIATORS

A further distinguishing characteristic of dispute resolution in China was that mediators were almost universally elected in their neighborhoods, production teams, factories, and organizations. They served for limited terms, could be recalled by their electorate at any time, and might change frequently. Some mediators, however, had been elected repeatedly for many years.

While I was unable to observe the election of a mediator, references by individuals were often revealing. One mediator stated that individuals were selected for their fairness and implied that they had remained uninvolved in previous disputes, or retained their equanimity when confronted, or had acted informally as mediators, or simply that a significant number of people liked them.

Another mediator commented that neighborhood mediators were chosen based on their availability and willingness to serve without compensation; another, that they were co-opted based on their successful performance of less crucial tasks. All the rank-and-file mediators we met appeared to enjoy their work, and like all mediators everywhere, took great pleasure in talking about their cases. They said there were often contested elections for mediation positions, but the percentages were not estimated. Mediators seemed to be held in very high esteem, and from the nature of their work one could well understand why.

Because mediators were elected locally, they were responsible to a community constituency that was more inclined to listen and follow their direction. Election was seen as more likely to produce mediators who are affable and fair, more devoted to their task, and better able to produce settlements than mediators who are self-appointed or appointed by the courts.

In a few cases, as with managers in factories, or at the highest administrative levels, or in prisons, mediators were selected by local administration or higher level officials based on recommendations from below. While there was no basis for comparison of data, it appeared that these individuals engaged in less mediation and implemented more policy than elected mediators. No clear reason was given why these positions were not also democratically elected.

## HOW MEDIATION WORKED IN CHINA

In 1987, there were approximately 10,000 lawyers for over a billion people (figures vary from 5,000 to 30,000), in 1987 there were over 6 million mediators nationwide who mediated over 9 million cases, not including a large number of traffic cases, arguments on the street, cases brought to notaries, and cases resolved informally by relatives, neighbors or my co-workers within enterprises and factories. For every civil case filed there were more than 5.7 mediations. The following charts illustrate the range and scope of Chinese mediation for 1987:

### Mediation Statistics for Urban Areas (1987)

| | |
|---|---:|
| Number of Mediation Committees | 980,325 |
| Location: | |
| Countryside | 736,678 |
| Neighborhoods | 77,420 |
| Factories & Enterprises | 131,113 |
| Misc. (Schools, hospitals, etc.) | 35,114 |
| Number of Mediators | 6,205,813 |
| Number of Cases Mediated by Committees | 6,966,053 |
| Type of Cases Mediated by Committees: | |
| Marriage | 1,188,353 |
| Family | 1,074,726 |
| Housing and Land | 1,024,296 |
| Neighbor | 889,502 |
| Production & Management | 667,409 |
| Number of Cases Successfully Resolved | 6,282,808 |
| Success Rate | 90.2 percent  overall |
| Cases Where Civil Disputes were Prevented | 68,858 |

| | |
|---|---|
| Cases Where Abnormal Death was prevented | 103,070 |
| Ratio of Mediations to Civil Cases | 5.7:1 |
| Professional (Judicial Assistant) Mediators | 42,615 |
| Mediations by Judicial Assistants | 1,019,097 |
| Mediations by Mediation Committees | 919,250 |
| Total Number of Cases Mediated | 8,904,400 (+) |

Over the past several years, disputes over marriage, family, housing, workplace, and economic conflicts had been rising, while neighborhood, injury, and compensation and property disputes had declined. In part, these trends can be explained by greater economic liberty, increasing privatization of the economy, a new civil law providing legal remedies for injury and compensation, and considerable grass-roots education in the neighborhoods. More legal options were now available due to the demands of entrepreneurs and foreign investors.

In the rural areas, mediation committees worked with legal service or assistance offices, which acted also as public notaries and gave legal advice. There was, in theory, at least one legal service officer located in each village and township. The functions of these officers were to:

- Provide guidance to local mediation committees and help them with exceptionally difficult cases, such as economic disputes;
- Give speeches and conduct propaganda work about mediation and other legal services;
- Help notarize legal documents;
- Act as counsel in minor civil litigation and help non-litigious parties arrive at a settlement;
- Conduct mediations referred to them instead of or through the local mediation committee.

The following chart details the mediation related activities of the rural legal assistance offices.

## Mediation Statistics for Rural Areas (1987)

| | |
|---|---|
| Number of Legal Service Offices | 23,737 |
| Number of Legal Service Officers | 61,823 |
| Number of Mediations on Economic Problems | 200,430 |

| | |
|---|---|
| Number of Civil Mediations | 705,363 |
| Times Conducted Propaganda on Mediation | 367,828 |
| Talks on Mediation and Legal Services | 575,674 |
| Number of Attendees  234,943,540 | |

The judicial assistants and legal service officers worked with the mediation committees and might mediate cases with them, or take over cases that had not been resolved successfully, or correct settlements that were inconsistent with the law, or eliminate mediators who were too old to function adequately (particularly in the countryside where travel was necessary) and generally helped the mediation committees solve their problems.

There were four requirements in China to becoming a member of a mediation committee:

1. Honesty;
2. Accessibility and a close relationship to people;
3. Enjoyment of mediation work;
4. Knowledge of law and legal requirements.

In 1987, about one half of all mediation committees experienced some form of corrective action by judicial assistants, mostly in the replacement of physically incapable mediators. The principal problems with individual mediators that prompt their replacement were listed as:

- Not abiding by the rules of mediation or with legal requirements;
- Age, if it interfered with being able to meet the demands of the work (mediators could be any age from 18 up);
- Ability;
- Education, primarily in relation to being able to understand the law.

At the time, there were only a small number of laws in China, and these, we were told, were written so that non-lawyers could understand them. Members of mediation committees were usually not lawyers and were not paid for their work. If they were required to take time away from work, the local government or their employer would compensate them, but these sums were generally quite small. As a result, most mediation committee mediators were retired workers between the age of 50 and

60. A certain percentage of mediators were required to be women, with exceptions based on local conditions, and women were preferentially selected to mediate disputes involving women and children. In the cities, women constituted more than 50 percent of the mediation committees. Mediations were conducted primarily under the following auspices:

1. Friends and Relatives Mediation: In family disputes, friends and relatives could intervene on their own to look for solutions.

2. Neighborhood Mediation: Conducted by mediators elected in Neighborhood Committees, they handled mostly conflicts regarding divorce, family disputes, assault, and property disputes. They followed three central principles:

   a. The mediation must be conducted consistent with applicable law.

   b. No one can be forced to participate in mediation. Mediation is voluntary and democratic in manner. No compulsory methods may be used. Persuasion and education are the methods to be used.

   c. Anyone can refuse mediation and go to court instead. This did not exist before 1949.

3. Factory Mediation: Factory mediators were elected by the workers to settle disputes between workers or personality disputes between workers and supervisors, but generally did not try to settle contract disputes.

4. Government Mediation: The judicial assistants were professional mediators and a minority in China, as the rest were lay mediators or judges. These professional mediators received two to three months of training, in some cases each year, depending on resources. Government mediators could resolve disputes between neighbors or relatives referred to them by the neighborhood committees, or between enterprises, or between workers and supervisors. They also mediated all civil cases before they went to trial.

5. Court Mediation: After a civil case came to trail and before pronouncing a verdict, the judges would attempt to encourage a mediated solution.

6. Institutional Mediation: In schools, these may be students

or teachers. Children were taught how to resolve disputes throughout their school lives, and might in later years act as mediators in conflicts between students, but generally without election or appointment. Other institutions such as hospitals had mediators to work with patients and relatives.

7.  Party Mediation: Occasionally, the Communist party would mediate disputes, and was sometimes seen as an ombudsman or "trouble shooter" to correct injustices or help parties agree on principles.

8.  Informal Mediation: A large number of disputes took place on streets and in stores, between merchants and customers, pedestrians and bicyclists, etc. Bystanders would generally intervene to prevent violence and try to cool tempers. Traffic disputes were also mediated informally, both by police and passersby.

The principal differences between mediation committee mediators, legal assistants (professional mediators) and judge mediators appeared to be the following:

1.  The "people's mediators," while not professionals, were often highly skilled individuals with very high prestige in their neighborhoods and workplaces and had a great deal of patience. They may take 10 or 20 days or longer to settle a case. As volunteers they were highly committed to the process and often co-mediated.

2.  The judicial assistants were professional mediators with a great deal more training and skill than most committee members and more understanding of the law. They were less accepted by the disputants and had less time to produce results. They generally mediated singly.

3.  The law judges were only partly trained in mediation and were the least active and independent as mediators. If one party objected, they did not press for a solution. They had the power to decide the outcome, however, and were often listened to.

If a case did not achieve resolution in mediation, the mediators would try to convince the parties to go to court to resolve the dispute. If the case was appropriate, a judge might recommend that the parties return to the mediation committee to resolve their dispute.

Judicial assistants were referred cases both by mediation committees and judges or approached directly by the parties. Most people thought judicial assistants had more power than attorneys, because they oversaw the work of the mediation committees.

As Chinese mediators viewed it, mediation consisted of the following steps:

1. Accept the dispute: Conflicts may come to mediation by application, referral, or on the mediator's initiative if they saw a problem becoming worse. They would not accept a case if:
   a. The parties refused.
   b. A major crime had been committed. Minor crimes included, for example, cases where a couple had been forced to get married, or where one of the parties was injured, but not seriously.
2. Investigate the dispute: The mediators investigate to obtain the facts and to tell "who is right and who is wrong." This may be done with the parties present or alone, depending on the circumstances.
3. Mediate the dispute: The mediators get the parties together so that the parties can understand the other, compromise, and produce "an atmosphere of friendship and understanding."
4. Make the agreement work: The mediators then become interested in the practical measures needed to make the agreement work, on specific action steps, and on writing down the agreement if the case is complex.
5. Follow-Up: The mediators check back with the parties to make certain that the agreement is working and fine-tune the details if it is not.

## ROLE AND AVAILABILITY OF MEDIATORS

Another important difference between Chinese and U.S. models lies in the immediacy of the process. Mediators in China were expected to be available 24 hours a day, and received payment only if they were taken from their regular work to solve a problem for their factory or production teams, but not for their neighborhood committees.

If a fight broke out, those nearest would step in to separate the combatants, and mediators—often teams would be called. They would generally arrive at the scene within minutes to investigate the facts, interview witnesses, deescalate the conflict, and possibly settle the dispute. There was a sense of average timing for the mediation process that seemed to number from several days to several weeks before final agreement would be reached.

Chinese mediators were far more active as investigators and fact-finders than their Western counterparts. Mediators and judges did not rely on the adversarial system to bring witnesses forward, even in criminal cases, but went into the community, examined the scene, and interviewed potential witnesses, including the direct participants—nearly always without benefit of counsel.

This expanded investigatory function, similar to the role of magistrates under the Napoleonic Code, makes the mediation process much simpler, more perfunctory and directed, and, in all likelihood, more accurate. It takes much longer from beginning to end to settle a dispute, but the mediator would be fully conversant with the facts by the time the parties meet.

A large percentage of what mediators do in the West is to listen to disputants argue their respective positions. In China, this was a smaller part of the settlement process. When the mediation was held, the mediators were cognizant of the facts and prepared to dispense with a great deal of superfluous rationale.

In factories and industrial concerns, the principal role of the mediator was to resolve conflicts between employees before they got out of hand. While factories were empowered to fire employees for violating factory rules—which were voted on by employees—terminations, even for fighting, were rare. Factory mediators would step in, acting partly as shop steward, partly as management, to solve problems and maximize productivity. The mediator might play the role of a social worker more often in the factory, seeking both to prevent conflicts from arising, and to help the employee resolve whatever personal difficulties may be obstructing their job performance.

# VALUES IN MEDIATION

A significant difference between mediation in China and the U.S. was the role of values. In China, the mediator spoke for society, counseled the parties regarding the law, acted as a moral force, and reminded participants of the value consequences of their actions. The mediator also acted as a political organizer, and brought the parties to a political or value-based understanding of their problems. Finally, the mediator acted as a peacemaker, creating a consensual settlement that worked not only on paper, but was expressed in the attitudes of the participants, and in their continued "good relations." Disputes were seen, discussed and solved, not as isolated incidents, but as social phenomena. The mediator might discuss class relations or socially irresponsible attitudes, or the importance of modernization and general social progress with the parties during a session.

The central goal, on which China was clearly united at the time, was modernization. A happy citizen was considered to be a productive citizen, and the right attitude at work meant fewer problems and faster modernization. This sense of social unity, of direction and priority, gave China a unified value structure on which community intervention, through mediators as social representatives, was based. This role required far more extensive monitoring than exists in the West, to ensure that the parties were implementing the letter and spirit of their agreements, and that there was feedback to the mediators on the effects of their interventions.

It is essential, in trying to understand this process, to gain a sense of what values meant in China, and in some cases, the Chinese have spelled, and even counted them out in detail. There were for example, five criteria for a good family, six for a good building, etc. These included, for a workers' village in Shanghai, such elements as loving and showing concern for one's country and one's family, courtesy to one's neighbors, cleanliness, security and order, frugality, and unity.

At a workers' residence in Chungquing, being a good family member meant studying hard and following residential regulations and disciplinary rules; respecting the elderly, maintaining love and respect between the husband and wife, doing a good job raising children, having courteous relations with neighbors, and helping keep a clean environment. These constituted the moral standards on which everyone agreed and became the basis for persuasion (their term) to accept a mediated solution.

Unity, social stability, and productivity were considered high values especially in the workplace. At the Yueyang production brigade, mediation was said to help society in six ways:

1. By solving problems and improving relationships;
2. By preventing rule violations;
3. By avoiding litigation in which courts become bogged down in minor matters;
4. By educating the public about the laws;
5. By increasing production;
6. By unifying the community.

At another rural production brigade, three values were cited:

1. To love one's country;
2. To build socialism;
3. To respect the Party.

People needed to be helped to "work in a communist spirit" and not to be "too selfish."

The mediator was also responsible for educating disputants in the law, sometimes by reading relevant passages from the recently enacted Constitution, which all sectors of society appeared to have had a voice in creating, or some other relevant legislation or factory regulation. Political literature was no longer routinely read to participants or cited as persuasive, as during the Cultural Revolution, but since the purpose of mediation was to reach agreement based on common principles, it would not be unusual for mediators, in searching for common ground, to mention political ideas that had common currency.

The mediator might also remind participants of their shared values, criticize wrongdoing, or praise ethical actions. This was not done indirectly or subtly, but honestly and bluntly, with a great deal of diplomacy and good will. A husband who had beaten his wife was criticized for his actions, while his wife might be criticized for leaving him, or complimented for her patience in not doing so. Considerable sensitivity to the feelings of the participants was evidenced in the cases we examined.

In the West, it is unusual for mediators to directly criticize or praise the actions of one of the participants, whereas in China this was seen as an important element in re-education, correction of problem-producing behavior, and prevention of further disputes.

# POLITICS IN MEDIATION

The mediator, at the time of my visit, might also have acted as a political organizer by connecting the individual elements of an isolated dispute with a discussion of Marxist principles, for example, by referring to social equality, the importance of the family, opposition to male chauvinism, equitable class relations, or even the principles of dialectical materialism.

The mediator-as-political-organizer cemented solidarity within the neighborhood, workplace, or group as a whole, imparting a broader awareness of what might have appeared as a historical problem, and indicating the practical steps that could be taken to solve it. All this was seen as important to accomplish through the mediation process, rather than outside, or in spite of it.

The mediator continued to act as a peacemaker between the parties after the dispute was settled, to ensure that conflict will be successfully resolved, and was seen as responsible for making sure that future relationships were improved. In one case, a mediator apologized for criticizing a worker, so that he could "save face" in spite of his wrongdoing and return to work with the right attitude. This would rarely occur among Western mediators.

According to Marxist theory, politics, morality, and values are relative rather than absolute, and vary with time and place. Yet in any one time and one place, certain values might become absolute. At the East China University of Law and Political Science, I asked how they went about determining what these values, even in relative terms, ought to be. I was told that the highest values at that time were a result of China's recent political history, and consisted of stability, consolidation of the socialist system, encouraging productivity, and raising living standards. As mediation was highly beneficial in producing these results, it was greatly encouraged—as much for the end product as for the process, and as much for resolving disputes as preventing future ones. A saying among mediators in China at that time, I was told, was: "Make big disputes into little ones, and make little ones disappear."

The truly extraordinary thing about these conversations was that mediators believed there was a clear, undisputed *answer* to the question of values, that people who were widely dispersed geographically, educationally and functionally had a clear notion of the value system for the nation as a whole and their own particular relationship to it. Nothing even remotely similar could be said of mediation in the West.

## CASE EXAMPLES

Some examples of mediated disputes that were reported to our group may help to illustrate these points.

1. In Shanghai, a mother and daughter-in-law did not get along. The neighbors noticed that they had many disputes over minor matters. They quarreled frequently over use of the kitchen, at one point coming to blows. Mediators were called in, spoke to the immediate family and their neighbors, and then criticized each party for not respecting the rights of the other. They articulated the rules and moral standards that, in the abstract, seemed to cover the situation, proposed a solution, and persuaded both parties to accept it. The serious consequences of their escalating rivalry were explained, some hidden agendas were discussed while others seem to have been avoided, and a schedule was proposed for use of the kitchen.

2. In Xian, a worker at an arts and crafts factory refused to help his wife with domestic chores. The couple came to blows, and the wife left to return to her family. Through mediation, the wife was persuaded to return, and the husband to help around the house, based on the principle of "mutual respect" between spouses.

3. In Chungquing, a woman refused to pay money to support her husband's elderly stepfather, claiming he had failed to fulfill his duty to raise his son. After investigation, it was determined that he had raised his stepson from age 12, and helped him form a family. The stepdaughter-in-law was persuaded to pay him a life pension of 10 Yuan a month plus pocket money.

4. In another case, a daughter-in-law was beaten for not returning early enough from work to complete her housework. The two mothers-in-law quarreled and the daughter-in-law tried to commit suicide. On investigation, it was revealed that

she was working after hours at the factory for extra income. The mother-in-law was told she had been wrong and was persuaded to apologize. Their misunderstanding was clarified and their relationship improved.

5.  In another case, a brother who was renovating his house placed a beam on his younger sister's house. The two fought and brandished knives. Mediators came to the spot and disarmed them, then listened to each side. After persuasion, the brother volunteered to move the beam.

6.  In a rural area, seven families bought a water buffalo that became ill. One of the farmers wanted out of the deal, but when the buffalo was cured, wanted to use it to plow his field. Mediators praised the farmer who had taken care of the buffalo during its illness, along with the other farmers who had remained united. They discussed various ways of using the water buffalo during the busy season, reached a new agreement, then discussed how future disputes might be settled before the busy season arrived.

7.  In Yueyang, a clear example of how this value system might be misused occurred. A girl and boy were engaged to be married. After spending some of his money, she fell in love with another man and refused to marry her fiancé. As there was no engagement law in China, only marriage law (somehow this group missed a provision in the new constitution that all marriages must be voluntary), resort was taken to Chinese customary law based on traditional morality. The girl was told she had to discuss this with her fiancé, who refused to release her, and she agreed to marry him. At the time the result was announced our translator commented, "I don't agree with that." Afterwards, she explained, saying the young woman should have been free to marry whomever she wished. A second translator who was present said, "I agree with her," and both were roundly applauded by the U.S. mediators, demonstrating that values may be strongly held, even among "neutral" Western mediators.

8.  Petty crimes were frequently mediated. In one case a 20-year-

old "boy" stole a watch, and instead of going to court, was sent to a local mediator for "education," consisting of a lecture and returned to his work brigade.

9. In a vegetable producing commune outside Guilin, economic liberalism had created an increasing number of quarrels and resulting mediation. Members who had stolen vegetables from one another, according to local regulations, were fined five Yuan per half kilo, or one Yuan for a single piece of fruit. If they quarreled or refused to accept mediation, they were fined five Yuan, and if they fought, they had to pay lo Yuan, a heavy penalty. Everyone democratically adopted these rules, and there were few violations as "no one wished to pay the fine." Sixty percent of the fines are given as a reward to the person who caught the violator in the act, and the rest to the brigade.

10. Two examples were given of disputes at a worker's residence involving marital problems. In the first, a young couple was watching TV with guests and the wife was wearing a short skirt, sitting with her legs open. The husband criticized his wife, who disagreed with his attitude and language. They quarreled, and, when the guests left, came to blows. The wife returned to her parents' home, and her family wanted to return with her and fight it out. Neighbors learned of this and summoned the mediators, who rushed to the parents' household. After calming their tempers, the mediators sought out the husband, and while being supportive, criticized him for failing to take a "gentle" attitude toward his wife. Together, they studied the residential regulations and provisions of the marriage law calling for mutual respect and unity between husband and wife. They criticized him for hitting his wife and convinced him to go to the wife's parents' house to apologize and bring her back. When he arrived he made a self-criticism, and seeing that he was sincere, the wife reciprocated admitting her part in the quarrel. They lived harmoniously afterward, and since have had a child. The wife was grateful and told one of the mediators that if it had not been for his intervention she

would have "destroyed" their family.

11. In a second example from the same workers residence, a young couple stayed together without registering as husband and wife, and the woman became pregnant. When her parents learned of this they were saddened, felt they had lost face, and scolded and beat their daughter. The man was saddened also and the couple left town without asking leave from work. No one knew where they had gone and all were worried. They were located after considerable efforts, but did not want to return and wished to commit suicide together. The mediator severely criticized their mistakes but showed warmth toward them and told them that if they admitted their errors it would be easy to correct the situation and all would be well. The mediator criticized the parents for their treatment of her. They had their marriage registered and were integrated into their family, factory, and neighborhood.

## ANALYSIS OF EXAMPLES

Each of these examples were related in Chinese and translated into English. Assuming there were some errors in translation, and that some selection principle affected their choice of examples to present, based on the facts reported and the words used by the mediators to describe their interventions, some conclusions can be drawn.

1. Many of the examples involved mediations to stop fights—particularly between family members and neighbors. Housing was in short supply throughout China, but especially in the cities where most of the acts of violence occurred. The dominant disputes in the countryside seemed to involve property rights more than over-crowding or flared tempers.

2. Mediation appeared to successfully calm tempers and prevent more serious results from occurring, particularly when mediators were immediately available.

3. While mediation was interventionist in China and did not rely on the parties to request it, mediators did not generally intervene until after violence had broken out or was clearly imminent, or until some genuine impasse had occurred. This

seemed to define some national sense of individual "privacy," a word that does not exist in Chinese, but could be essential in such tight living and working quarters as the Chinese occupy.

4. No one seemed to object to the mediators' presence once they arrived, nor was there any sense that their intervention was unwelcome. Some of this may have been cultural, some political, in a collectivist society where problems are seen as arising primarily from selfishness.

5. There seemed to be widespread acceptance of the belief that social responsibility had to be exercised by everyone, and that while individualism might flourish within generally responsible attitudes, anti-social individualism was intolerable and almost unimaginable as anything more than an example of improper education or upbringing.

6. No one was forgotten or "given up on," everyone was included, regardless of how hostile or violent they might have been and allowed to "save face" (which seems no more important in China than in the West.) No one was considered incorrigible or worthless, and there appeared to be an equal willingness to criticize as to praise. No doubt many disputes were settled by this technique.

7. No matter was considered too insignificant or unimportant for mediation. On a boat trip down the Yangtze, a meeting was held among representatives elected or chosen among all groups of passengers. These representatives were told to be careful of the sick and elderly and send special cases to the ship's doctor, to watch out for their possessions, not to sit on rails, where not to buy souvenirs because the prices were too high, and to remind the passengers the following morning to come out on deck and see the gorges, so their spirits could be lifted. All problems should be mediated, so that "a good trip would be had by all." This attention to feelings, attitudes, and spirit was refreshing.

8. Nearly all the cases cited were successfully mediated. While less than lo percent are unsuccessful, it was a fundamental principle of mediation that recourse to the court system was

available at any time and the parties could choose to avoid mediation altogether. In one unsuccessful case that was cited to us, the injured party wanted more in monetary damages than the party at fault was willing to pay and recovered a larger amount by a court action. Many commercial disputes end up in court, or are unsuccessfully mediated—in part because there is some law-testing taking place and the amounts in controversy are more considerable.

By way of contrast and to point out what happens in unsuccessful mediations, it is useful to examine how civil trials were conducted in China. According to an article in the February 13, 1984, *Beijing Review*, between 1980 and 1982, over 1.6 million civil suits were tried at first hearing; 100,000 went on to second hearing, and 23,000 were appealed. The percentage of civil disputes ran at 53 percent in 1977, 67.2 percent in 1978, 74.4 percent in 1981, and 76.1 percent in 1982. There was an increase in the number of cases relating to foreign trade, from joint ventures to property loss, insurance, and copyrights, and an increasing number dealing with support of elderly people and fighting, but fewer dealing with marriage and inheritance. From 60–70 percent of civil cases were said to be resolved by mediation—about 11 percent fewer than were resolved by neighborhood mediation committees.

In stark contrast to the simplicity and unpretentious directness of neighborhood and workplace mediations, I observed a civil trial with uniformed judges, an elevated bench, and silver-tongued counsel. A widow attempted to sell her house to a co-worker. The contract was signed, the money was paid, but the sale was not registered with the government department in charge of such matters. Within a few days, the seller's daughter discovered the sale and protested. As the husband had died without a will, the property under Chinese law went equally to the widow and any surviving children.

The widow contacted the buyer, attempted to return the purchase price with interest and rescind the sale, but he refused, saying she had agreed and should be bound by her contract. She claimed she had not known the house also belonged to her daughter, and when she found out it was illegal she immediately contacted the purchaser; and in any event, the sale had not been recorded and was therefore illegal.

Under China's Russo-European based "inquisitorial" system (as opposed to the U.S. "adversarial" system) the judges had already spent considerable time investigating the case and gave every appearance of having already made up their minds. Attorneys were allowed to cross-examine parties and witnesses, but written declarations were admitted without formal proof of unavailability, and counsel were permitted simply to comment. They argued back and forth, and then the judges announced they would try to mediate the dispute, even though previous efforts had failed. They clearly indicated to the purchaser that the law was not on his side and took a 15-minute recess.

While the mediation was being conducted, we were told by one of the judges that it would proceed according to three points: placing friendship first, endeavoring to find a better solution for everyone, and adhering to the facts and the law of private housing. The failure to register the sale was seen as decisive against the purchaser.

After court reconvened, to no one's surprise, it was announced that a mediated solution had been reached according to the principle of mutual respect, based on an agreed upon set of facts, which were summarized, and the law, which stated that the children also owned the house. It was therefore illegal for the mother to sell it, and the failure to register the sale also made it illegal. The parties agreed that the money should be returned with interest, the house should be surrendered to the original owners as soon as possible, but since it would be difficult to find another house, the purchaser was allowed to remain in the house for six months rent-free.

The trial took place within five to eight months of filing, as highest priority is given to pension cases involving the elderly. It was reported that 80-90 percent of all cases referred to mediation by courts were successfully mediated. No mention was made during the trial, so far as we were informed, of legal terms such as bona fide purchaser without notice, rebuttable presumption based on recordation, capacity to contract, ministerial duties, hearsay evidence, or the like. The law seemed simple and clear, though the parties did not appear to be focused on it, except as an afterthought. The pomp was more than circumstantial, and the total effect was as intimidating as any courtroom in the West, with coercive force plainly in evidence.

# THE CHINESE MODEL

Morality, values, ethics, and politics all seem vague and indefinable in the West, or are given formal definitions that avoid any substantive debate over meaning. In China, normative interventions in mediation are direct, open, and legitimate. They are considered the responsibility of everyone and are shared throughout society. They are openly discussed in settling disputes, so that principles and values will inform and clarify the results and help the parties arrive at a successful solution. Far from being the province of philosophers or intellectuals, the criteria for a good family seem to be understood broadly, and like common sense to the parties.

China, though increasingly prosperous, was still desperately poor at the time of my visit, painfully overcrowded, and technologically so backward that a trip there felt like a journey to the 19th century or earlier. Yet there was a quiet dignity, an honesty, and an affection that were quite remarkable, from the quiet, humble face of a factory manager to the dignity of a hospitalized prisoner, or the admiring applause of a group of schizophrenic patients.

Loving kindness, a care for others' feelings, a sense of refusal to quit or give up on anyone, were abundant in the mediations in China, producing a profoundly effective, and broadly popular form of social intervention. The values of cooperation, individual responsibility for social improvement, denigration of selfish advancement at the expense of others, unity, harmony, mutual respect and trust, were not just words but real elements in China's dispute resolution system.

At a time when values and ethics in the West seem in eclipse, when hypocrisy and pretense appear so endemic; when "me first," "look out for number one," and "I'm all right" values often defeat the sense that each of us is responsible not only for our own lives, but for those of others, this sense that China created something different, which may well be exaggerated, is nonetheless intriguing. The direction is right, the sentiment is positive, and the result is one we would do well to examine with an eye to how we might encourage similar processes here.

Mediation was developed in China over several thousand years. It was promoted by Confucius and the imperial court, and then implemented by the Fourth and Eighth Route Armies under Mao. It was Mao's theory of non-antagonistic contradictions that gave the go-ahead to advance mediation as the acceptable method of handling "contradictions among the people." Mediation may be the most advanced form of pacification and social control since bread and circuses (or their modern equivalent—television), but it is also an effort to return control over disputes to the people who created them.

Mediation is not obviously oppressive because it is taking place in a socialist environment. If anything, mediation evidences significant gains in democratic participation, social cooperation, and individual rights, and suggests that considerable personal autonomy must nonetheless have existed within the Chinese socialist system. No social system tolerates serious antipathy to its basic principles, or open disregard for its rules, and liberty within cannot be fully measured by examining the rights of those who find themselves outside it. There is no doubt that China would grant swift justice to anyone who challenged its political administration without following established rules, but in this respect it is unexceptional among the world's nations. Where it *was* exceptional was in the national use of locally based and democratically elected mediators who intervened instantly to minimize and resolve conflicts, and who brought to that process a sense of social and political direction, ethics, and values, and a sense of social responsibility that increased its effectiveness and prevented minor disputes from escalating into major ones.

Mediation saved China what must be conservatively estimated at millions of dollars annually in reduced medical costs, property damage, court salaries, attorney fees, imprisonments, lost wages and tax revenues, declining productivity, and similar costs that are all by-products of unresolved social conflict. There is no reason to suppose the West could not benefit from a similar program.

## LESSONS FOR U.S. MEDIATORS

It would be pointless and rather silly to suggest that other countries simply copy the Chinese model. Several proposals may be made for mediators in many nations, however, based on the Chinese experience, including these:

1. *Electing Neighborhood Mediators:* Everyone admits local government is a good idea. The problem is often that it is not local enough. Yet there is no reason why cities could not be subdivided into tracts, then into blocks or neighborhoods in

which residents could elect conflict resolution committees to represent their neighborhood's interests, prevent threats to security, and mediate disputes between neighbors and family members.

2. *Workplace Committees*: There is no reason why every organization and institution could not elect mediation committees to resolve workplace disputes. Unions represent a declining percentage of U.S. employees in disputes with management, but rarely use grievance mediation or intervene in fights between their members. In most cases, employee-employer disputes can be resolved far more rapidly by mediation, without violence or termination. Employee-employee disputes should all be mediated, and only later arbitrated. This would lead to far greater harmony and productivity, fewer terminations and disciplinary actions, less expense, and more rapid resolutions. Mediation can be used for all employees, including those who are unprotected by union contracts or civil service.

3. *Rapid Intervention Teams*: Mediators in many areas could be organized, on call, and available for immediate crisis interventions on a rotating basis.

4. *Mediating By Walking Around*: Mediators should consider not confining their work to their offices, but going out directly to investigate the causes of disputes. Where invited, they could become more active in discovering facts, rather than waiting for them to be presented by the parties.

5. *Values in Mediation*: Mediators should openly acknowledge their values and belief systems. To say that one is apolitical or without values is simply to say that one's politics or values are not discordant with those of the dominant group. While disagreements may occur, discussion and debate over values and politics would transform the mediation process, making values concerns legitimate and explicit. It would help turn false consensus into honest disagreements, stasis into growth, and manipulation into genuine discussions. The intrinsic nature of dispute resolution automatically

promotes values of consensual decision-making, equality, mutual respect, minimization of interpersonal violence, stability in relationships, compassion and kindness to others, compromise, honesty in expressing needs, and democratic decision-making. Rather than being hidden and denied, values among mediators should be admitted and discussed openly. Disagreements over values will at least reveal areas in which, as a society, we should focus our attention, and in which, as mediators, we should respect opposing points of view. We should recognize that we *can* be "unbiased" and at the same time human; non-judgmental, yet have beliefs.

6. *Multi-Door Mediative Courthouses*: Courts could easily appoint professional mediators under conditions of confidentiality to settle disputes before and during every trial. Judges could be specially trained in mediation and interrupt court proceedings to refer cases to mediation whenever it may appear fruitful, no matter when that might be during a trial. Mediation could be introduced early in the legal system to reduce attorneys' fees and costs, and be mandatory for at least one session.

7. *Victim-Offender Mediation*: Mediation could be used far more extensively in criminal cases, where arrest is already a substantial punishment, through victim/offender mediations, sentencing circles, and restorative justice.

8. *Peer Prison and School Mediation*: Peer mediators could be selected in prisons, schools, and similar institutions to minimize interpersonal violence and resolve grievances.

9. *Cross-Cultural Conflict Competency*: More effort could be made to learn from other countries' conflict cultures and experiences, while removing the cultural biases and technological smugness we in the West often display toward poorer nations' achievements.

10. *Mediator Internationalism*: In spite of our many differences, conflicts are human and similar worldwide. Therefore, mediators can join forces globally to share techniques and ideas and work together in international teams to assist each

other in developing our capacity to resolve conflicts without being restricted by national borders or political boundaries.

In relation to our culture and history, our traditions, social values, and political goals, these lessons may allow us to expand the effectiveness of our mediation systems internationally and dramatically reduce the social and economic costs of conflict.

# CHAPTER 12

# THE DANCE OF OPPOSITES

## Dialectics, Philosophy, and Dispute Resolution

*Wherever there is light, there is shadow; wherever there is length, there is shortness; wherever there is white, there is black. Just like these, as the self-nature of things cannot exist alone, they are called non-substantial.*

~ Buddha ~

*The problem and the means for its solution arise simultaneously.*

~ Karl Marx ~

*The opposite of a correct statement is a false statement. But the opposite of a profound truth may well be another profound truth.*

~ Neils Bohr ~

I T IS AXIOMATIC THAT opposition is essential to conflict. Without polarization, antithesis, contradiction and antagonism, there is merely disagreement, which lacks the personal hostility and ill will, the distrust and antipathy, the energy of personal antagonism, and the negative emotional experiences that are indispensable to conflict.

Our focus as mediators is on overcoming these sources of conflict, bridging the gaps, searching for commonalities, quieting negative emotions, and unifying the disparate interests that draw people into more effective communications, negotiations, and relationships. In doing so, we have spent considerable time and energy over the last several decades trying to understand the sources and dynamics of conflict, and developing interventions and methods that enable people, often with great success, to settle and resolve their disputes.

But we have spent considerably less time seeking to understand the abstract, formal characteristics and laws of motion of opposition itself, discovering what all antagonisms have in common, or analyzing the characteristics of contradictory phenomena in order to discover better ways of transforming and transcending them, turning them in a synergistic direction, and transmuting them into something new.

As a result, we have not been focused on learning from a number of highly developed, widely disparate bodies of thought and experience regarding the nature of oppositional phenomena. These range from ancient wisdom texts such as Daoism and Zen koans, to a variety of dialectical philosophies, to core principles in math and physics. Each of these bodies of thought and experience can add to the skill of our interventions, offer insights into the interplay of opposites in mediation practice, assist us in developing a better understanding of the forms of opposition without regard to their content, and illuminate the complex ways that divergent forces polarize and combine.

By considering the abstract nature of conflicts in general and attempting to derive the rules of contradiction and laws of motion of unity and opposition from first principles *without* regard to their subject matter or issues in any particular dispute, we will be able to strip individual conflicts down to their essence and not be diverted by superficialities or specifics.

This will require us to investigate and mine a variety of dialectical traditions for insights without regard to their religious, political, philosophical, or scientific content, in order to transform their insights into deeper truths about the nature of conflict and lead us to more profound and effective methods of resolution.

## WHAT IS DIALECTICS?

Dialectics, as I view it, is a set of insights, theories, and understandings regarding the tensions and interactions between conflicting ideas or forces. It includes the nature and forms of opposition, the rules for combining inverses or opposites, the movements typical of contradictory phenomena, and the different ways of shifting, shaping, transforming, resolving, synthesizing, and transcending conflicts.

Together, this body of knowledge can be thought of as the dance of opposites, or referred to simply as dialectics or dialectical philosophy. Together, this set of ideas rests on an assumption that regards unity and opposition as inextricably linked and views the interplay of opposites, including thesis and antithesis, form and content, emergence and cessation, as pointing in the direction of a taxonomy of combinations, that is, of potential syntheses and transformations, synergistic and emergent phenomena, and personal and organizational transcendence.

It is possible for us to identify within the purview, even of abstract religious, philosophical, political, and scientific traditions, not only a sophisticated set of analytical tools that can be adapted and applied to the practice of mediation, but an inescapable element of *action* that describes ways of developing practical applications and altering these phenomena in fundamental ways.

Dialectics is therefore, as Karl Marx recognized early in his life, not only a philosophical device that is useful for understanding the world, but also a method of changing it. My object in initiating this brief examination of dialectical thought is to locate within insight traditions and philosophical analysis, as well as within nature and mathematics, improved ways of mediating and negotiating; in short, to learn through the laws of opposition how we might resolve conflicts more effectively and become better able to transform and transcend them.

## FOUR STREAMS OF DIALECTICAL THOUGHT

Over the course of several centuries, many widely divergent thinkers have developed important ideas regarding the nature of oppositional dynamics. These, it seems to me, fit into the following historical categories:

1. *Spiritual dialectics*, as represented by the writings and practices of Taoism, Confucianism, and Buddhism;

2. *Philosophical dialectics,* as represented by the dialogues of Socrates, the writings of Aristotle, Democritus, and others, and more recently in the explicitly dialectical philosophies of Hegel, Fichte and Marx;

3. *Mathematical and scientific dialectics,* as represented in mathematical and scientific discoveries from ancient times to the present, from elementary number theory to complex particle interactions in physics and the science of chaos and symmetry;

4. *Conflict resolution dialectics*, as represented by the theory and practice of mediation, collaborative negotiation, dialogue, and allied dispute resolution techniques, all of which seek to ameliorate human hostilities through a variety of conflict resolution practices.

It is not within my expertise or purview to develop each of these topics in detail. Instead, I will search for what I consider the most significant contributions among the first three, the places where they overlap and reinforce each other, and attempt to introduce some fresh sources of understanding of the forms of opposition and their evolution that may be relevant to the practical experience of mediators, negotiators and conflict resolvers. To begin, it will be useful to briefly summarize the essential contributions to dialectical methodology in each of these areas.

# SPIRITUAL DIALECTICS

By spiritual dialectics, I refer principally to a number of classical Taoist and Buddhist "pre-philosophical" writings that describe the inner life and ways of experiencing the world, and point toward wisdom, insight, awareness, illumination, and enlightenment.

In Taoism and Buddhism, the universe is seen as consisting entirely of opposites. Lao-tse writes, for example, in the Tao te Ching:

> When people see some things as beautiful,
>
> other things become ugly.
>
> When people see some things as good,
>
> other things become bad.

And again, in a more practical vein,

> He who stands on tiptoe
>
> doesn't stand firm.
>
> He who rushes ahead
>
> doesn't go far.
>
> He who tries to shine
>
> dims his own light.
>
> He who defines himself
>
> can't know who he really is.
>
> He who has power over others
>
> can't empower himself.
>
> He who clings to his work
>
> will create nothing that endures.

These examples of opposition in ancient wisdom traditions are always paired, defining a complex, contradictory, paradoxical reality that always contains two opposing truths. It is necessary, therefore, in the words of Lao Tse, for us to ...

> Take time to listen to what is said without words,
>
> to obey the law too subtle to be written,
>
> to worship the unnamable and to embrace the unformed.

In conflict resolution, this translates into recognizing as mediators that what people in conflict say to each other is not their deepest truth, and that between "good" and "evil," "this" and "that," or what is sometimes referred to as "the ten thousand things," there is a place of unity that exists simultaneously within, around, and between these opposites.

In the ancient Chinese manual for living, the I Ching, or Book of Changes, the following advice is offered to those who are in conflict:

Conflict develops when one feels [oneself]
to be in the right
and runs into opposition.
If one is not convinced of being in the right,
opposition leads to craftiness
or high-handed encroachment
but not to open conflict.
If a man is entangled in a conflict,
his only solution lies in being
so clear-headed and inwardly strong
that he is always ready to come to terms
by meeting the opponent halfway.
To carry on the conflict to the bitter end
has evil effects
even when one is in the right
because the enmity is then perpetuated.

This attitude toward internal and interpersonal conflict reaches its highest level in a variety of Buddhist practices that focus on compassion, loving-kindness, gratitude, tolerance, and patience. For example, the Dalai Lama advises people to be thankful for their enemies for giving them the opportunity to practice these skills:

Now, there are many, many people in the world, but relatively few with whom we interact, and even fewer who cause us problems. So, when you come across such a chance for practicing patience and tolerance, you should treat it with gratitude. It is rare. Just as having unexpectedly found a treasure in your own house, you should be happy and grateful to your enemy for providing that precious opportunity.

An example of this practice, especially useful in conflict resolution, is offered in this short anonymous Zen haiku:

When the quarrel over water
reaches its highest pitch

—a sudden rain.

Or the following poem:

> Now that my house has fallen down
>
> I have a much better view of the moon.

Buddhism, Taoism and similar wisdom traditions share a recognition that paradox and contradiction are not occasional or accidental, but the essence of things, and it is through their combination that higher forms may be achieved. I-tuan writes, for example: "Speech is blasphemy, silence a lie. Above speech and silence there is a way out."

In the second century, the Buddhist monk Nagarjuna described the realization that points toward the way out, and summarized the expressly paradoxical Buddhist philosophy of opposition:

> Anything is either true,
>
> Or not true,
>
> Or both true and not true,
>
> Or neither true nor not true;
>
> This is the Buddda's teaching.

In relation to dialectical philosophy, these wisdom traditions contributed, among other ideas, the following three essential principles that we can regard as forming the fundamental theory of dialectics:

1. The Universality of Opposition: All things exist and arise as opposites. This is referred to in Buddhism as "dependent origination" or "mutual arising."

2. The Interpenetration of Opposites: All opposites contain each other, as in the yin/yang symbol, so that there is always a little bit of good in every evil, and vice versa.

3. The Transience of All Things: Everything changes and change is constant. This is commonly known in Buddhism as "impermanence."

The application of these principles to internal and interpersonal conflict can be seen as giving rise not only to the idea of nonviolence, but to the Four Noble Truths of Buddhism: the truth of suffering, the origin of suffering, the cessation of suffering, and the path leading to the cessation of suffering, all of which can be identified in analogous forms within the entirely secular practice of mediation, as described earlier in the chapter on mediation and meditation.

A simpler approach to conflict resolution within this tradition can be found in the writings of the extraordinary, unparalleled Sufi poet Rumi, who poignantly and beautifully reminds us how we might behave in conflict:

> if your beloved
> has the life of a fire
> step in now and burn along
> in a night full of
> suffering and darkness
> be a candle spreading light till dawn
> stop this useless
> argument and disharmony
> show your sweetness and accord
> even if you feel
> torn to pieces
> sew yourself new clothes
> your body and soul
> will surely feel the joy
> when you simply go along
> learn this lesson from
> lute tambourine and trumpet
> learn the harmony of the musicians
> if one is playing a wrong note
> even among twenty
> others will stray out of tune
> don't say what is the use
> of me alone being peaceful
> when everyone is fighting
> you're not one
> you're a thousand
> just light your lantern
> since one live flame
> is better than
> a thousand dead souls

There is also a considerable body of dialectical wisdom in the Mishnah Torah, the New Testament, and especially the Gnostic gospels, and the

Koran, each of which invites research and elaboration. To cite just one example from this vast literature with great relevance for mediators, Jesus is alleged to have said in the Gospel According to Thomas in the Nag Hammadi Library, as cited by Elaine Pagels:

> If you bring forth what is within you, what you bring forth
> will save you. If you do not bring forth what is within you,
> what you do not bring forth will destroy you.

In all the wisdom traditions, internal and external conflicts are viewed as linked, causing those who have not paid attention to their own spiritual growth and development to behave in ways that are destructive to themselves and to others.

## PHILOSOPHICAL DIALECTICS

Philosophical dialectics emerged in its modern form in ancient Athens, where its principal goal was the discovery of truth through dialogue, or "talking between" opposite views. In the modern world, "dialectics" is more frequently used to describe Marxist political philosophy, or to suggest manipulation, sophistry and deception, but in classical Greek philosophy, it was used to describe the interplay of opposites, albeit in a variety of different ways, including:

- As a method of argument in Socratic dialogue (Plato);
- As a technique of disputation and refutation in debate and eloquence in conversation (Cicero);
- As a way of systematically evaluating definitions in natural philosophy (Aristotle);
- As an approach to disputing mathematical continuity (Zeno);
- As a method of formal logic (the Stoics);
- As an analysis of change (Heraclitus);
- As a means of mathematical proof and analysis (Euclid and Archimedes).

Greek dialectics included several key notions that continued to inform philosophical discourse, for example, the philosophy attributed to Heraclites, that change is eternal and endemic; to Socrates, that truth emerges out of contradiction; and to Zeno, that continuity and discontinuity in mathematics lead to contradictory outcomes that defy rational explanation.

Dialectics were also limited and defined by the Greeks, as in Aristotle's *Logic*, which established three fundamental propositions or laws:

1. The Law of Identity: "... every thing is the same with itself and different from another." This is essentially the same as the principle of the universality of opposition in Taoism and Buddhism.

2. The Law of Non-Contradiction: "... one cannot say of something that it is and that it is not in the same respect and at the same time." This is the opposite of the ancient principle of the interpenetration of opposites. It is possible, for example, to say of someone that they are intelligent and unintelligent; profound and ridiculous; good and bad at the same time.

3. The Law of the Excluded Middle: "... there cannot be an intermediate between contradictories, but of one subject we must either affirm or deny any one predicate. ... To say of what is that it is not, or of what is not that it is, is false, while to say of what is that it is, and of what is not that it is not, is true; so that he who says of anything that it is, or that it is not, will say either what is true or what is false ..."

It is this third law that gives us the greatest difficulty, not only in conflict resolution where it is manifestly untrue, as people are often midway between right and wrong at the same time; but in Buddhist and Taoist philosophy and dialectics generally, where it is possible for many things to be both true and untrue at the same time.

In more modern times, the Copenhagen Interpretation of quantum mechanics contradicts this view by defining elementary particles as waves and particles at the same time, or as "entangled," or as having "superposition," or as neither and both simultaneously, until they are measured.

Clearly, there are situations in which the middle is excluded. This is true, for example, in mathematics where two is two and not four, or in set theory, where something is either a member of a set or it is not, and there is no in-between state. Yet it is easy to tie this assumption in a knot by presenting it with a paradox, as in the classic example offered by the Cretan philosopher Epimenides, who is reported to have stated, "All

Cretans are liars." Yet it is clear that if the statement is true then it must be false, and if it is false then it must be true. A similar example was given by mathematician Bertrand Russell, in what is known as "Russell's paradox," which defines R as the set of all sets that are not members of themselves. If R is not a member of itself, then by definition it must contain itself, and if it contains itself then it contradicts its own definition. A similar paradox formed the basis for Kurt Godel's famous "incompleteness theorem" in mathematics.

It is possible, however, to redefine the law of the excluded middle as an argument against simply merging, or mixing up truths, or compromising them, as by adding opposites together and dividing their sum by two, without any synthesis or creative search for higher order possibilities. This approach in mediation, often born of a fear of opposition, seeks a middle ground that in fact denies the truth of both sides and seeks settlement for the sake of settlement, rather than struggling through the opposition of the parties to discover deeper or higher orders of truth.

What is most important for us as mediators is to recognize that conflicts often reflect multiple truths, even those that contradict each other, suggesting the possibility that a higher order of truth could emerge in dialogue through new ways of thinking about the problem, or emergent ideas, or syntheses, and that all conflicts in fact are gateways to a greater, far more subtle and nuanced truth, which is the truth of both/and, rather than either/or.

There are many examples in life of non-excluded middles, but the easiest to explain and most relevant for our purposes appear in mediation: which party's story is true and which is false? In reality, both stories are true, and both are false at the same time—true because they express one person's experience, and false because they do not also express the other person's experience.

Perhaps it was in order to overcome this and other logical difficulties that Immanuel Kant invented the term "transcendental dialectic" to describe the idea that it is possible to use philosophical principles to speculate beyond the bounds of any given phenomena or experience and to transcend or rise above the somewhat trivial problem of contradictory phenomena. However, it was Georg Wilhelm Friedrich Hegel, rather than Kant, who fully developed this idea and turned it into the modern dialectical method.

What is known today as the "Hegelian dialectic," (which Hegel attributed to Kant but was actually developed by Johann Gottlieb Fichte and used in a different form by Hegel) can be found in several interrelated ideas, theories, and formulations. Briefly, the first begins with movement from an "Abstract" *thesis*, to a "Negative" mediating *antithesis*, to an "Absolute" *synthesis* that "negates the negation," overcomes the negative nature of the initial proposition, raises it to a higher level, and re-initiates the process.

By negation of the negation, Hegel imagined that things are only what they are in their relation to "other" things that are different from themselves, and through their negation incorporate these others into themselves. This dialectical movement integrates two elements that negate each other, a Thing and an Other. In the negation of the negation, "something becomes its other; this other is itself something; therefore it likewise becomes an other, and so on ad infinitum."

In *The Science of Logic*, to simplify, Hegel elaborated a dialectic that moved from Being or existence, to Nothing or non-existence, to Becoming, which combined being and non-being in a new, complex, higher order form. Thus, initially, existence is abstract pure Being, but pure Being is the same as Nothing, so everything that comes into being (i.e., is born) returns to nothing (i.e., dies), and as a result, Being and Nothing unite or combine in the concrete form of Becoming.

Hegel used this dialectic to describe the whole of human history, which he saw as a dialectic of being, proceeding from slavery to its highest form in the modern German state. Hegel also wrote about the transition from quantity into quality, using the phase transition of water turning into steam or ice as an illustration of how small quantitative changes can produce a deep alteration in the qualities of things, or how adding grains of wheat will gradually create a pile.

Hegel described the movement from abstract to negative to concrete as a "mediation," which Karl Marx found exactly backwards. Marx turned Hegel's abstract dialectic into highly useful instrument for analyzing social, economic and political ideas, but since it was idealistic and mystical, had to be done by standing it on its head:

> The mystification which dialectic suffers in Hegel's hands, by no means prevents him from being the first to present its general form of working in a comprehensive and conscious manner. With him it is standing on its head. It must be turned right side up again, if you would discover the rational kernel within the mystical shell.

> My dialectic method is not only different from the Hegelian, but is its direct opposite. To Hegel, the life-process of the human brain, i.e. the process of thinking, which, under the name of 'the Idea', he even transforms into an independent subject, is the demiurgos of the real world, and the real world is only the external, phenomenal form of 'the Idea'. With me, on the contrary, the ideal is nothing else than the material world reflected by the human mind, and translated into forms of thought.

Dialectics, for Marx, always expressed a transformational potential and a possibility that nature and society could evolve to higher levels of order. Marx followed Hegel in applying dialectics to history and politics, but came to a radically different conclusion. For example, consider his use of dialectical technique in his analysis of the relationship between private property and communism:

> [C]ommunism is the positive expression of the abolition of private property, and in the first place of universal private property... [T]he positive supersession of private property, i.e., the sensuous appropriation of the human essence and of human life, of objective man and of human creations, by and for man, should not be taken only in the sense of immediate, exclusive enjoyment, or only in the sense of possession or having.

> Private property has made us so stupid and partial that an object is only ours when we have it, when it exists for us as capital or when it is directly eaten, drunk, worn,

inhabited, etc., in short, utilized in some way; although private property itself only conceives these various forms of possession as means of life, and the life for which they serve as means is the life of private property—labor and the creation of capital.

Thus all the physical and intellectual senses have been replaced by the simple alienation of all these senses; the sense of having. The human being had to be reduced to this absolute poverty in order to be able to give birth to all his inner wealth ...

The supersession of private property is therefore the complete emancipation of all the human qualities and senses. It is this emancipation because these qualities and senses have become human, from the subjective as well as the objective point of view. The eye has become a human eye when its object has become a human, social object, created by man and destined for him... Need and enjoyment have thus lost their egoistic character, and nature has lost its mere utility by the fact that its utilization has become human utilization."

What is important for mediators in this passage, from the point of view of dialectical methodology, is the idea of a positive negation that leads to supersession and emancipation through a transformational synthesis or resolution of antagonistic social relations. In mediation, the idea of positively reframing otherwise negative emotions, antagonistic positions, and other oppositional statements has proven quite useful, as William Ury demonstrates in his book, *The Power of a Positive No*, which offers a number of useful ways of shifting negative communications in a positive direction during negotiations.

## TRANSFORMATIONAL AND NON-TRANSFORMATIONAL SYNTHESES

More theoretically, it is possible for us to distinguish syntheses that are additive or non-transformational from those that are multiplicative or transformational in any oppositional system. If we consider, for example, the relationship between order and anarchy, or centralization and decentralization in any system, be it familial, organizational, or societal, we can derive the following diagram, based loosely on the Hegelian dialectic:

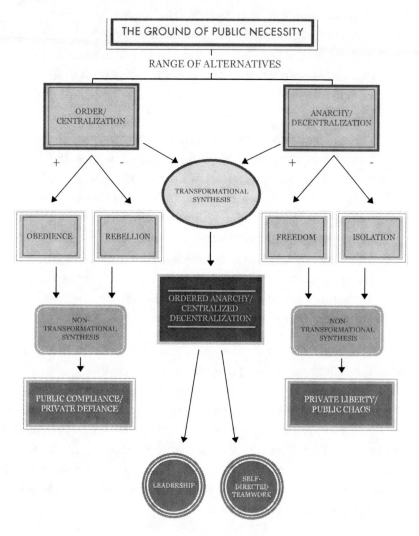

In this example, a transformational synthesis is one that produces outcomes that are qualitatively new and different, giving rise to higher order, more complex, interdependent, collaborative, and emergent solutions that could not have been imagined or achieved simply by placing opposites in polarized juxtaposition or adding them together. Instead, their creative reformulation results from integration, re-imagination, and combined use of complexity and opposition.

In summary, a part of what philosophical dialectics, as developed by Kant, Hegel, Fichte, Marx and others, contributed to the basic laws of opposition, in addition to reaffirming the three essential contributions derived from ancient wisdom traditions, are the following core ideas:

1.  The Movement toward Synthesis: There is a movement from thesis to antithesis to synthesis, which represents a higher, more complex, and progressive form of opposition.

2.  The Unity of Opposites: While opposites are polarized in appearance, they are unified in essence. Thus, there is a unity of sameness and difference, continuity and change, inner and outer, good and evil, etc.

3.  The Transition from Quantitative to Qualitative Change: There is a sudden transition from minor, incremental changes to major, systemic ones, introducing the ideas of revolution and transformation.

4.  The Possibility of Non-Transformational Synthesis: Opposites can be combined in non-transformational ways, as by adding or averaging them, as through compromise. Thus, hot water and cold water can be combined to create lukewarm water.

5.  The Possibility of Transformational Synthesis: Opposites can also be combined in transformational ways, as by creatively merging or multiplying them, as through collaboration, thereby producing something qualitatively new. Thus, water can be combined with flour, yeast, and heat to create bread, which is a fundamentally different quality from all of its constituent elements.

6.  The Application of Dialectics to Economic, Social, and Political Forces: The dialectics of opposition apply not just to nature, but to economic and social phenomena as well, including social conflict.

# MATHEMATICAL AND SCIENTIFIC DIALECTICS

In its purest form, dialectical philosophy arises directly from the laws of mathematics, which describe the interactions of symbols and operations that represent natural phenomena in their simplest and most abstract formulations. As a result of the development of this symbolic formalism and the discovery/invention of positive and negative numbers, entirely new number systems were created, including natural numbers, rational numbers, integers, transcendental numbers, imaginary and complex numbers, entire sets of infinite numbers, and other fascinating entities, together with the development of complex operations to differentiate and integrate them.

More deeply, it is possible to find in the mathematics of calculus, symmetry groups, matrices, topology, and similar fields, a variety of operations that can be performed on opposites whose consequences can be felt all the way from quantum interactions to grand unified theories, black holes, vacuum space, and the most advanced forms of string theory and quantum gravity in physics.

The basic rules regarding mathematical operations provide, for example, multiple ways to negate an outcome by conducting simple inverse operations, but more important for our purposes was the development of a rich variety of methods for transforming and solving algebraic equations. Many of these methods, like adding, subtracting, multiplying, and dividing both sides of an equation by the same number, simplifying numerical expressions, and using imaginary numbers represented by the square root of minus one to solve higher order equations, can be analogized to mediation interventions that treat conflicts as analogous to equations and solutions as unknowns, or as a combination of real and imaginary constituents.

A practical example is the Poisson distribution formula, which relates the probability of random phenomena through a single elegant formula, including the deaths of cavalrymen from horse kicks, the number of radioactive decays, cancer clusters, tornado touchdowns, mutations in DNA, Web server hits, cars arriving at a traffic light, goals in sports by competing teams, and the probability of wars breaking out, among others.

Another example is the idea of mathematical dimensions, which can be defined either as the number of coordinates needed to locate any point inside a given space, or as the number of ways one can move, or as "degrees of freedom." It is possible to move from a lower to a higher dimension simply by dragging its coordinates 90 degrees in a brand new direction. This new, "orthogonal" direction can be analogized to mediation, where impasse may be avoided by creating a new direction for adversarial or conflicted conversations to flow in. [For more on dimensions, see discussion in chapter 10.]

Within the natural sciences, dialectical principles can be found in an immense variety of forms, raising a question as to whether the forms of opposition are not in fact representative of higher truths about the natural world. Ralph Waldo Emerson, from the point of view of the mid 19th century, described the relationship between dialectics and the natural sciences in this way:

> As there is a science of stars, called astronomy; a science of quantities, called mathematics; a science of qualities, called chemistry; so there is a science of sciences—I call it Dialectic—which is the intellect discriminating the false and the true.

Physicist Neils Bohr followed this tradition describing many of the paradoxes of quantum physics with the highly useful dialectical phrase: complementarity, which he defined as "a great truth whose opposite is also a great truth." By this he made reference, for example, to the truth that electrons are particles, together with the truth that they are waves; the truth that they occupy a fixed position in time and space, alongside the equal truth that possess a momentum, and the synthesized truth that, on a small enough scale, these become collectively uncertain.

Some recent work in quantum mechanics suggests that even Bohr did not go far enough in capturing "quantum weirdness," since elementary particles do not have fixed or defined positions in space or time, and waves display a spectrum of probabilities, so that all we are left with is relations and properties, whose dialectical interactions create things.

While the principles of dialectics were originally based on observations of nature, this connection has largely been lost. Today, science is undergoing a revolution in its understanding of natural phenomena, yet there has been little philosophical generalization of this new scientific knowledge in terms of the dialectical method. It is exceptional, for example, to find within dialectical philosophy today, a discussion of the philosophical significance even of the basic physical principles of general and special relativity, quantum mechanics, elementary particle physics, cybernetics, chaos, fractals, dimensionality, etc., and an analysis of their implications for the "laws of motion" of society, politics and conflict resolution.

To illustrate, a considerable body of physics is devoted to the problem of wave propagation, which can be discerned in particles of light, sound, magma under the Earth's crust, even probability. Scientists have learned a great deal about the mathematics of wave propagation and the geometric patterns that are created by interference. But what about wave phenomena in human behavior, in consciousness, dispute resolution, and other social, economic, and political processes? Has wave/particle duality any corollaries in social psychology? Would it be useful to regard parties in conflict as somehow "entangled," by analogy with quantum physics where particles lose their individuality to the larger system that entangles them? Are there laws of conflict behavior that can be derived from catastrophe formulas in mathematics? Does a Heisenberg uncertainty principle express limits that operate by analogy in mediation?

This is not to suggest that there is a one-to-one correlation between discoveries in the physical sciences and various aspects of conflict or social behavior. Rather, it is that the original basis for dialectics in philosophy was the application of scientific or mathematical understanding to human activity, and while science has changed paradigmatically in many areas, dialectical philosophy has not always continued to learn from science, or followed closely enough behind.

It is therefore possible for us, on this basis, to suggest as metaphors, based on dialectical principles, that the progress of dialectical understanding in dispute resolution, as well as in science, can be thought of as helical rather than linear; that the patterns of opposition in dialectical philosophy can be seen to correspond to fractals, or a meander, or a "drunkard's walk" in mathematics; and that conflicts can be regarded as analogous to infinite quantities that can only be described in finite terms.

## THE DIALECTICS OF CHAOS

A useful analogy for mediators to consider can be drawn from the field of "chaos." The physics of dynamic systems suggest that as a system moves farther from equilibrium, bifurcations start to occur, indicating that the system is undergoing a rapid change, and that a phase transition from one state to another may be beginning. As the phase transition approaches, fluctuations become more powerful and unpredictable, driving the system forward.

Once a critical value is reached, new forms of self-organization begin to emerge as the system continues to bifurcate and degenerate into chaos. There is an inherent uncertainty about chaotic outcomes, which are "sensitively dependent on initial conditions." Yet under these conditions, small, ordinarily microscopic fluctuations can produce macroscopic results due to increased sensitivity during the phase transition, in ways that are completely unpredictable, yet follow deterministic patterns.

Using this process as an analogy, we can describe the ways that new structures and systems in a range of relationships start to self-organize during the chaos of conflict, are sensitively dependent on initial conditions and cannot be predicted or prepared for in advance. At the same time, during criticality, as the phase transition approaches, even minor interventions by the parties or the mediator can have a profound impact in creating new, emergent, and higher order forms of relationship and organization.

We can also apply these scientific ideas by analogy to dialectical philosophy itself, allowing the Hegelian movement from quantitative to qualitative change to be understood as a movement away from equilibrium and toward chaotic conflicts, leading to a phase transition to a higher level of understanding.

As opposed to Newtonian mechanical reductionism, which views the change from quantity to quality as inherently predictable, a modern abstraction of scientific categories that includes human behavior would require a recognition of the rules of chaos as impacting transitional states, and a focus on the probability of outcomes, rather than on their predictability.

In this way, the science of chaos reveals the presence of a dialectical relationship in nature between spontaneity and organization, chaos and equilibrium. The fact that spontaneous self-organization emerges in non-linear systems that are far from equilibrium where there is a high degree of feedback can help us understand the origins of social and interpersonal conflict and identify alternative approaches that might be taken to the crises they generate.

In similar ways, entropy and thermodynamics, evolution and adaptation, special and general relativity, quantum mechanics and a variety of other scientific ideas can be seen to reflect dialectical principles, and may find analogous application in conflict resolution, as well as in philosophy and politics. Not only may conflict resolution theory be enriched, as dialectics originally was, by scientific discovery, science may gain by identifying the general principles that describe oppositional dynamics and searching for applications to a variety of natural and social phenomena.

## SYMMETRIES AND CONFLICT

Another significant contribution made by math and science to dialectical methodology can be found in symmetry and the mathematics of symmetry groups. Another word for symmetry is invariance, meaning that a thing does not change in appearance, or vary as a result of its movement when compared with some element in its environment. In 1915 mathematician Emmy Noether discovered that for most varieties of physical symmetry there is a corresponding law of conservation.

Thus, energy is conserved when an action does not change with respect to *time*, and is therefore invariant, or appears the same, whether it is moving backward into the past or forward into the future. Momentum is conserved when an action does not vary in *space*, and looks the same whether it is moving up or down. Angular momentum is conserved when an action does not vary with *direction*, and appears the same whether it is spinning clockwise or counter-clockwise. Information is conserved when an action does not vary in *scale*, and looks the same whether it is small, medium, or large, etc..

Applying this metaphor, we can identify symmetries in conflict that represent a relational conservation, as for example, when a conflict appears the same regardless of its content, or the substantive issues people are fighting about. We might also identify a conservation of meaning, for example, when a conflict looks the same even when people switch sides in an argument; or a conservation of polarity, for example, when a conflict appears the same even after the issues people are arguing about have been settled.

## ENTROPY, CONFLICT, AND COMMUNICATION

Entropy, or the Second Law of Thermodynamics, is a measure of the amount of disorder or randomness in a system. Since work is required to create order, entropy is also a measure of how much of a system's energy is unavailable for work, including the work of ordering and the work of change. Entropy is a measure not only of the loss of energy due to random motion, but the loss of information as well.

When an isolated system makes a transition from one state to another, entropy always increases. A system cannot spontaneously become more ordered, but it can easily become more disordered. Work can produce "negative entropy," which results in disorder being transferred, "dissipated," or "exported" from the thing that is worked on to the work itself. When entropy is exported, a higher form of complexity and order can arise, giving rise to what is referred to as "emergent phenomena."

Because agreement is a more highly ordered state than conflict, it requires far greater energy to bring it into existence. Entropy predicts that, because there are many more ways and of being in conflict than there are of being in agreement, without any additional effort, it will always be easier for communication and relationships to break down and produce conflicts, than if will for communication and relationships to be successful and conflicts to be resolved.

One of the functions of language is data compression. The science of information tells us that to achieve accuracy, it is necessary to simplify communications, and that, to avoid mistakes and the confusion created by inevitable background noise, it is necessary to build in a certain amount of repetition or redundancy. Entropy in adversarial conflict communications can therefore be regarded as a kind of static that diminishes the integrity of the communications and distorts the integrity of messages for the receiver.

Because communications are organized and take effort to generate meaning, and because there are many more ways of expressing no meaning than of expressing a particular meaning, communications are easier to destroy than to create, and are vulnerable to entropic deterioration. This is especially true of conflict communications, which often turn intelligible messages into garbled, misunderstood, and unintelligible ones, creating dissonance between speakers or senders and listeners or receivers.

Negative entropy occurs where, for example, trust in a relationship allows incomplete, blurred or negative emotional messages to nonetheless be received positively and intact, perhaps because the listener or receiver is trusting and is therefore able to fill in the missing details, or recognize the real meaning and content of the communication in spite of its distortion. Redundancy, or the use of selective repetition to reinforce the elements that define the meaning of a communication, is an antidote to entropy. Successful conflict communications are therefore quite often redundant—i.e., repeated, summarized, and reassuring, perhaps by going over the same material to ensure that its meaning gets through.

Feedback, especially in its positive form, is also an antidote to entropy in communications. Certain forms of communication require little feedback, while others cannot succeed unless the sender is able to calibrate the distortion of the communication and its effect on the listener, and find ways to counter it. Feedback can also dramatically decrease the amount of entropy in subsequent communications, building trust over time that reduces the impact of entropy.

By analogy, we can see that entropy helps us explain how conflict results in the loss of socially important information regarding, for example, the human nature of our opponents; the potential usefulness of collaborative approaches to problem solving; what it is we really want or need from others; anomalies and defects in our family, organizational or social systems; our ability to accept responsibility for solutions; or our capacity to detect and prevent destructive conflicts before they occur.

In these ways, conflict resolution allows individuals, families, organizations, and societies to avoid the natural entropy and deterioration of their communications, preserve socially important information, adapt to changes in their environment, and reach higher levels of communication, relationship, development, and social order. At the same time, conflict resolution can protect against social entropy by dissipating the energy of conflict into more complex interactions and communications, learning processes, and higher levels of systemic unity and cohesiveness. Conflict resolution can therefore be regarded as a hedge against social entropy, and a means for translating the chaos of conflict into personal, relational and social evolution.

# THE EVOLUTION OF CONFLICT AND RESOLUTION

Another key scientific idea that contributes to our understanding of dialectics originates in Charles Darwin's idea of evolution based on natural selection. The combination of variation or diversity as a result of random genetic mutations; competitive oppositional pressure as a result of scarce environmental resources; selection based on sexual recombination; and advantages conferred as a result of social cooperation, combine to produce adaptations that can improve chances for survival or result in extinction.

Over time, this combination of opposite forces, of competition and cooperation, survival and extinction, isolation and combination, results in adaptations that produce more complex organisms capable of higher order functioning. In a similar way, conflicts within families, organizations and social systems can result in adaptations that strengthen the relationships between their members, or unresolved antagonisms that undermine and end them.

What is most important in the idea of evolution from the point of view of dialectical philosophy is the realization that oppositional forces can turn any system in a circle, or produce a spiral that moves the system upward or downward in its ability to function within a given environment, either advancing or retarding its development.

As a result of these developments in math and science, we can add to our list of dialectical principles at least the following main ideas:

1.  The Emergence of Equilibrium and Chaos: Each of these movements and shifts can take place in predictable patterns reflecting equilibrium, or chaotic and unpredictable patterns reflecting a sensitive dependence on initial conditions.

2.  The Symmetry and Conservation of Opposition: Opposition, antagonism, and contradiction reveal a variety of symmetries that are invariant under various forms of translation, reflecting a conservation of polarity.

3.  The Entropy of Conflict: The amount of disorder or randomness and therefore conflict in an oppositional system always increases, unless it is exported or ordered through work.

4.  The Evolution of Conflict and Resolution: Through the interaction of competition and cooperation, organisms and

systems are able to evolve from simple to more complex forms that experience higher forms of conflict and resolution, and adapt to their environments in new ways.

5. The Orthogonal Dimensionality of Transformational Syntheses: Transformational syntheses take place by shifting the dimensionality or "degree of freedom" of phenomena at right angles to their prior arrangement, or orthogonally. Thus, shifting a number system in a brand new direction, as with the invention of imaginary or complex numbers; or in mediation, altering a dialogue by shifting the conversation in a new direction, or increasing the degrees of freedom, or raising an issue to a higher power.

Clearly, these are not the only contributions to dialectical method that can be drawn from math and science, but they are illustrative of the range and kind of contributions that can be derived from the study of conflict and opposition in natural phenomena.

Indeed, the contributions of each of these areas to dialectical philosophy are so numerous, important and widespread that they are difficult to summarize briefly. Below, I have selected a few additional ideas that seem to me most likely to improve our understanding of how conflict and resolution might be organized, and help us identify a set of general principles that could lead to more advanced methods of resolving disputes. They are presented in my own words and in an order that is less logical or historical, let alone mathematical or scientific, than might be required to make them logically or philosophically rigorous. In essence, they include the following core ideas, in addition to those I have already stated:

## ADDITIONAL DIALECTICAL PRINCIPLES OR RULES OF OPPOSITION

1. The Movement from Unity to Differentiation: In the beginning, there is unity and change, which produces differentiation. Before differentiation, number and shape, one and many, conflict and resolution do not exist.

2. The Movement from Differentiation to Polarity: Differentiation gives rise to opposition, antagonism, contradiction, and

polarity. Once differentiation occurs, so do zero and one, space and time, existence and non-existence, light and dark, sound and silence, here and there, conflict and resolution.

3. The Differentiation of Form and Content: The presence of opposition, antagonism, contradiction, and polarity between phenomena produces tensions, conflicts, and vibrations between them. These generate energy that can be understood in relation to their form and their content, their quantity and their quality.

4. The Numeric Nature of Quantity: When phenomena are regarded solely from the point of view of their form or quantity, they assume an objective, extrinsic, numeric, or particulate shape. The laws, characteristics, and interactions that govern forms or quantities include those that apply to arithmetic, algebraic, geometric and topological operations.

5. The Wave-Like Nature of Quality: When phenomena are regarded solely from the point of view of their content or qualities, they assume a subjective, intrinsic, geometric, or wave-like form. The laws, characteristics, and interactions that govern content or qualities include those that apply to relationships, behaviors, properties, and waves.

6. The Negation or Cancelation of Opposites: If there is a quantity A, such as four, there must also be an opposite quantity B, such as negative four, which when added to the first negates and cancels it. In mathematics, this is the inverse, or "conjugate." If there is a quality A, such as hot, up, good or love, there must also be a quality B which is the opposite of A, such as cold, down, bad or hate, which when added to the first also negates and cancels it.

7. The Opposition of Contradiction and Complementarity: Opposites are either contradictory, in which case they become antitheses that conflict with or cancel each other; or complementary, in which case they express dual truths that add to or multiply each other.

8. The Forms of Contradiction and Complementarity: Complementary qualities can exist as A and B, A or B,

and neither A nor B. Quality A, however, does not exist independently without reference to quality B. Therefore, these qualities are opposites (two), and at the same time unified (one). In this case, they are entangled, and their individuality is exported to the system. Their simultaneous opposition and unification make them capable of combining to produce something new (three). To consider A or B without its opposite is to regard it narrowly, locally, reductively, and incompletely. To understand qualitative phenomena, it is necessary to simultaneously understand them both in their opposition and their unity.

9. The Integration of Oppositional States: Transformational syntheses do not simply combine, but integrate oppositional states in ways that can no longer be fully characterized by either of them alone. These new qualities can be described as transcendent, or "emergent phenomena."

10. The Emergence of Transcendence: Transformational syntheses result in transcendence, which occurs when their combination causes them to evolve to a higher state of complexity, so that new phenomena emerge and become independent, leaving behind their earlier antecedents.

11. The Movement from Non-transformational to Transformational Syntheses: Non-transformational syntheses may increase quantitatively or incrementally until they reach a phase transition, a point where their quantity achieves a new, emergent, qualitative dimension, and a transformational synthesis occurs that can result in transcendent outcomes.

## CONFLICT RESOLUTION AND DIALECTICS

We started with the idea that opposition is an essential element in every conflict, beginning with the opposition of Self and Other. Yet dialectical principles suggest that self and other are "complementarities," in Bohr's sense of the word, truths that cannot exist without each other, exactly in the way that front and back, top and bottom, good and evil, negative and positive oppose each other, yet are unimaginable without each other. The disappearance or transformation of one is automatically the disappearance and transformation of the other.

In dialectical reasoning, there cannot be a completely isolated Self, which does not exist without an Other; nor can the Self be defined without acknowledging the countless ways it has been shaped by others from conception to death. Higher order self-determination therefore does not consist of dividing these into neat little piles, but in finding synergy in the interplay and constantly fluctuating relationship between them. People interacting with each other *jointly* reveal the deeper places where each of their "separate" selves gets defined, invented, and transformed. Indeed, Self and Other continually inform and shape each other, and are the limits at which each begins to transform into the other, much as one begins going North at a certain point by heading further South. Instead of a purely personal self-identity and self-determination, mediation can be seen as the agent of a *collaborative* self-determination, revealing the places where "I" is transformed into "We."

As Mary Parker Follett pointed out in the 1920s, opposition and differences between self and other need to be regarded not as problems, but as fertile sources of enrichment and creativity:

> The basis of all cooperative activity is integrated diversity. ... What people often mean by getting rid of conflict is getting rid of diversity, and it is of the utmost importance that these should not be considered the same. We may wish to abolish conflict, but we cannot get rid of diversity. We must face life as it is and understand that diversity is its most essential feature ... Fear of difference is dread of life itself. It is possible to conceive conflict as not necessarily a wasteful outbreak of incompatibilities, but a normal process by which socially valuable differences register themselves for the enrichment of all concerned.

In their modern form, dialectics in conflict resolution can be regarded as a theory of the ways of transforming polarity into unity, and how mediators can turn two antagonistic, hostile, or contradictory ideas, forces, perspectives, or positions into one. We can imagine, for example, a number of theoretical ways of turning two opposing views into one, each with a conflict resolution analogue, for example, by:

- Selecting one and suppressing the other (power-based solutions);
- Accepting one and rejecting the other (rights-based solutions);
- Adding them together and dividing by two (compromise, non-transformational syntheses);
- Pretending they are actually one (denial);
- Selectively combining only parts of them (manipulation);
- Identifying one thing they both have in common (unification);
- Finding their lowest common denominator (minimal commonality);
- Agreeing on either, both, or a third option (consensus);
- Discovering where they intersect (triangulation);
- Discovering why they are important (interest-based solutions);
- Affirming them both as equally true (complementarity);
- Multiplying them together (transformational syntheses);
- Asking deeper, more profound or poignant underlying questions that do not have a single correct answer (transformation);
- Learning, evolving, and rising above the conflict (transcendence).

Clearly, if we wish to help parties move in their mediations from conflict suppression to resolution, transformation, and transcendence, considerable effort will be required to overcome the entropy in their communications and bring their opposing views into alignment, allowing us to use the energy of their opposition to identify new directions and design synergistic outcomes.

## ADDITIONAL WAYS OF APPLYING DIALECTICS IN CONFLICT RESOLUTION

Conflict resolution is dialectics as a *practice*. We can enlarge this idea by examining in greater detail the relationship between dialectical ideas and conflict resolution. Here are a few ways of thinking about the dance of opposites that may help explain how we can improve our skills by applying dialectical principles in dispute resolution, including some I have not mentioned before that are drawn from math and science:

1. Conflicts are places of impasse where two or more people, or sides of the same person, become stuck and unable to move, except in a circle.

2. By analogy with the physical law of inertia, those who become stuck in conflict often remain stuck until something happens to get them unstuck.

3. It is possible to suppress conflicts and punish those who engage in them, or settle them through compromise, without altering either their form or their content. Beyond suppression and settlement lies resolution, in which the underlying issues that gave rise to the dispute and will continue to generate new disputes, are addressed, transformed (changed in form), and resolved.

4. Every genuine resolution requires a movement into some new idea, process, understanding, proposal, or "conflict space" that did not exist beforehand. This implies the creation of a new conversation and a new relationship. For example, moving people from position A and position B to some new position C requires the acceptance of at least three truths: the truth of A and of B, plus a recognition that these two truths contain some larger third truth, C.

5. We are able to discover this larger third truth by means of an orthogonal movement into a higher dimensional conversation, perhaps by digging deeper into underlying emotions or surfacing unspoken interests, i.e., through an integral calculus of infinitesimal movements that map the transition of A and B onto some new C. This transition can take place in three distinct ways:
   - Interactionally, through emotionally open conversation, reciprocal feedback, or interest-based dialogue;
   - Internally, through awareness, wisdom, or insight;
   - Externally, through systems design, collaboration, or change.

6. Since there are two in every conflict, each movement toward a new understanding takes place as a result of some

communication or interaction, some dialogue or dialectic between opposing views, emotions, positions, or perspectives.

7. Transformation, by definition, is a change in the form of a conflict. Yet changing its form automatically changes its content, just as changing its content necessarily alters its form. Thus, moving from yelling to discussing issues automatically reduces the level of hostility between people and makes resolution more likely, while discovering the underlying reasons for the dispute allows them to discuss and find solutions that will not occur to them when they are yelling.

8. Transcendence, on the other hand, is the discovery that there is a more successful way of being in conflict. It implies learning, substantive change, and the birth of something new. Thus, the realization that the reason he became angry had nothing at all to do with who she is, but perhaps with the way she behaved, allows them to rise above the conflict and transcend it. In that moment, two starts to become one again, and the conflict begins to disappear.

9. If forgiveness consists of forgetting, including the behaviors that gave rise to the conflict, learning and transcendence cannot occur. Instead, it is necessary for people to transform their conflicts by correcting the behaviors that triggered it and re-experiencing the people who engaged in those behaviors in a new way, thereby striping the issues of polarization and revealing the unities that could not be grasped while they were feeling powerless or oppressed.

10. To do these things, it is necessary to learn to apply higher order resolution skills that are superior to the sources of conflict and thereby require it to evolve, giving rise to newer, higher order, emergent conflicts that represent more complex challenges and a need to develop ever-higher orders of skill at uncovering unity in the midst of polarity.

By applying these and other dialectical ideas to conflict resolution, we begin to reveal its immense transformational potential. We may then discover that our own personal growth and learning, together with our ability to create higher order family, organizational and social systems and evolve beyond war and violence, are all dependent on our ability to identify what unites us in our opposition. Doing so frees us to enjoy our diversity, and our dance of opposites.

# CHAPTER 13

# CONFLICT AND MOVEMENTS FOR SOCIAL CHANGE

## The Politics of Mediation and the Mediation of Politics

*If you cry, "Forward!" you must be sure to make clear the direction in which to go. Don't you see that if you fail to do that and simply call out the word to a monk and a revolutionary, they will go in precisely opposite directions?*

~ Anton Chekhov ~

**M**OVEMENTS FOR SOCIAL CHANGE are products, producers, and resolvers of conflict. By joining together to bring about change, their members affirm the positive, creative role that conflict can play in calling attention to injustices, applying pressure to support needed social changes, reinforcing progressive values, halting censorship and retaliation, and resolving the chronic, systemic sources of social conflict. Yet these same movements are often plagued with their own internal conflicts, which are routinely handled in negative and socially regressive ways.

Internal conflicts in social movements are commonly resolved using a range of highly destructive methods, including avoidance, apathy, accommodation, screaming, suppression, enforced silence, personal insults, mass resignations, gossip, ostracism, unnecessary splitting, sectarian behaviors, angry denunciations, and public humiliation, none of which maintain unity, encourage principled opposition, or demonstrate an ability to solve larger social problems.

The emotions that occur naturally in the course of these conflicts are frequently repressed—partly in deference to a higher goal, political ideal, or principle, or immediate practical priorities; partly out of disrespect for subjective weakness, which can be seen as a form of political vacillation; and partly out of a fear of co-optation and capitulation.

Personal needs are then equated with selfishness and self-indulgence or a lack of commitment, or identification with opposing political interests, so that toughness and insensitivity can come to be regarded as positive attributes and essential accommodations to the rough-and-tumble of political activity.

## WHY MOVEMENTS EXPERIENCE CONFLICT

Internal conflicts are endemic and natural to progressive political and social movements, in part because it is difficult to agree on how to define and change highly complex, volatile and evolving social problems. As a result, over time, different definitions of the problem and perceptions about the nature of those who defend and represent it result in radically different notions about what needs to be done to change it.

Moreover, these alternately reinforcing and contradictory definitions and ideas are not fixed in time, but fluctuate dramatically with events, shifting perspectives, hardening or softening commitments, and an evolving, uneven understanding about the kind of organizational structures and decision-making processes needed to overcome the obstacles that are periodically placed in the way.

For this reason, debates over means versus ends and goals versus process are a part of the history of all social movements, which are simultaneously fixed on achieving specific goals or demands, and at the same time searching for principled ways of achieving them that do not replicate the worst of what unjust and alienated social practices have created.

At the same time, maintaining unity in the face of an organized and repressive opposition is of paramount importance. In decisive moments, everyone understands that nothing is achievable in the absence of unity, and that everything is possible with it.

## VARIETIES OF UNITY

Internal conflicts, if handled incorrectly, unnecessarily undermine this unity. But how, exactly, is unity formed? One type of unity derives from having a common purpose, goal, vision, idea, or source of inspirational energy. We can think of this as a unity of substance or content. A second type of unity emerges from affection, community, struggling together against great odds, friendship, or empathy. We can think of this as a unity of relationship. There is also a third type of unity, which we can think of this as a unity of process, that emerges from open and honest communication, dialogue, circles, and other collaborative processes.

Unities of content are fleeting, limited, conscious, intellectual, future-oriented, and externally directed. Unities of relationship are enduring, unlimited, subconscious, emotional, past-oriented, and internally motivated. Unities of process are situational, transformative, largely unconscious, intuitive, present-oriented, and group inspired. Each of these impacts the others, and is able, even in tiny, unnoticeable ways, to strengthen or weaken them.

In any movement or organization that seeks to strengthen its internal unity and capacity for common action, it is critical to build all three, and move, wherever possible, from the first, which is widely acknowledged, to the second and third, which are largely ignored. In political movements, it is especially important to rescue the principles of human affection and collaborative process from the demands of political expediency and abstract content.

There is a historic tendency among political groups to dismiss concerns with relationship building and collaborative process as unnecessary and time consuming, or as diversions from political substance, or "touchy-feely" and bourgeois in nature. Each of these judgments could be accurate, depending on the circumstances. Yet to regard relationships and processes in general as secondary or unworthy of concern is to ignore their extraordinary impact and transformative power.

Process encodes relationships and recapitulates content. The process of bowing to a monarch or saluting a superior officer reveals and reinforces their hierarchical content. Whenever people stand in line or sit in rows before a speaker, or dance on tabletops, relationships are created through process that reinforce relational and political content. Similarly, if ideas are expressed using mathematical proofs, footnoted pages, oil painting, ballet, or rhymed poetry, different kinds of content will emerge from each form.

The same idea extends to political organizations and their approaches to resolving conflict. It makes an enormous difference whether a group acts in lockstep with the will of its leader, or by majority vote, or by consensus. And it matters equally whether internal disputes are handled by silencing dissent, mass expulsions, power struggles, avoidance, acrimonious debates, mediation, or open dialogue.

Progressive organizations have a particular interest in encouraging the use of collaborative, relationally constructive methods of resolving internal disputes that do not recreate the same negative, adversarial techniques that characterize the unjust, internally divided societies they seek to improve. Once it becomes permissible to treat allies and internal members in the same ways we treat external opponents, the movement has taken a huge step backward and diminished what it will be able to achieve.

To succeed in creating more just societies, we need to begin with ourselves, and encourage not only substantive unity regarding core ideas and political principles, but the caring relationships and collaborative processes that are needed to support them over the long term, by improving the levels of skill and understanding in these areas.

## THE POLITICS OF CONFLICT

Every conflict takes place not only between individuals, but within a context, culture, and environment; surrounded by social, economic, and political forces; inside an organizational system, structure, and technological setting; among a diverse community of people; at a particular moment in time and history; on a stage, milieu, or backdrop; within a relationship.

None of these elements is conflict-neutral. Each contributes—often in veiled, unspoken, yet significant ways to the nature, intensity, duration, impact, and meaning of our conflicts. And each element, depending on circumstances, can play a determining role in the conversations, interventions, and methods required to settle, resolve, transform, or transcend it.

Every conflict, no matter how petty, therefore possesses hidden social, economic, and political elements that inform and influence its evolution and outcome. More critically, social inequality, economic inequity, and political polarization raise the intensity of even the least significant interpersonal conflicts, and these forces are experienced personally as conflict. Nonetheless, it is rare that any of these systemic background elements are noticed, analyzed, discussed, or subjected to problem solving, negotiation, or conflict resolution by those whose daily activities bring them into existence.

In addition, social, economic, and political dysfunctions trigger or aggravate interpersonal and organizational conflicts, and these conflicts contribute to the maintenance of oppressive, social, economic, and political systems, in part by generating chronic conflicts, and with them, a culture of avoidance and aggression, and a set of adversarial attitudes and behaviors that limit the ability of individuals and groups to work together to improve their lives.

We can identify a number of sources of chronic conflict throughout history, and among these are social inequality, economic inequity, political autocracy, and environmental change. Therefore, every effort to end or ameliorate these sources of conflict by individuals or movements for social change can be regarded as a form of conflict resolution.

## WHAT CAN BE DONE?

These observations lead us to three threshold questions:

First, can we become more skillful in preventing, resolving, transforming, and transcending conflicts in social movements by addressing the systemic, contextual, and organizational influences that trigger or aggravate them?

Second, is it possible to apply conflict resolution principles to the inequalities, inequities, and dysfunctions that fuel chronic social, economic, political, and environmental conflicts?

And third, can we learn to interact with each other socially, economically, politically, and environmentally in more humane, compassionate, and collaborative ways, while uniting to bring about social change? These questions suggest deeper ones:

- What is our responsibility for the conflicts that are taking place within our own movements?
- Are we not implicitly responsible for learning better ways to address and resolve them?
- Is it possible for us to use our knowledge and experience in conflict resolution to do a better job of preventing, resolving, transforming and transcending chronic conflicts inside and outside our organizations?
- How could we redesign the organizational processes, relationships, cultures, and systems that routinely and globally give rise to them?

## THE POLITICS OF MEDIATION

Mediation, like every process, has a political content. It is voluntary and radically democratic, since it uses consensus rather than coercion, and therefore produces a maximum of unity and a minimum loss in energy, time, commitment, and resources within organizations. These same characteristics allow mediation to also be seen as a model for social interactions and a goal for more just future societies.

Mediation encourages empowerment in both substance and process. When successful, it allows conflicting parties to reach settlements that are satisfactory to both sides, while creating more effective communication and identifying what can be done to improve ongoing relationships.

In mediation, there is no hierarchy or power elite dictating results, encouraging non-adversarial forms of negotiation and creative informal problem solving. Empathy and mutual understanding are supported, as are the purposes or goals that the parties share.

Even where fundamental political disagreements separate conflicting parties, these can be clarified and discussed honestly, respectfully and openly through dialogue that supports the frank and honest discussion of disagreements. A rich array of problem solving techniques can identify creative solutions that seek to satisfy both sets of interests.

Through mediation, dialogue and other collaborative processes, progressive movements can also model methods for resolving deeper social conflicts and an acceptance of diverse races, genders, nationalities, sexual orientations, communities, and political perspectives, which is a part of their reason for existence.

## THE MEDIATION OF POLITICS

The goals of peace, equality, democracy, and justice require collaboration, respect, honesty, fairness, and empathy—not only in abstract political theory, but as integral parts of practical problem-solving, negotiation, and conflict resolution that allow diverse communities to unite and co-exist.

Mediation, together with dialogue and other collaborative processes, should therefore, be a long-term goal of progressive movements, for at least the following reasons:

1.  Mediation is the modern version of an ancient tradition invoking wisdom and fairness to heal the repairable rifts that divide people. Indigenous tribal elders, representing forgiveness and regeneration, empathy and wisdom, are represented today by mediators.

2. Mediation is the reconciliation principle and a means of social repair for people whose disagreements are beyond their ability to resolve.

3. Mediation is the most democratic method of conflict resolution possible, as the parties control both the process and the outcomes.

4. Mediation encourages responsibility for one's actions. It is problem solving without hierarchy, power without autocracy, structure without bureaucracy, and justice without the state.

5. Mediation is the transformation of external into internal constraints. It is individual and group self-determination in practice.

6. Unresolved conflicts are costly to any society, whether they are social conflicts that arise from inequality and empire; economic conflicts that arise from scarcity and a hierarchical division of labor; or political conflicts arising from autocracy, graft, and the corruption of elites. Mediation, dialogue, and conflict resolution systems design offer ways of discussing, addressing, and resolving all of these.

7. Pretending that there is no conflict or that it will resolve itself is like ignoring an illness and hoping it will go away. Mediation is the ounce of prevention that is worth a pound of cure.

8. Mediation is entirely without coercion. It *is* the "withered-away" judicial state, and the judicial future of civil society.

9. Principles of political and social democracy as a whole can benefit substantially from large and small scale peer mediation programs that use elected volunteers from neighborhoods, work units, schools, and communities to settle disputes voluntarily, quickly, and confidentially.

10. The obstacle is the path. By resolving conflicts at their chronic sources, we make it possible for individuals, groups, and societies to evolve to higher levels of conflict and more advanced techniques for resolution.

11. By affirming and creatively combining complex, contradictory, paradoxical truths, we make it possible to identify complex, higher order, synergistic solutions.

A living organism, like a social movement, cannot exempt itself from the cumulative effects of its decisions regarding process, and sooner or later these effects begin to show themselves in burnout, fatigue, in-fighting, destructive relationships, apathy, cynicism, and a loss of effectiveness and unity. Valuable contributions in time and effort then predictably decline as money is not donated and a cycle of blame and recrimination begins, ending in a hardened, adversarial exterior for those who remain, and bitterness and enmity against their former comrades for those who leave.

Much of this is avoidable. Through mediation, conflicts can be surfaced, discussed, and acknowledged, and in most cases amicably resolved. Communication can be improved and working relationships strengthened, preferably before they become dysfunctional.

While there are clear limits on the mediation process, and while it can be misused to suppress genuine political differences, a positive attitude toward conflict, disagreement, and diversity is more common to the mediation process and its outcomes are consistent with the democratic aims of progressive movements, as well as with social equality and community empowerment.

For these reasons, mediation allows conflict to be seen as positive and a source of change, rather than as something to be feared and avoided. Conflicts then become opportunities, challenges, learning experiences, useful adjuncts to the political change process, and sources of unity within the movement and within society as a whole.

# CHAPTER 14

# MEDIATION, LAW, AND JUSTICE

*So long as society is founded on injustice, the function of the laws will be to defend injustice. And the more unjust they are the more respectable they will seem.*

~ Anatole France ~

*No one can say
That the trial was not fair. The trial was fair.
Painfully fair by every rule of law,
And that it was [fair] made not the slightest difference,
The Law's our yardstick and it measures well
Or well enough when there are yards to measure.
Measure a wave with it. Measure a fire.
Cut up sorrow in inches, weigh content.
You can weigh John Brown's body well enough,
But how and in what balance weigh John Brown?*

~ Stephen Vincent Benet ~

*Each time someone stands up for an ideal, or acts to improve the lot of others, or strikes out against injustice he sends forth a tiny ripple of hope.*

~ Robert F. Kennedy ~

"JUSTICE" IS THE GREAT catchword, the past's promise to posterity, humanity's hope. It is the indignant cry, the lost illusion, the selfless dedication, the bitter and the sweet. It is the last word of millions who suffer and the first demand of those who seek change. It has stood for revenge and forgiveness, punishment and rehabilitation, compensation and closure, mercy and terror.

Justice has been cited in support of integrated schools and supporters of racial segregation, on behalf of gay marriage and by those who would outlaw homosexuality, by spokespersons for pro-choice and pro-life, by defense attorneys and by the prosecution. It graces the facades of law schools and decorates courthouses, but is rarely explored or sought after inside. It is a fixture in the rhetoric of politicians the world over, including the most right-wing supporters of dictatorship and the most left-wing proponents of democracy.

Shakespeare wrote that "mercy seasons justice," while Robespierre declared that "Terror is nothing else than justice, prompt, secure, and inflexible." Plato recalled a dialogue in which Thrasymachus debated Socrates over whether justice was simply "the interest of the stronger," while Aristotle argued that justice was "the highest virtue of the state." Franz Kafka believed that justice was "a fugitive from the winning camp," while comedian Lenny Bruce quipped that "the only justice in the halls of justice is in the halls."

Aristotle believed that justice could be regarded as a "due proportion," for example, in the meting out of rewards and punishments. More intriguingly for mediators, he also asserted that it could be thought of as "someone else's self-interest." From a mediation perspective, we might modify this definition by describing justice as a synergistic, consensual combination of our own and someone else's self-interest.

In the *Nicomachean Ethics*, Aristotle goes further and *expressly* connects justice with mediation, writing,

> This is why, when people dispute, they take refuge in the judge; and to go to the judge is to go to justice; for the nature of the judge is to be a sort of animate justice; and they seek the judge as an intermediate, and in some states they call judges mediators, on the assumption that if they get what is intermediate they will get what is just. The just, then, is an intermediate since the judge is so. Now the judge restores equality; it is as though there were a line divided into unequal parts, and he took away that by which the greater segment exceeds the half, and added it to the smaller segment.

For all this diversity in definitions and beliefs about justice, the word is not a without content or meaning that goes beyond Aristotle's idea of the middle or intermediate as just. It is important to notice, for example, that justice has an internal ratchet, which prevents it from being claimed equally, for example, by those who demand equality and those who defend discrimination, genocide, and privilege; by those who support liberty and those who advocate its suppression; by those who favor health care for the poor and those who favor tax benefits for the rich.

In Thucydides' account, in his *History of the Peloponnesian War,* of a conversation between Athenian envoys representing the island of Melos, a colony of Sparta which had resisted Athenian rule, the Athenians declared that "right, as the world goes, is only in question between equals in power, whereas the stronger do whatever they can and the weaker must suffer what they must." The Melians replied: "You debar us from talking about justice and invite us to obey your interest."

Nearly identical views of justice appeared in the classic debate between Socrates and Thrasymachus in Plato's *Republic,* where Thrasymachus is said to have stated:

> Justice is nothing else than the interest of the stronger ... The different forms of government make law democratical, aristocratical, tyrannical, with a view to

their several interests; and these laws, which are made by them for their own interests, are the justice which they deliver to their subjects, and him who transgresses them they punish as a breaker of the law, and unjust. And this is what I mean when I say that in all states there is the same principle of justice which is the interest of the government; and as the government must be supposed to have power, the only reasonable conclusion is that everywhere there is one principle of justice which is the interest of the stronger.

To which Socrates is said to have responded, claiming justice consists of obedience to the will of the ruler, which may or may not be in his interest,

... you acknowledged justice not to be for the interest of the stronger, when the rulers unintentionally command things to be done which are to their own injury. For if, as you say, justice is the obedience which the subject renders to their commands, in that case, O wisest of men, is there any escape from the conclusion that the weaker are commanded to do, not what is for the interest, but what is for the injury of the stronger?

Socrates later comments:

There is no one in any rule who, insofar as he is ruler considers or enjoins what is for his own interest, but always what is for the interest of his subject or suitable to his art; to that he looks, and that alone he considers in everything which he says and does.

Justice, then, can be thought to represent a specific *direction* in political history, one that expands the reach of liberty and equality, rather than contracting or suppressing them; one that finds a home with those who have been oppressed, cast out, or excluded, rather than with those who possess power and rarely exercise it entirely in the interest of their subjects, who in Athens included slaves whose freedom was not thought to be required by justice. For this reason, ruling elites have always tended to refer instead to law and order, obedience, and rights and responsibilities, without inquiring:

- Whose laws?
- What kind of order?
- Obedience to whom?
- Responsibility for what?"

Respect for "legally constituted authority" appears to be just, but what of the legally constituted authority of slave owners, not only in Athens, but before the Civil War; respect by the slave for the authority of the master, "obedience to the law" of slavery; and "acceptance of the rights and responsibilities" of the slave? These signify acquiescence in continued oppression by the slave masked as obedience to the law, a law created and designed to protect the master and perpetuate what we regard today as injustice.

As an illustration, consider the Fugitive Slave Act that allowed Southern slave owners before the Civil War to claim that ex-slaves living in a Northern free state were runaways and petition the courts to have them returned to servitude. At issue was whether, in federal courts, the slave had a right to speak and raise objections, as any citizen of a free state might, to being returned to slavery. If not, slavery was recreated procedurally within the courts, even in Northern abolitionist states. But if the slave could speak freely, slavery was abolished procedurally, even in courts in slave-owning states. What appeared on the surface to be a simple procedural rule took on a transformational character and challenged the justice of slavery as a legal institution. In this way, the Fugitive Slave Act threatened to turn the entire nation into a slave state and abolish the rights of Northern states to grant manumission.

If we examine in more detail the role of justice in 19th century slave societies, we can recognize a number of additional ideas that may prove useful in exploring the importance and meaning of justice in mediation. In the first place, justice was not abstract or academic, either to the slave or the master, from the birth of slavery to its demise, but was immediately practical and political, with genuine life consequences for each.

Second, justice was seen in fact to be not unitary, as claimed by lawyers and politicians, but conditional and relative, with a content that differed based on the personal, socio-economic, political, racial and historical circumstances of the person who was claiming injustice. For a while, it was assumed that a single legal rule might unite all the states and parties. Yet, as William Blake recognized, and the abolitionist movement agreed, "The same law for the lion and the ox is oppression." Especially when the lion makes, interprets, and enforces the laws, and writes them as though the ox were an equal partner.

Third, as the end of slavery approached, justice was increasingly seen by each side to represent only its substantive, procedural, and relational interests, and therefore became partial, "biased," more aligned with one set of views, and incapable of representing those of the other. In general, within any group, time, or set of circumstance, what is regarded as just may therefore cease being relative and become absolute, and appear to reside more in one side than in the other.

At this point, the law began to fall apart, as it became clear that it could not continue pretending to represent the slave while in fact representing only the master. It finally became obvious in the Supreme Court's Dred Scott decision that the law was incapable of uniting a house that was so deeply divided. In the conflict between slavery and free labor, and ultimately between law and justice, one side had to lose.

Fourth, virtually all of the efforts to find a mediated solution, including historic compromises dating back to the Constitutional Convention and before, were seen to be predicated on giving slavery a legal right to continue. While we have no problem today recognizing that slavery is unjust, the efforts of many well-meaning mediators at the time were based on the premise that laws must enforced even if they were unfair, and that peace might prevail in the absence of justice.

The difficulties with this approach, from the point of view of mediation today, are many, beginning with the universal exclusion of slaves and abolitionists from the electorate, as well as from the negotiating table. All the mediations and compromise solutions, especially those proposed by "the great compromiser" Henry Clay, arose out of conversations between wealthy representatives of Northern industries and wealthy representatives of Southern slave plantations.

What suddenly made slavery appear unjust to the rest of the country? Nothing other than the growing recognition that slaves were human beings and equally entitled to dignity, respect, and self-determination; to life, liberty and the pursuit of happiness. But if slaves and masters were equally entitled to the same rights, the adversarial and unequal assumptions on which the *law* of slavery was based could not be sustained.

Indeed, in every society, the dramatic rise of allegations and concerns over injustice can be seen as the hallmark of a need to transition to a higher order of social relationship. Similarly, frequent attempts at mediation can be regarded as a reflection of the increasing internal polarization within a society that is experiencing a profound transition, whose internal divisions over what is just are becoming increasingly acute.

These issues continue to the present day, and can be found, for example, in the efforts of the recent Occupy movement to raise the issue of justice in relation to the unequal distribution of wealth between the top one percent and the remaining 99 percent; or the claims of politicians and judges battling over the marriage equality; or to recent political divisions between liberals and conservatives in the US Congress, which have become increasingly hostile and intransigent.

Here, as with slavery before, defining justice abstractly in terms of "fairness," or "natural law" brings us no closer to understanding what substantive, procedural, or relational justice might consist of within any particular circumstance or society. What is "fair," "just," or "natural" in a society based on slave labor is manifestly unfair, unjust, and unnatural in one based on wage labor. Yet considerable efforts have been expended in searching for absolute standards by which all earlier outrages against "modern" common sense could be measured and found lacking, for understandable reasons. If right and wrong are no more than relative categories, might mass enslavement not be regarded as just, or genocide, or torture? Might not any law be considered "just," no matter how contrary to innate "fairness" or "natural law" principles?

John Rawls, in *A Theory of Justice,* asserted in response that there are two "fairness" principles:  (1) everyone has a right to the most extensive liberty compatible with a similar liberty in others, and (2) social and economic inequalities and privileges must be so arranged as to be equal toward all, and that liberty had to be considered a lexical priority over equality. Rawls argued that inequality would be just if equal liberty and fair opportunity principles were not violated, and if class distinctions, however great, nonetheless benefited the least advantaged. Yet liberty without equality ultimately undermines liberty as well. As Martin Sklar commented,

> Liberty becomes the power and privilege of the few, an instrument for the manipulation and exploitation of the many. As the mask for narrow self-interest destructive of community and mutuality of social responsibility, liberty divorced from equality discredits genuine liberty itself and places it in jeopardy to disillusion and cynicism.

It is precisely here that mediation parts company with the law in its approach to justice. Rather than proclaim abstract universal principles, or assert the priority of liberty over equality, or impose one approach or set of ideas on both parties equally, as the law does, mediation seeks to resolve the practical issues that encourage each side to believe that what is happening is unjust, and allows the parties to decide for themselves what is fair or just, using procedures that invite everyone who is touched by the problem to come to the table and collaboratively negotiate how it should be solved, and in this way, preserves both liberty and equality as interconnected aspects of justice.

Historically, we can see that laws are created when their violation becomes socially inevitable; in other words, that they arise when, where, and to the extent that societies are internally conflicted. For example, the law of theft comes into existence only with the rise of moveable private property and a division between rich and poor, i.e., as a result of an increase in social inequality and the social need to steal. The resolution of this conflict through laws that favor property owners, enforced by criminal courts on which the propertied serve as judges, can only create a continuing series of chronic conflicts, and with them, the need for a growing number of police, attorneys, trials, judicial decisions, and prisons, all for the purpose of keeping the private property of the wealthy out of the hands of the impoverished many.

It is not merely a concern for protecting the private property of owners that reveals this injustice, but the absence of an equal or stronger concern for the lives of the poor who seek to survive and raise their wealth and status. The same points can be made regarding the legal recognition of corporations as people, the laws that protect banks and creditors and permit foreclosures, the eviction rights of landlords in opposition to the rights of tenants, and similar legal assumptions.

Injustice succeeds partly by collapsing justice into law, and making it synonymous with the requirements of order. It does so by subsuming subjective emotions into what is claimed to be objective, universal rationality, and by turning practical, particular, historically grounded, relative ideas about justice into abstract, universal, ahistorical, absolutist principles.

Mediation represents a significant, transformational departure from the law and its relationship to justice, not only by seeking to equalize the role of all parties and offering them a veto power over whatever is proposed, but more subtly by seeking justice first, then creating law through the negotiation and writing of agreements; by inviting conversations that are based on interests rather than on rights or power; by acknowledging emotions, listening closely and encouraging respectful communications, and building consensus in collaborative relationships. In these ways, mediation allows the parties to write their own laws based on what they believe to be just, rather than allowing legal principles to determine in advance and for everyone what is just. Rather than law-driven justice, there is justice-driven law. Like in mediation, as Albert Einstein wrote, "In matters of truth and justice, there is no difference between large and small problems, for issues concerning the treatment of people are all the same."

## NO JUSTICE NO PEACE

It is a truism, yet no less true as a result, that we cannot create lasting peace in the absence of justice. Merely attempting to do so validates anthropologist Laura Nader's stinging critique of settlement-driven forms of mediation as "trading justice for harmony," and turning peace into something fleeting, fragile, and phony. Novelist Toni Morrison offers a more useful definition of peace:

> There is a certain kind of peace that is not merely the absence of war. It is larger than that. The peace I am thinking of is not at the mercy of history's rule, nor is it a passive surrender to the status quo. The peace I am

thinking of is the dance of an open mind when it engages
another equally open one ...

We cannot achieve either a sustainable peace or an integrated, equitable, and just social order that makes such a peace possible, unless opposing sides are enabled to listen, learn, and genuinely seek to understand each other. There can be no lasting justice without peace, or lasting peace without justice. Without both, we become unable to solve our common problems, collaboratively negotiate our differences, seek genuine truth and reconciliation, and dismantle our prejudices and hostilities toward one another. More importantly, we become unable to prevent, resolve, transform, or transcend chronic conflicts by unlocking them at their systemic social, economic, and political sources. This truth applies not only to large-scale, global conflicts, but to the small-scale, interpersonal conflicts we experience every day.

If we are to successfully reduce injustice and engage disputing parties in communication, dialogue, and negotiation, it is important for us to recognize that the deepest form of evil *is* injustice. And as long as it continues, peace will be fleeting, fragile, and a disappointing, yet potent reminder of everything people have suffered and lost.

For this reason, where injustice prevails, peace becomes merely a way of masking and compounding prior injustices, impeding necessary changes, and rationalizing the continuation of domination, aggression, and war. As the Trappist monk Thomas Merton astutely observed:

> To some men peace merely means the liberty to exploit other people without fear of retaliation or interference. To others peace means the freedom to rob others without interruption. To still others it means the leisure to devour the goods of the Earth without being compelled to interrupt their pleasures to feed those whom their greed is starving. And to practically everybody peace simply means the absence of any physical violence that might cast a shadow over lives devoted to the satisfaction of their animal appetites for comfort and leisure ... [T]heir idea of peace was only another form of war.

Where millions lack the essentials of life, peace lends legitimacy to continued suffering, while compromise offers a rationale for capitulation, passivity, and tolerance of injustice. True peace requires a search for justice and a dedication to harmoniously satisfying fundamental human needs; otherwise, it becomes the self-interest of the satisfied, the ruling clique, the oppressors, the victors in search of additional spoils. For this reason, Gandhi believed that peace and justice required not just non-violence, but resistance and *satyagraha*, or "speaking truth to power."

For peace to be achieved, it is essential that we neither trivialize the sources of conflict nor become stuck in the language of good and evil, but work collaboratively and compassionately to redress the underlying injustices and pain each side has caused the other. One of the immense contributions made by the South African Truth and Reconciliation Commissions was the invitation to *both* sides to seek forgiveness and an end to bloodshed by telling the truth about what they did – not just the defenders and enforcers of Apartheid, but the revolutionaries and supporters of freedom within the African National Congress as well.

Ultimately, justice requires a sharing of power and resources, of advantages and disadvantages, successes and failures, and efforts to satisfy both groups' or individual's legitimate interests. As Eleanor Roosevelt commented, "Justice cannot be for one side alone, but must be for both." This means collaborating and making decisions together. It means giving up the assumption that what is legal is necessarily just. It means taking time to work through differences, and making our opponent's human interests our own. It means standing up for the rights of others as though *our* lives were affected.

Wherever shantytowns coexist with country clubs, peace cannot be lasting or secure. Wherever some go hungry while others are well fed, terror and violence will be nourished. In the end, it comes down to a question of equalization of status, wealth, and power, based on the realization that we are all part of a single human family, and the understanding that an injury to one is genuinely and truly an injury to all.

Making the search for justice an integral part of conflict resolution therefore means not merely *settling* conflicts, but resolving, transforming and transcending them, and turning them into levers of dialogue and learning, catalysts of community and collaboration, and commitments to egalitarian social, economic, and political change. By failing to take these steps, we make justice secondary to peace, undermine both, guarantee the continuation of chronic conflict, and lay the groundwork for more to come.

As global problems extend their reach and increase in importance and severity, it is essential that we continue to discover improved ways of responding to contentious social, economic and political issues, and come together across and beyond borders to improve our ability to listen, ask questions, discuss, understand, and act together in solving them. It is essential that we build bridges across divided political and cultural spectrums, and not allow ourselves to become silent or passive as difficult, dangerous and polarizing events drag us into their downward unjust logic.

As a result of climate change, economic crises, political corruption, racial and religious intolerance, economic inequity, and great injustices, many people around the world are searching for better lives. As a consequence, political antagonisms, violence, hatred and intolerance have greatly increased, fracturing once stable communities and alliances, escalating conflicts and bringing misery to many.

The unimaginable is now stirring, and we are moving toward a watershed in world events, a crossroads where values, ethics and justice are put to a very real test, creating a flashpoint that could lead either to greater hatreds, violence and war; or to increased dialogue, respect and collaboration. The outcome depends partly on us.

No country is immune from these problems, and no country has discovered a surefire way to solve them. What we require is not war or litigation or well-meaning official pronouncements; not rhetorical speeches, denunciations or apathetic silence, but courageous conversations, authentic engagement, genuine listening, creative problem solving, mediation, and dialogue.

If we can discover how to successfully collaborate across the borders that divide us and build the capacity of local communities to collaborate in addressing these difficult and dangerous issues, we may be able to significantly increase understanding, collectively create new possibilities, reach consensus on recommendations for action, increase understanding, and reduce the growing threat of hatred and violence. And if we can do this in countries where violence and hatred are at a high, perhaps we will be able to do so elsewhere in the world as well.

After centuries of suffering and turmoil, we now have available the tools we require to produce radically different outcomes. Through the dramatically increasing power and reach of dispute resolution techniques, we can now begin to build the capacity of people around the world to resolve their disputes based on interests, rather than on power or rights; based on justice, and not merely on law.

As a result, it is uniquely within our grasp to *integrate* law and justice, to achieve a more lasting peace, and to prevent conflicts by solving the most egregious problems that compel people to engage in them. In the process, regardless of whether we succeed, the dance of opposites will really be something to behold. As Allan Watts advised, "The only way to make sense out of change is to plunge into it, move with it, and join the dance."

# INDEX

CPSIA information can be obtained at www.ICGtesting.com
Printed in the USA
LVOW07s1556120114

369099LV00002B/4/P